Popovers and Candlelight

Popovers and Candlelight

Patricia Murphy and the
Rise and Fall of a Restaurant Empire

*To Ellen
with much love,
Marcia*

MARCIA BIEDERMAN

excelsior editions

AN IMPRINT OF STATE UNIVERSITY OF NEW YORK PRESS

Cover image: Patricia Murphy at her popover oven with her husband, James E. "Rosie" Kiernan, 1954. Photo courtesy of the Photography Collection, Harry Ransom Center, University of Texas at Austin.

Published by State University of New York Press, Albany

Excelsior Editions is an imprint of State University of New York Press

For information, contact State University of New York Press, Albany, NY
www.sunypress.edu

Library of Congress Cataloging-in-Publication Data

Names: Biederman, Marcia.
Title: Popovers and candlelight : Patricia Murphy and the rise and fall of a
  restaurant empire / Marcia Biederman.
Description: Albany : State University of New York, 2018. | Series: Excelsior
  editions | Includes bibliographical references and index.
Identifiers: LCCN 2017058365 | ISBN 9781438471549 (pbk. : alk. paper) |
  ISBN 9781438471563 (ebook)
Subjects: LCSH: Murphy, Patricia, 1905–1979. | Restaurateurs—United States—
  Biography. | Patricia Murphy's Candlelight Corporation.
Classification: LCC TX910.5.M8 B54 2018 | DDC 647.95092 [B]—dc23
LC record available at https://lccn.loc.gov/2017058365

10 9 8 7 6 5 4 3 2 1

For my sister, Phyllis, who sets a beautiful table

Contents

Acknowledgments

This book would not have been possible without the help of many individuals and institutions. Paul Murphy never met his great-aunt, Patricia, but he was instrumental in the writing of this book. Paul was close with his grandfather, James F. Murphy, Patricia's brother and a successful restaurateur. In Paul's view, Patricia's refusal to reconcile with the four siblings who left her business to start their own was "over the top, pure Patricia." His sharing of family lore, articles, and menus, and his encouragement of my project, helped bring the pure Patricia into focus.

Patricia's former manager, Greg D. Camillucci, provided crucial perspectives on the woman and her business. It was a thrill to talk to a man I had seen on screen in my repeated viewings of the film *Tootsie*—he plays a maître de at the Russian Tea Room, where in real life he was a manager and vice president.

Owen T. Smith, the son of Patricia's sister, Lauraine, offered tremendous assistance as the oldest member of his generation of Murphys. Jim E. Rogers, a son of John E. Rogers, had thought of writing his own book, a fact-based novel based on his father's eventual ownership of Patricia's business and its unfortunate outcome. Tragically, his life was prematurely ended by illness soon after he spoke to me. I hope I have done his story justice.

The famed decorator Carleton Varney gave me a lively, quotable view of his former client. Patricia's pilots—Alexander E. Cabana, R. John Bates, and Dr. Richard A. Strauss—offered impressions and anecdotes. I contacted them with the intention of debunking Patricia's flight credentials. Their reminiscences convinced me that her fibbing, probably prompted by a publicist, was far less important than her warm relations with them. Peter and Andy Kern painted a vivid picture of Patricia's continued connection with her first Candlelight restaurant in Brooklyn.

Diane Carlson Phillips, daughter of Patricia's head gardener in Westchester, offered insights and photographs; Nader James Sayegh, a son of a Candlelight chef, shared his father's reflections. Kevin J. Gonzalez helped me visualize the last of the Candlelights in Deerfield Beach, Florida, which he once managed. Paul A. Gore, the attorney who handled the probate of Patricia's estate, and Dr. Greg J. Harrison, her fellow orchid collector, shed important light on her final days.

Merrilyn Rathbun of the Fort Lauderdale Historical Society answered my lengthy questions by phone and in person. Tom O'Keefe waited an hour for me at the Placentia Area Historical Society when my travel plans went awry, and his colleague, Anita O'Keefe—my Canadian counterpart in the Patricia Murphy fan club—steered me to Anne Marie Murray and her memories of Patricia. In typical Newfoundland style, a manager named Wanda at Placentia's Ocean View motel drove me hours out of her way when I couldn't rent a car. I'm grateful also to the Culinary Historians of New York and the Biographers International Organization for egging me on.

Patricia left few letters and documents behind. I'm thankful that some were preserved in the Archives and Manuscripts division of the New York Public Library and the Archives and Special Collections of Barnard College. New York University preserved important letters written by John Rogers; Yale's Beinecke Library collected the papers of Patricia's lighting designer, Richard Kelly; and Harvard's Schlesinger Library on the History of Women in America holds the restaurant management lesson books she studied. Librarians at these institutions and at the Memorial University of Newfoundland were enormously helpful, as were employees of the New York City Department of Finance offices in Manhattan and Brooklyn and the records office of Broward County, Florida. Special thanks to Kevin Bailey, an archivist at the Dwight D. Eisenhower Presidential Library, for unearthing papers related to Patricia's investment in the film *John Paul Jones*.

Warm embraces to my brother, Alan, who explained mortgages and deeds to me. No repayment is possible to my sister, Phyllis, and others who listened to my endless Patricia anecdotes, especially Jonah and Michael Quinn and Paul DuCett.

My deepest appreciation to my agent, Matthew DiGangi, for believing in Patricia and me, and to my editor, Amanda Lanne-Camilli. Without them, this book would not be possible.

Introduction

Joan Crawford, an Oscar winner for her portrayal of the fictitious Mildred Pierce, was fascinated by Patricia Murphy, said the decorator Carleton Varney, a friend of both. The star and the restaurant owner may never have met, but Crawford knew Patricia Murphy's Candlelight Restaurants. In 1961, at the pinnacle of her success, Murphy published her partly concocted memoir, but a plunge lay ahead. Uncannily, she followed Mildred Pierce's trajectory.

Murphy's life, unlike the 1945 film noir *Mildred Pierce*, was not a murder mystery. It more closely resembled the plot of the movie's source material, written four years earlier, a novel by James M. Cain. Like Cain's Mildred, Patricia launched her chain of restaurants at an inauspicious time, the start of the Great Depression. Mildred was a suddenly single mother of two; Patricia was a daughter of a bankrupt Newfoundland merchant. Products of the middle class but desperate for cash, both initially spurned waitressing work. Mildred surrendered, donning the uniform but hiding it from her children. Patricia, fired from cashier and cafeteria jobs, would not hoist platters. Instead she enrolled in a storefront restaurant management school and learned how to be a boss.

Men helped both of them, and later helped to ruin them. A convenient bedmate bankrolled Mildred's first chicken-and-waffles joint in Glendale, California; Patricia opened a Brooklyn tea room with a small wad of cash from her hard-pressed father. Mildred Pierce, Inc., blew up when its founder stopped minding the store; a gold-digging second husband had distracted her, in league and in bed with her monstrous daughter. Patricia Murphy eventually relinquished control of her business to a reckless male manager who destroyed both the chain and himself.

And, at least in Patricia's view, two brothers betrayed her by setting up a rival restaurant, copying her format and menu while recruiting two sisters to their side.

Both Mildred and Patricia luxuriated in their temporary wealth. In this case, the film version of Mildred more closely resembled Patricia. Clad in fur and dripping with jewels, Patricia reveled in visiting the New York and Florida restaurants where her name flashed in lights. In a flourish Hollywood failed to imagine, she loved arriving unannounced in her private plane. But just as Glendale-bred Mildred failed to win acceptance in Pasadena society, Irish-descended Patricia failed, by a hair, to breach the inner social circles of Palm Beach or Manhattan.

The life stories of Mildred Pierce and Patricia Murphy raise issues of economics, class, gender, and ethnicity in midcentury America. They are compelling stories about two remarkable women—one of them real.

CHAPTER I

Truth or Dare

Avoid flurried manner, even when you must work fast.

—Patricia Murphy's manual for employees, 1930

It was exactly one week before Thanksgiving, 1961. The windows of Macy's flagship store in New York's Herald Square would soon be festooned with more than 100,000 red and green Christmas ball ornaments and three miles of tinsel. Store holiday displays all over Manhattan were going to be unabashedly traditional, ending years of experimentation with modernist and Asian-inspired trends, prompting a newspaper to declare, "It's Chic to Be Corny."[1]

For now, other delights enticed passersby from behind the plate glass. Mannequins wore Botany knit jackets over knee-length skirts, the Jackie Kennedy look. Guitars and Hammond organs were arranged under a banner announcing that the kids from *The Sound of Music* would take part in the Macy's Thanksgiving parade. Two windows on Broadway showcased washer-dryers, hi-fi systems, and TV consoles. The one-stop-shopping craze had seized the suburbs, and even here in Manhattan, Macy's boasted of carrying everything from rings to refrigerators.

On this day, November 17, Macy's had something extra. An entire window on Thirty-Fourth Street was devoted to the display of a single book whose author would autograph copies at Macy's that evening. The title was *Glow of Candlelight*, and the author was Patricia Murphy, a restaurateur—or "restauratrice," as her publisher described her—who over the previous three decades had opened five restaurants in Greater New York and Florida and financed one in London. All had thrived, particularly the Patricia Murphy's Candlelight Restaurant in Yonkers, recently

1

expanded to thirteen acres of hills, gardens, artificial ponds and enormous parking lots. Still, an entire Macy's window was a lot of hoopla for the autobiography of a woman known best for her popovers—airy rolls served from bottomless baskets by roaming, attractive "popover girls."

By 4:30, two hours before the autographing session in the book department, Kay Vincent, the author's publicist, was a smartly dressed mass of nerves. Not that she displayed any as she left the department store's executive office. Everything was ready for the 5:30 press conference that would precede the book signing. Patricia's catering staff had laid out china, silver, a sumptuous buffet, and, of course, orchids.[2]

The author, Kay knew, would be oh-so-slightly late for the press, though her Manhattan penthouse was just a short limo drive from the store. As one of Patricia Murphy's pilots would later say about her penchant for flying short distances more easily driven, with Patricia it was all about The Arrival.[3]

Kay passed the typing pool, blowing kisses to the clerks. Everybody knew her; she had headed up Macy's public relations department until the previous year. Patting her chignon to check for wayward hairs, she rode the escalators down to the fifth floor, digging in her purse for the notes given her by Patricia, a warm friend and congenial drinking buddy, but a demanding client. Even the *Trib*'s horticulture editor, though mesmerized by Patricia's gardens, found her to be "an intense lady."[4]

There were the notes, green scrawls, and doodles. Proudly Irish and still steaming from an ancient and ambiguous anti-Irish slight she mentioned twice in her book (Howard Barnes, Kay's left-leaning husband and the book's ghostwriter, had egged her on there), Patricia always wrote in green.

Green ink! Would there be enough in Patricia's fountain pen for ninety minutes of autographing? Suppressing an urge to scramble up the moving escalator and grab one of those typist's phones, Kay instead looked out at the store and admired her handiwork. She had done enough—an entire Macy's window dedicated to the book, full-page ads in *The New York Times* and other papers announcing the event, and, floating past Kay as she descended, posters bearing Patricia's image in a dozen departments.

"MEET AN ALMOST-LEGENDARY LADY IN AN ABSORBING AND INSPIRING BOOK," the posters demanded.[5] Maybe that "almost" had been a mistake, but it was too late to change it now. And, frankly, Patricia was no William L. Shirer or Theodore White, whose *Rise and Fall of the Third Reich* and *The Making of a President, 1960* filled large swaths of the bookcases lining the walls of the book department. Hell, she wasn't even that doctor who wrote *Calories Don't Count*, which one ample-figured Macy's shopper was at this moment taking to the register.

However, Patricia Murphy was rich. She had invested sixty dollars in a failing Brooklyn restaurant at the start of the Depression and turned it into a fortune, exactly as the posters and book ads said. Plus, she threw fabulous parties, and knew people like Kay Vincent. The press would show up for Patricia's book launch to gobble jumbo shrimp and to say hi to Kay, who for years had been fashion editor of the *Herald Tribune*. When the *Trib* pushed her aside for that snarky young editor who wrote the Christmas-is-corny headline, Macy's snatched her up. It was Kay who decorated Macy's model home for the trade exhibition in Moscow, where Nixon and Khrushchev held their 1959 Kitchen Debate.[6]

Today she faced a tougher challenge: decorating the dowdy book department to Patricia Murphy's exacting standards. Piles of *To Kill a Mockingbird* were swept off tables. Damask tablecloths were laid down and topped with candelabra and orchid arrangements. These, as well as popovers, were the signature emblems of Patricia Murphy's Candlelight restaurants. Candles and flowers, along with costumed employees and a constant round of seasonal celebrations, gave her eateries "atmosphere," a feeling that one had stepped into a world beyond everyday experience. That's what kept the public coming.

They were coming here, too. Kay, after moderating the well-attended press conference upstairs returned to a mobbed book department. An announcement was made, and a short, middle-aged woman took a seat at a table, between an elaborately carved candelabra and a tall vase of orchids. Interlocking gold hexagons marched across the woman's white jacket, worn over a sheath of the same brocade. The top of her small pillbox hat echoed the pattern in miniature.[7] Kay had been wondering why Patricia insisted that the candles be lit. They were a fire hazard, and the flames were barely visible in the dull wash of Macy's fluorescents. Now, however, they worked their magic, brightening the gold of Patricia's clothes and jewelry.

A typical Patricia stroke of genius, Kay thought, to choose precisely the right outfit for the debut of a book titled *Glow of Candlelight*. The effect also softened her face, which on bad days—and there had been plenty of those since Patricia's second husband had suddenly died four years earlier—bore little resemblance to the portrait Patricia had commissioned for the book-jacket cover. Patricia was a failure at posing for pictures. The back of the jacket featured a nice candid of her with her dog. But the minute she became aware of the lens, she froze.

So instead of a photo, a painting dominated the cover of her book. It showed an elegant blond woman sitting among orchid plants in a full-skirted white evening gown. The person in the portrait resembled the screen goddess Lana Turner, whose stardom was then just beginning to wane, though the eyes were Patricia Murphy's. The artist was Jon Whitcomb, by that time a high-priced magazine and advertising illustrator, more accustomed to portraying glamorous young actresses like Debbie Reynolds and Natalie Wood than businesswomen who had just turned fifty-six—not fifty, as the dates and ages in her book suggested. She had been lying about her age since her first humble Brooklyn Heights tea room attracted press coverage with its enormous success.

The Patricia Murphy signing book after book for her adoring fans was somewhat heavier than the one in the portrait, although the real Patricia had been dieting like mad. She'd been subsisting on breakfasts of tomato juice and half a cup of coffee—half, because once sipped midway, a full cup failed to meet her exacting temperature standards.[8]

Whitcomb had captured, though idealized, her heart-shaped face with high forehead and semi-circles of brow over eyes set so wide they appeared serene, though that was not an adjective to describe Patricia, who invited comparisons to a hummingbird.[9] She had a decent nose, but candlelight and lipstick couldn't help the small, taut mouth. That's where all the tensions of running her businesses showed. When Patricia needed a drink, lines formed and made her jaw area look sectional, like the face of a marionette.

Kay stood to the side of her friend and client, enduring Patricia's rearrangement of stacked books already carefully arranged, and praying, if that was the word for it, that Patricia would not cross herself in secular Macy's, where God took second place to Mammon. Patricia was not particularly religious, but incurably superstitious, and her behavior could verge on the eccentric.

But Patricia looked fine, beaming at the adoring fans who had waited patiently in line, first at the register and then in front of her table. She was in her element, as was her audience. Folks intolerant of long lines were unlikely to have dined at a Patricia Murphy's Candlelight Restaurant, which at times sat ten thousand people on a single day. When tour buses jammed the parking lots, and there was no hope for tables, meals were beautifully plated and served on the buses.

Unwound, she more closely resembled her portrait, the image she had cultivated for decades. "It was a glamour picture, and it was somewhat different from what she looked like," said her interior decorator, Carleton Varney, "but Patricia Murphy was a fantasy. She was the hostess in the restaurant."[10]

She also had astounding commercial instincts. Sentimentally, the book linked her midlife interest in horticulture to memories of her mother's rock garden in Newfoundland. It also cloaked her profitable restaurant gift shops in family tradition. Her father had run a general store in a fishing village, selling everything from needles to anchors.

Like much of the book, that was partly true. But in business, Patricia looked forward, not back. She had anticipated middle-class flight from city to suburbs and the jet-age potential of Florida. The Fort Lauderdale restaurant was smaller than the one in Yonkers, but she had grand plans for it. Having already invested heavily in renovating and landscaping the Fort Lauderdale restaurant, she planned to persuade the city to let her develop the marina with a hotel and shopping center.

A reporter once called her "five feet of Irish dynamite." True enough. Wherever Patricia went, explosives and earthmovers followed.[11]

Meanwhile, in Fort Lauderdale and Yonkers, gardens and gift shops, not to mention the bars, gave people something to do and a reason to spend while they stayed on site, ready to refill the table seats. Patricia had fixed things so that hundreds, even a thousand, were often waiting for tables, ensuring a steady stream of revenue.

Kay watched the stacks of *Glow* disappear as Patricia bent forward to listen to her fans give their names or the names of intended gift recipients. She scrawled as they talked about their grandfather's birthday, celebrated in the Yonkers restaurant back in the fifties when it first opened, or asked if the live animals would be in the Christmas crèche again this year.

Two older women had taken the IND train from Brooklyn. Oblivious to the crush of people behind them, they were regaling Patricia with their memories of the first Candlelight as it looked in its infancy. Those early months, when it was down in the Henry Street basement, before all the expansions upstairs—how tasteful and artistic Patricia had managed to make it look. And how surprising to read in the Macy's ad that she'd been juggling twenty cups and saucers among thirty-six seats. That didn't mean the cups hadn't gotten a thorough wash, did it? They had been so pleased that Patricia, a girl with manners and refinement, had taken over that dreadful place so they could be sure it was clean, not like when that man was running it, that Italian . . .

Kay chuckled to herself as Patricia interrupted and deftly changed the subject. Even with Kay mediating, ghostwriting the book had not always gone smoothly for her husband. But Patricia's views on working-class people and oppressed groups had met with Howard Barnes's approval. That, along with friendship, had prompted Howard to take the task on. For four decades Howard had been the film and theater critic for the *Herald Tribune*, but he was also the son of an unschooled farm boy who had managed to become a Stanford professor. With Patricia's schedule allowing no time to keep a journal or write letters too fat for a small baronial envelope, this book was her only chance for a literary memorial.

Patricia's story wasn't quite the rags-to-riches tale the ads and jacket copy promised. Her merchant father had done well and sent her to Catholic boarding school before the family fell on hard times, so it was more like Frances Hodgson Burnett's *A Little Princess*, about the English girl whose wealthy father died in India, leaving her to starve temporarily in her former private school's attic. Still, for all of Patricia's furs, jewels, and lap dogs, she bristled at injustice. Howard had happily crafted sentences from her complaint about the real estate broker who, on learning that "Pat Murphy" was no burly Irishman but rather a tiny female, laughed her out of his office.

"Aside from being young and tiny, I was blackballed in advance by my sex," Howard quoted Patricia, perhaps slightly radicalizing her late-1930s anecdote. "The fact that women are discriminated against has always made me mad, and I've championed scores of girls and women who were looking for careers ever since that time."

Or at least, Kay thought, girls and women attractive enough to be relish girls, who like their popover counterparts, visited tables with condiments and pickles. And Patricia had certainly courted women restaurant-goers. She'd defied the East Side snobs who initially spurned her second restaurant, on Manhattan's East Sixtieth Street. The clubwomen claimed that the salad bar—eighty-five cents for half a lettuce head crammed with salmon and topped with hard-boiled egg, plus beverage, and dessert[12]—attracted the so-called riff-raff, namely salesgirls and secretaries working in the area.

"I encouraged the patronage of white-collar working girls, who were just becoming a factor in the restaurant luncheon trade," is how Howard helped phrase Patricia's whiskey-fueled recollections. Patricia could match Howard and Kay drink for drink.[13] Her book boasted that she spiked watermelons for unsuspecting guests. She never made cracks about the Barnes's alcohol intake or that time Howard had wrapped his car around a tree in Connecticut.[14] Patricia liked a good time.

Beaded, bejeweled, and doused with her own brand-name fragrance, Patricia also liked to flaunt her wealth and accomplishments. To enter the Fort Lauderdale market, she flew its mayor up to Yonkers on her private plane. Patricia had bid nearly a third of a million dollars for a ten-year lease on a city-owned yacht club, and Mayor John V. Russell boarded the small aircraft to verify her credentials. The young Democrat, friendly with JFK, wished to see with his own eyes the floral-fabulous Westchester dining place pictured on hundreds of thousands of postcards.[15] Patricia's business dispensed the cards to queued-up patrons and spent $10,000 a year on three-cent postage. Many mailed the cards to friends hoping to instill envy.

Kay didn't envy Patricia's restaurant staff that day. They swore that Patricia could simultaneously count the house while noticing the customer in a distant corner who needed butter.[16] Yet her employees seemed more respectful than terrified; Patricia treated others with dignity. Howard pointed out that Russell was on the right side of the civil rights struggle in Florida. The Candlelight hosted Urban League dinners and catered wedding receptions for black couples. A black church had chosen Patricia's restaurant for a celebration of the first anniversary of school desegregation.[17] The young Floridian may have found this remarkable, coming from the segregated South.

Well, the popover girls were still lily white, and Negroes were just another market, mused Kay. Between them and the Filipino waiters, Patricia was probably providing plenty of conversation for the out-of-towners who took tour buses to the Westchester Candlelight, the official name of her Yonkers location because the county name carried cachet, while the city suffered stigma. As for Patricia, Kay knew that, despite the green ink and the all-out St. Patrick's Day celebrations at her restaurants, she was dying for WASP acceptance and buying her way into Palm Beach society.

Kay noticed that the pair from Brooklyn had emerged from the autograph line and were now browsing the wall shelves. Would they choose something by J.D. Salinger, perhaps? Kay doubted it. She shared Patricia's dim view of this pair's "staid borough of churches," as Howard wrote, quoting her almost directly, but she was happy that as publicist, she'd forced the two of them to omit the worst jabs. Patricia could nurse a grudge like nobody else—that's why she was still speaking to only one of her six siblings—but you couldn't publish this stuff and expect folks from Brooklyn to buy your book.

Kay recalled the passage she'd noticed in the final manuscript, right before the book went to press. She and Howard were at their weekend home in New Hartford, Connecticut, when it leapt out at her. It was well worth the cost of a prolonged long-distance call. The Prentice-Hall editor had been persuaded to soften Patricia's final kiss-off to Brooklyn, calling it "provincial" and "prejudiced."[18]

As for Patricia's telling of her love–hate relationship with the nuns, Kay let it stand. Kay, too, had been educated by the Sisters of Mercy before engaging in antics like racing a horse around the ballroom of the Hotel Astor for a Newspaper Woman's Club event. For Manhattan-born Kay, Catholic school academics had laid the foundation for journalism. For Patricia, a convent school for middle-class Newfoundland girls had created a restauratrice who played classical piano and arranged flowers, skills that endeared her to the Brooklyn Heights burghers.

Patricia could not only ride horses but buy them. She had a show jumper, Treaty Stone in Ireland, as well as a rented castle in County Mayo, part of her self-prescribed rehab regimen after the death of her beloved second husband, Captain James E. "Rosie" Kiernan. Oh, the parties they hosted when the captain was alive! There had been the one at their Florida estate when Rosie—nicknamed for his rosy complexion, extra rosy *that* night—filled the swimming pool with orchids and topped it with Plexiglas for a dance floor. What a loss that had been for Patricia, finding a man secure enough not to mind becoming "Mr. Patricia Murphy," then losing him after only nine years of marriage.

Patricia was rapping out one of her requests, which, no matter how politely phrased, always sounded like a close-drill order. This one was something like, "May I have another pen, Mrs. Fitzgerald?" Patricia always used the honorific with her front-office employees, and many of them called her Mrs. Kiernan. Not her general managers, though. Not her right-hand man, John Rogers, who called himself her brother-in-law, though he was related only to one of her estranged brothers, nor Greg Camillucci, who had worked his way up from busboy to general manager. Both were listed, along with Kay and Howard, on the acknowledgments page of the book, though Greg's last name was misspelled, Kay had noticed earlier in the day.

There was nothing to be done about that, and it wasn't significant like the Brooklyn gaffe. That one would have cost sales. The Camillucci misspelling was not an entirely wrong name, as when Howard somehow typed "Edward Cabana" instead of "Alexander Cabana, Jr." for the name of Patricia's pilot. Kay had fixed that, too. Maybe the mistake revealed Howard's unconscious discomfort with the Big Lie: that Patricia, along with running restaurants and raising flowers, often flew the plane herself.[19]

Kay and Howard were her co-pilots on that fib, letting it stand because it helped sell the publisher on the book. They were news people, and they knew what made a story. Restauratrice wasn't enough, no matter what obstacles Patricia had overcome. They also had to make her an aviatrix. It was in the book, which opened with Patricia surmounting her grief at the loss of her husband by flying in the clouds, and in all the publicity materials which, as Kay knew, most newspapers would copy verbatim.

There had been one more last-minute manuscript fix. Howard had Patricia writing, "ours was a large family" after fifty-odd pages in which she had mentioned only one of her three sisters—the youngest, Sheila—and none of her three brothers.

Right now, Kay wished she could bunch up Patricia's table linen to gag a threesome from Long Island's North Shore, who for some reason were Christmas shopping at this Macy store instead of the one near them in Roosevelt Field and had recognized the name on the posters.

"We were at your Manhasset restaurant last Mother's Day. Just lovely as usual,"[20] said one, referring to a Patricia Murphy's Candlelight Restaurant that Patricia had sold seven years before and had nothing more to do with, as she made clear in a message printed on her menus. That line of text had spawned lawsuits, appeals, and enmity. Kay held her breath, as the Long Islanders waded deeper into yet more perilous waters.

"Of course, we love your sister Lauraine's place, too. We're there even more, maybe twice a month."

"Only because it's closer to Lord & Taylor," interjected one of the speaker's friends. She was, perhaps, a more intuitive sort who had seen the flicker of irritation pass over Patricia's face, looking a little tired now from the labor of inscribing books, the shedding of facial powder, and the mention of the Lauraine Murphy restaurant.

Kay hovered as Patricia recovered her composure, asked the Long Islanders for their names, and gave them her autograph. She had never spoken to her siblings again, but Kay knew they were always with her, gnawing at Patricia's gut. In the Murphy family's version of the Cold War, the dueling siblings practiced industrial espionage on one another, pumping their mother and Sheila for news of the other side, or visiting Patricia's Yonkers restaurant when they knew she'd be away. Her brother Vincent, managing Westchester at the time, had given them the all-clear. He was a double agent—staying on with Patricia for several years while secretly investing in Lauraine Murphy's before eventually joining the others in Long Island.

The mutinous quartet couldn't have missed the ads for this event, and the press conference had been well attended, ensuring plenty of reviews. The women's page writers and book reviewers had closed their notepads and left after the conference, but Kay spied an editor from the industry trade bible, *Publishers Weekly*, still lurking on the fringes of the thinning crowd. He had already taken some pictures. Did he plan to stay until the bitter end?

"It could be setting a record of some sort," was his answer to Kay's query.

As it turned out, it had. At eight o'clock, the last autograph seeker straggled out of the department. The cashiers began proofing their registers, and while Patricia's private secretary and other minions imported from Yonkers moved the furniture back into place and packed away candlesticks and table cloth, Patricia personally counted the few books remaining before they went into boxes. As always, Kay admired Patricia's swift calculations.

Between chatting, accepting compliments, and fending off uncomfortable questions, Patricia had autographed 400 books in ninety minutes. Added to the 950 she'd signed for pre-publication mail orders, plus 200 more for Macy's to keep on hand, she'd made history.

The man from *Publishers Weekly* confirmed the numbers with the department manager. Yes, it was indeed a record for autographed copies sold by the store. Yes, this made it the number one bestseller at Macy's, over Shirer, Turner, Lee, and the diet doctor.

On December 18, his trade weekly ran a piece that placed Patricia's accomplishment alongside others who had broken records for sales of autographed book copies. Those others included former President Harry S. Truman, who had signed four thousand copies of his autobiography, *Years of Decision*, at a hotel in his native Kansas City and baseball Hall of Famer Bob Feller, who had inscribed three thousand copies of *Strikeout Story* in Cleveland, where he was then playing for the Indians. And at Macy's rival, Gimbels, Democratic Party kingmaker and former U.S. Postmaster James E. Farley had equaled Patricia's numbers with his 1948 autobiography.

But, remarked an astonished *Publishers Weekly*, "what seems to be unusual about the sales of the Murphy book is the fact that the author is neither a nationally known nor even a well-known local figure. . . . She is a restaurateur whose hobby is gardening." The report—perhaps trying to unravel the mystery—went on to mention that her book included not only her life story, but also gardening tips, recipes, and full menus for meals and entertaining.[21]

In truth, the throngs had shown up for the woman, not the recipes. Patricia Murphy had built herself into a brand, so valuable that the buyers of her Brooklyn and Long Island restaurants continued to use all or part of her restaurant name, paying handsomely to do so. It was a name that sold not only meals—"luxury dining at budget prices," as her menus put it—but also her Patricia Murphy's Green Orchid bath oils and perfumes, on display at her New York and Florida gift shops.

The packing up was almost finished, but Patricia conferred with her Westchester staff for a few minutes. She wanted to make sure the new menus had come back from the printers, listing her book above the soups and appetizers to tell customers they could buy it in the gift shops, the restaurant lobbies and the Yonkers greenhouse.

Was it on the Florida menus, too? Patricia's weary secretary nodded. Kay put her arm around Patricia and steered her toward the elevator.

Macy's hired elevator operators long after self-service elevators became available. That was the kind of touch that pleased Patricia. "She was a socially conscious gal, wouldn't be seen in Manhattan without a hat and gloves," recalled Camillucci, her former manager. Referring to an upscale store that had once competed with Macy's, he added, "She wouldn't go to Best and Company when they got rid of the elevator girl and you had to push the buttons yourself."[22]

They ascended to the executive offices on the thirteenth floor so Patricia could retrieve her fur and get some rest. One of the men from Yonkers was already trotting down chilly Seventh Avenue in search of the limo that had been circling Herald Square for hours. The driver was waiting to take Patricia back to Sky High, her penthouse at 1136 Fifth Avenue, later to become the fictional residence of the rich girl in the twenty-first-century book and television show, *Gossip Girl*.

Kay had even worked Sky High into the book publicity campaign, convincing gardening columnists to cover Patricia's stupendous terrace gardens. As far back as July, Patricia was getting coverage of her hibiscus, azaleas, her many national and international gardening awards and, by the way, her upcoming book.

There would be many articles and honors to come. Patricia had already been named Woman of the Week by a New York paper, the *Journal-American*, and Woman of the Month by the American Woman's Association of New York. *Life* magazine had run a full-page photo of the Miss Patricia Murphy dahlia. A few months after her book appeared, American Express would select the Westchester Candlelight as Restaurant of the Week. *Current Biography 1962* would devote one of its rare slots for women to a profile of her. Papers across the nation would run features about her and the book, and no one would question her pilot's license.

The book would soon cede its number one sales slot at Macy's to national bestsellers, but it remained a favorite in small-town women's book clubs. Two years after publication, it was still the top nonfiction title in Amsterdam, New York. Even five years later, a woman in Statesville, North Carolina, chose to review the book for her club, never mind that times had moved on and Jacqueline Susann's *Valley of the Dolls* would be another choice at the same meeting.

But there was none of that to temper the triumph of the two women basking in the afterglow of the *Glow* party, kicking off their shoes in an office shortly before the notorious Macy's Dobermans were due to start patrolling the empty store. A dog lover, Patricia hoped her limo wouldn't be located too fast because she wanted to meet the Dobermans.

One of her first extravagances had been to rent the yards adjacent to her own in Brooklyn for a dog run.

Almost every family in Newfoundland had dogs, Patricia thought, as she shrugged into her mink and pulled on her gloves. Newfoundlanders used dog sleds in the winter if they couldn't afford horses. There had been no roadmap to point her toward success. In fact, she came from a place that barely had roads.

CHAPTER 2

Patricia of Avalon

Never stand idle like a wooden doll.

—Patricia Murphy's manual for employees, 1930

Everyone knew the Newfoundland Reid Company never should have built a railway through the Gaff Topsails, but here was young Patricia Murphy, trying to get home from her boarding school for Christmas, stuck on a train. The year was 1920, a record-setter for fierce winter weather, and a blizzard had been raging for days. The conductors said they must stay put until the rotor plow could come out from Bishop's Falls and ram through it with steam. In the meantime, there was plenty of coal for the furnaces on the passenger cars, so no one was going to freeze. Or so the passengers had been told, though some were growing skeptical.

The railroad was equipped for delays here because they happened all the time; the Topsails were knobby promontories, 1,700 feet high, and deep snow was the norm. Plows attached to the coal-fired locomotives cleared much of the track as the train looped its way across Newfoundland, from Port aux Basques in the southwest to the capital, St. John's, in the southeast. Above the Barrens, regular plows were of no use. Here, nature issued the train orders.

Patricia had celebrated her fifteenth birthday two months earlier. She'd spent three years as a boarder at St. Michael's Convent and Academy in St. George's, on the wild western coast of the island. In the fall, the 450-mile trip from her village to her school had taken the scheduled nineteen hours. Patricia wrote that this journey back for the Christmas holidays would last twenty-one days, but the truth was probably closer to one week. The blizzards of 1920 created a series of crises for the passengers, including food shortages, but the most notable train delay lasted days, not weeks.[1]

Patricia was only six hours into her journey before reaching the infamous Topsails, where the winds screamed like banshees, and the train seemed to slip into a long icy tunnel. It had halted there and not budged since. The winds had since died down, but the train remained encased in snow. Patricia looked up from the cup of tea she was idly stirring. The chief steward in his black pants and white linen tunic—not quite as starched and clean as it had been a few days ago—was taking bets on whether this run would go slower than the legendary one in 1900. Back then, when he was a young pantry man, winds had blown the train right off the track. Miraculously, no one was injured, but the mail and baggage cars had been torn apart.

He was using one of the order books to record the bets. Patricia exchanged smiles with the St. Michael's classmate sitting across from her and politely declined to place one. What would the nuns say? At any rate, she'd run out of pocket money. But teenaged Patricia did not mind being included with the adults in the games, distractions, and near-death experiences that were part of growing up in early twentieth-century Newfoundland.

The tea and her seal-skin coat were warming her. The train crew had taught her how to snowshoe, and today the chief steward had taken her on a tour of the nearest village while some of his colleagues hunted in the subfreezing barrens. One of the trainmen had brought down a caribou, some men in second-class had helped dress it, and the cook was now converting it into a menu item.

Thanks to the railway workers' marksmanship, the dining car could continue to feed twenty-four people at a time. Melted snow provided water to wash the crested china and silver that Patricia admired. Soon she would vacate her seat for other diners and return to the coach car, maybe to join those traveling salesmen in a round of casino, which they'd taught her to play.

Before taking her last sip of tea, Patricia plucked the menu from its sterling-silver prongs to study it again. The fresh fish, sirloin, ham, mutton, and eggs had long since run out, and the vegetable selection, always scant, was now nonexistent. There were still sardines, though, for twenty cents, and the tab for these many extra meals would be paid by "H.D.," as the crew referred to Harry Duff Reid, president of the railroad. Playing cards, priced at twenty cents on the menu, had been given out as a holiday gift.

The air in Patricia's second-class sleeping berth was stale except where cracks let in the chill winds. In her autobiography, she wrote that her father was "the leading citizen of Placentia, sharing high honors of course with the priest, the doctor and the magistrate."[2] Nonetheless, second class satisfied most passengers for a trip that was usually completed overnight, and Patricia's father, Frederick Francis Murphy, was acutely aware of prices.

Patricia would never forget this arduous journey, and how she and her fellow Newfoundlanders made the best of it. Books about the cross-island train tell how the baggage car was sometimes cleared during delays, with passengers and crew producing guitars and accordions for hours of dancing.[3] Patricia wrote:

> Physical hardship, desolate wastes, even being alone, were things I grew up with, things I accepted as a matter of course. It was a tough training, but it stood me in good stead when I had to fend for myself and survive in a grueling and hazardous occupation. Many years ago people talked about the virtues of a log cabin background on the American frontier. My own beginnings were not very different.[4]

There were, in fact, log cabins in Newfoundland then—locals called them "tilts"—but Patricia didn't live in one. Her house no longer stands, but by ranking her father socially alongside the magistrate, William F. O'Reilly, she left evidence of what it looked like. Today the Placentia Area Historical Society has turned the O'Reilly House into a museum. It is a large, handsome Victorian house built in the Queen Anne style, with huge double bay windows, a handcrafted staircase, stained-glass windows, and decorative moldings. Placentia has a rich history of European settlement dating back to the 1500s and was once the French capital of Newfoundland. By the time Patricia was born, most residents were of Irish descent.

The O'Reilly and Murphy families were bound by class and heritage. When Patricia's grandfather, James, died in 1911, Magistrate William O'Reilly assessed the value of the Murphy home and business at $2,750, a considerable sum at the time. Patricia's family home would have been comfortable even during that snowy winter holiday, with four fireplaces roaring.

Patricia yearned for those fireplaces as she finally stepped off the train at a junction station nearly a week after boarding it. Dirty and disheveled, she braced herself for a wait of several more hours in the drafty station until the Placentia Branch Line train would take her the final fifty miles home. But railway telegraph operators had kept her family informed of the train's movements, and her father had come to meet her in his horse-drawn sleigh. He embraced her in a bear hug and spun her around, his customary expression of enthusiasm.

Snuggled under layers of fur harvested by the sealing expeditions sponsored by her father, Patricia chatted easily with him about the trip as the horses pulled them home. It was a journey of several hours by sleigh, but Patricia delighted in it. She wrote of being her father's favorite child.

Entering the house, Patricia was greeted by two sisters, Lauraine and Maude, relatively close to her in age. Less than two years younger than Patricia, Lauraine was her close friend and confidante. Nicknamed "Lonnie," Lauraine was also home from a boarding school, though not a very distant one. Both Lonnie and Maude, five years younger than Patricia, attended a convent school only eighty miles away, in St. John's. They could easily take the train home on weekends.

A boisterous crew of little brothers joined in the homecoming celebration. The oldest, James, was nine when Patricia arrived from her prolonged train adventure. Barely one year younger than Maude, Jim had a close, if somewhat abrasive, relationship with her. His preferred playmate was Vincent, then six, who idolized his older brother.

The Murphys' school-aged sons were attending classes locally, knowing they would eventually join the boarders at St. Bonaventure's. Jim and Vincent already knew which of the Jesuit brothers to fear or revere; their father and Uncle Phil were St. Bon's alumni. Packing children off to boarding school was customary for the middle class in Newfoundland, then a British dominion not yet confederated with Canada.

The small boys of the family were Shannon, four, and two-year-old Kevin. Passionately devoted to her mother, though never quite certain of her approval, Patricia hugged Nana, as she called her mother, tearfully. Despite the demands of children, Nana always managed to look impeccable, bandbox-perfect. As quickly as possible, Patricia extricated herself from the crowd to rush off and attend to her own grooming.

Of the 120 households in Placentia, the Murphys' home was one of the few with indoor plumbing. Most families lived in cramped two-story homes huddling around the kitchen in winter, as there were no upstairs fireplaces. With luck, some fathers found work in the long cold months as seal hunters or lumberjacks. Families raised animals and planted gardens to feed themselves. Even into the twentieth century, women sewed their family's clothes and sometimes spun their own yarn.

For their livelihood, most families depended on fishing. Back then, Placentia Bay swarmed with cod. Its early twentieth-century summers were a whirl of activity. Nearly every male villager went out in small boats with lines or traps, returning several times daily with cod to be salted and cured by small communities of workers. Women and children pitched in, feeding the fishing crews and helping to dry the cod, which had to be processed—"made," as the local people said—before sale. Wooden structures erected for fish processing dotted a rocky shore that is now a quiet beach.

A fisherman's fate depended on the price his catch fetched from the local merchant. In Placentia, that person was Patricia's father, Frederick Francis Murphy, known to all as Frank.

In August, the carts of fish arrived at James Murphy & Sons, founded by Patricia's grandfather, now run by her father and her Uncle Phil. Perhaps sensing that small-scale fishing and curing would be eclipsed by global events like international competition and centralized fisheries, Phil departed in 1920 to open a clothing store in St. John's. That left Frank to export the fish. The working class gave him dried cod, and he gave them store credit. Currency was scarce in Newfoundland, not incorporated into Canada until 1949. The store minted its own coins, for use only in the store.[5]

Patricia's father did not send his children to school to learn commercial skills. The sisters at the western Newfoundland convent did offer classes in typing and stenography, but Patricia never spoke of taking them. However, her father unwittingly taught her to be a boss.

The merchant was not a beloved figure in those parts, but Frank sought respect, not love, from the fishermen. A representative of the fish importers—the companies that would pay Frank, the middleman, for the catch—graded each cured fish by quality and paid for it accordingly. It was widely believed that the cullers, who were supposed to be independent of the merchants, in fact conspired with them to lower prices.

The government virtually insinuated such collusion years later, when Frank was called to testify before a commission investigating the collapse of the small-scale fisheries. His response was, "I am no man's servant." This did not really answer the question, as no one was suggesting that Frank had worked for the culler, but rather that the two had collaborated. Still, it was a dramatic statement that probably rang out over the room. It halted the line of questioning.[6]

Patricia would eventually supervise far more employees than Frank did, figuring out how to work with people of diverse backgrounds. The daughter who stepped off the train was not the same village girl who had enrolled in St. Michael's three years before, becoming the youngest of their boarding students. The rigorous train trip had filled her with admiration for the self-reliant Newfoundlanders who hunted for food and eventually dug out the train in a blinding snowstorm. However, Patricia's three years at the school had turned her into a bit of a snob, polite and gracious to the coach-class passengers she had met, and even danced with, on the train, but acutely conscious of their rough manners and lack of handkerchiefs. She had never spent so much time exclusively with people of her own class.

Once bathed and dressed in clean clothes, Patricia made a beeline for the piano in the parlor, eager to show off her improved musical skills. St. Michael's Convent and Academy had a strong teaching staff. The music teacher, Sister Xavier, invited examiners from Trinity College of Music in London to evaluate her students, with results released to the press.[7]

Food service is a tough business with a polished veneer, and Newfoundland turned out to be an apt training ground. Patricia's family lived in a rugged place where the middle class went to great pains to remind others of their refinement, whether this took the form of their dining-room china or the results of a music exam published in a local paper.

During vacations, Patricia loved helping her father in his business. Domestic life with her siblings lost its charm after a day or two. Restless after a morning helping her mother with the little ones, Patricia relinquished her duties to her younger sisters. Lena Foley, a servant two years younger than Patricia,[8] did the cleaning and most of the cooking. Patricia herself was a disaster in the kitchen, as she wrote in her autobiography. She was destined to become a restaurateur, not a chef. Bundling up against the cold, she made her way to her father's store, where she'd be of more use.

Though only a short distance from the house, Murphy & Sons was situated on a wharf on the other side of the Gut, a narrow opening to the harbor where the tides were fierce, and which had to be traversed by ferry. Today a lift-bridge connects the two sides, but back then Patricia had to wait for Thomas Kemp's ferry to take her across. The bay tended not to freeze over, an attribute that had attracted Basque, French, and English settlers since the 1500s.

Patricia crowded into the boat with some twenty other townspeople. They saluted her warmly, calling her "m'dear" and joking about her escape from the nuns as the waters raged around them. It was worse in late winter when large pieces of ice clogged the Gut, and the ferries couldn't run. To deliver shoes needed for a funeral, Frank Murphy once traversed the Gut by jumping from ice patch to ice patch, like the hero of a silent movie.

Patricia wondered what job her father would give her today. He had mentioned at the dinner table that a ship had arrived with goods from abroad, sabadilla powder for killing insects and Jamaican ginger. She might help check the quantities against the orders. But she hoped instead to work on *Murphy's Good Things*, a monthly publication that had served as the town's newspaper of record since Murphy & Sons had bought out the local paper and its printing press. In truth, it was just an advertising circular preceded by one page of news and opinion, written by her father. Her favorite job was writing obituaries—usually the top stories of the month and often the only ones.

Arranging interviews with survivors of the deceased was easy. This month's obituary was about a man who lived on this side of the Gut, so Patricia paused from her writing and typesetting duties to visit the family at their home. They were about to sit down to a meal of beans and seal flippers, the only food that many in Placentia could afford. The smell of cooked seal nauseated Patricia, but she smiled, graciously declined to share in the repast, and sat down to complete her reporting duties.

The task required the multi-dialectical skills that Patricia had acquired in her Placentia upbringing and honed at St. Michael's Academy. For the high-sounding words she liked to scatter around obituaries, she consulted the dictionary, but life itself taught her to comprehend the local variety of English. Today tourist shops are stocked with glossaries of Newfoundland sayings with their Standard English translations, meant to provoke laughs. "Oh me nerves," translates into "you're driving me crazy, "the arse is gone right out of 'er" means that things aren't so good, and "long may your big jib draw" is a wish for your good fortune. Patricia and other islanders of her class could negotiate between worlds.

As a busy restaurant owner, Patricia enlisted Howard Barnes's help with her book, but surviving documents show her own facility with words. In addition to teaching music, art, and needlework, St. Michael's Academy had a reputation for preparing students well for university admissions exams. In 1930 Patricia told the U.S. Census she'd attended some college. That was a stretch, but the rigors of her education gave it some basis.

The academy also offered windows on the world. Two of the nuns were Americans who had transferred to the Newfoundland convent from Providence, Rhode Island.[9]

Although isolated—it was so far from a hospital that it served as the area's infirmary during the 1918 Spanish flu outbreak—St. Michael's was a virtual Athens for young Patricia. Here she won praise for her piano playing and started to dream of a musical career and a life beyond her native fishing village.

She designed, landscaped, and populated her dreams with the help of society magazines lent to her by the Mother Superior of St. Michael's Convent and Academy. Before taking vows, Mother Aquinas had been a fine lady in her native Ireland, and she had brought a stock of Irish society magazines to Newfoundland. The pictures of Irish gardens and lavish homes left a lasting impression on Patricia, who wrote in her autobiography about risking punishment to hide them from a priest.

Soon after Patricia's latest issue of *Murphy's Good Things* had gone to press, it was time for her to leave. The return rail trip to St. Michael's was less catastrophic than the one that had brought her home. Patricia made the trip many times over the next few years, sometimes partly by steamship, as did other students from all over Newfoundland. Many families saved for years to send their daughters to St. Michael's because the school was so well regarded.

Patricia completed her secondary schooling there, returning during vacations to scenes of domestic warmth and security. Her youngest sister, Sheila, was born in 1921. Seven Murphy children survived early childhood.

Unlike Patricia and her other older siblings, Sheila would never enjoy comfort and leisure in Newfoundland. In fact, there were times when little Sheila had to go without shoes. In the 1920s, Newfoundland was rocked by devastating economic changes. For reasons involving global competition and technological changes in food processing, the price of salted fish plunged. All along Placentia Bay, families abandoned the fishing and curing that had sustained them for generations. A Newfoundland diaspora scattered through Canada and the United States, as islanders left in search of work.

In 1927, Patricia's younger brothers were outside playing when Charles Lindbergh flew his plane, the *Spirit of St. Louis*, over Newfoundland on his way to completing the world's first solo transatlantic flight from New York to Paris. Patricia's brother, Jim, would always remember pausing from a game with younger brothers Vincent, Shannon, and Kevin to raise eyes to the sky.[10]

It was a luminous, inspiring moment for a family in deep trouble. Two years earlier, Frank Murphy had dissolved his business. The price for a hundredweight of cured cod had plummeted from fifteen to two dollars, and he could no longer pay his bills. His brother, Phil, once an equal partner in the business, had sold out earlier and departed for St. John's, where he operated a successful dry goods business in a prime location across from the post office.

But success eluded Frank Murphy after the fishing collapse, no matter how many schemes he tried, and there were many. Setting a model for his more fortunate, entrepreneurial daughter, he took bold risks. After dissolving Murphy & Sons, he tore down the store and shipped the salvaged lumber to Corner Brook on Newfoundland's west coast, not far from Patricia's former school. The government had invested in a pulp and paper mill there, and it was thriving, the island's sole pocket of industrialization and prosperity.

If Newfoundland then was the Wild West, Corner Brook was its Dodge City. Frank wanted part of this boomtown. Leaving his family in their Placentia home, now mortgaged to the hilt, Frank left them to use the lumber he'd shipped to build a new store on one of the streets that had sprung up in Corner Brook overnight. He hoped to be storekeeper to the former fishermen and seal hunters who had rushed there to seek fortune.

Patricia and the rest of her family joined Frank in Corner Brook for a summer. They would never return to their house in Placentia. The store failed, and the house was sold for barely enough to pay off the mortgages. Frank sent what was left on his shelves to St. John's, where he rented a storefront for his business and a place for his family to live.

So, as she had done during so many vacations, Patricia went to work at her father's store. But work was no longer a recreational activity. As her parents continued to send her siblings to their parochial schools in St. John's—perhaps paying tuition in the form of merchandise, as other families at the time did with agricultural produce—Patricia's labor became essential to her family's survival. Lauraine, who had also finished school, worked alongside her.

Their mother helped out when not occupied with the younger children. During these troubled years, the second-youngest child, Kevin, died. He had been named for another son lost to them previously.

Jim, the oldest surviving son, was still in high school but burdened by adult responsibilities. When not attending class, he worked with Patricia and Lauraine at the store, which eventually expanded into larger quarters. Jim also had a second job: searching for his father almost every night in the taverns of St. John's. Despondent after his business failure, Frank Murphy spent half the week sober and half of it drunk, Jim told his grandson. Nana habitually woke her oldest son in the middle of the night to send him out on this sad errand. "He was the nicest guy in the world," Jim said of his father, "but he went to pieces when things went bad."[11]

In bursts of manic energy, Frank would start yet another enterprise. In what would become a pattern, he again separated temporarily from his family, moving thirty miles outside St. John's to start a soda-bottling operation. Pumping an aeration device with his foot, Frank produced his own beverage line, one bottle at a time. With Jim joining him on a few weekends for seventeen-hour pumping shifts, the father and son produced a homemade concoction they labeled "Coca Cola," though it tasted more like ginger ale.

They made root beer, too, labeling it, "Budweiser," a name Nana remembered from a pre-Prohibition trip to New York. The Murphy family knew that names mattered in business.

With a truckload of soda finally pumped, Frank hired a driver to market it to Newfoundland's small towns, where deliveries of goods were rare, and people were starving for novelty if they weren't simply starving. Nonetheless, the driver returned three days later with no soda and no money. No explanation is available, but Jim's recollections of the event include a mention of problems with the unauthorized use of the Coca-Cola brand name.

Just one month short of graduation, Jim fell ill with typhoid fever. He recovered and got a summer job as mess boy on a Norwegian ship that plied the Great Banks off the Newfoundland coast, where the *Titanic* had sunk. Jim expected to resume school in the fall, take his final examinations, and receive his diploma.

That never happened. The Murphys could no longer afford to have all their children in school rather than working. Young Vincent, too, took a weekend job on the ship, despite his propensity for seasickness.[12]

For Patricia, these grim years in St. John's were lightened by visits to a luncheonette jammed between a pharmacy and a store near a streetcar stop. This unimposing place was called The Blue Puttee, a nickname for the Royal Newfoundland Regiment, the island's infantry, which suffered heavy losses during World War I. In addition to the emotional costs, the war had nearly bankrupted Newfoundland, contributing to its economic collapse in the 1920s.

However, worries were checked at the door of The Blue Puttee. Inside, there was always "a party atmosphere," as Patricia wrote in her autobiography, describing it as the template for her first restaurant. Though owned by a man, it was managed by Mary Powers, a native of Placentia. The St. John's of this era had more impressive eateries, like Wood's Candy Store and Dining Rooms, with its smartly uniformed staff and tall display windows heaped with delicacies. Nonetheless, Patricia took the shabby-genteel Blue Puttee as her model, perhaps thinking, "I can do that."[13]

In January of 1928, however, she was thinking not of restaurants but of music. Eager to escape the drudgery of store work and resume her piano studies, she accepted an invitation—arranged with some difficulty by her parents—from her father's uncle, Frank J. Murphy. This older Frank Murphy was a wealthy real estate investor who lived in Staten Island, New York. She could stay with him while she found some way to pay for piano lessons.

In the meantime, there would be one less mouth to feed. Unmarried at twenty-two, nicely built but not a raving beauty, Patricia had already overstayed at the family hearth. As impractical as a music career may have seemed to the Murphy family, Patricia's departure was an occasion for hope and optimism.

She left on a Saturday, January 21. Jim, peeling potatoes on the Norwegian ship, was at sea and could not see her off. The rest of the family put a "closed" sign on the store and walked down the hilly streets of St. John's to see her off on the *S.S. Nerissa*. In four days, it would arrive in New York. The crew, in dark double-breasted jackets adorned with brass buttons, was bustling around the deck, tending to the needs of passengers returning home after holiday visits to Newfoundland relatives.

As Patricia took her place on the deck, Nana, Lauraine, and Maude raised gloved hands, waving tear-soaked handkerchiefs at her. The youngest children, Shannon and Sheila, pestered their father with questions about icebergs and the *Titanic*. The *Nerissa*, built locally, had a reinforced hull, an icebreaker stern, and a crew of Newfoundlanders accustomed to facing nature's challenges. Icebergs were the least of the Murphy family's worries.

After the ship had steamed away, fourteen-year-old Vincent said his goodbyes and walked alone to another part of the harbor. It was Saturday, and Jim's ship, a much smaller vessel with a thirty-man crew, was due into port. Vincent would work in the mess and return late the next day. He knew that Jim, who hated the vulgar speech and rough manners of the sailors, would be glad to see him.

The ship lurched into view. Seized by the anticipation of seasickness, Vincent threw up. Patricia was lucky to get away from this, he thought as he wiped his mouth. The only good reason for a sea voyage was to go to the States, the land of the real Coca-Cola.

CHAPTER 3

New Girl

Do not risk insulting the dignity of a child, making him feel too young or too small.

—Patricia Murphy's manual for employees, 1930

Patricia descended upon America at gale force.

The wind had roared out of the west beginning around midnight on the third day of the voyage. By early morning of day four, it was breaking records and confounding new weather bureau instruments with speeds exceeding one hundred miles per hour.[1] The S.S. *Nerissa* rocked crazily over swollen seas, reversing direction to head for the nearest harbor. Until then, the ship had been steaming steadily along the New England coast, scheduled to reach New York the following day. Mainly a mail ship for much of the year, it was carrying only thirteen passengers, divided nearly evenly by gender. Patricia's female companions on that terrifying voyage included a domestic servant, two nannies, and two nurses.

The oldest of the women, a forty-one-year-old housewife named Ida Wilansky, was a native of Poland who had lived in St. John's for five years. Several Newfoundland-born passengers gave Brooklyn or Manhattan addresses as their permanent residences, including an iron worker, perhaps one of the many Newfoundlanders braving dizzying heights to chart new points along the evolving New York skyline. Other men on board were middle-aged buyers from St. John's, and a lone male U.S. citizen from New Jersey.

Patricia, who had spent the past few years toiling at her father's failed stores in Corner Brook and St. John's was the only passenger to give her occupation as "none." Conscious of her elite schooling, and proud of her musical skills, she was not about to peg herself as a shop girl. The whole point of going to New York was to turn nothing into something.

But all class and ethnic divisions blew away as the Atlantic reached a rolling boil that threatened to gulp down all vessels. Below deck, some passengers huddled in fear as captain and crew struggled to keep the ship righted. Patricia, often separated from her large family during her boarding-school years, envied the nannies. They were sisters, who, if the worst came, at least would go down together. She crossed herself continually, as she always did when death seemed near, but she did not huddle.

Danger was part of life in the small coastal communities of Newfoundland, known as outports. The news her father had printed in his Placentia gazette was often grisly. A neighbor returned from pallbearing duties at a funeral, set to work gathering firewood, and was discovered frozen to death on the forest floor.[2] Fishermen and seal hunters failed to return from expeditions. Lumberjacking had its own perils.

Hence, Patricia Murphy was well suited to brave the record-breaking gale of January 25, 1928, which ripped down the seacoast from Halifax to Baltimore. It tore cornices and roofs off buildings in New York, sank a dredge off Staten Island, and sent a water tower crashing down four floors of a book bindery in downtown Manhattan, miraculously sparing the lives of all 153 workers, most of whom were out at lunch.

Forty-two people were reported injured in New York, most by flying glass. The tempest smashed in some store windows and formed vacuums that sucked others off. News accounts noted a similar windstorm had occurred a generation earlier, but this one caused more bodily injury in New York City because of the proliferation of plate glass.[3]

Patricia wanted the things behind all that plate glass. The wind died down, the *Nerissa* arrived just one day late, on January 27, and she debarked at Ellis Island, enthralled by the Statue of Liberty, the majestic bridges spanning the East River, and the new art deco buildings with their novel setbacks flanking the older towers. New York had already swept up the broken shards and was glittering only with its customary marvels.

Patricia had ample time to enjoy the view. On Wednesday, customs officials had met only one ship before the high winds sent water spraying over the seawall of Manhattan's Battery, and all revenue cutters scurried back to their pier. Even now, Saturday, the lines for processing passengers and paperwork were longer than normal.

Patricia fashioned her world for the immigration officials, while they shaped theirs to prevailing prejudices. In the column of the passenger register headed "race or people"—defined by the U.S. government as a "stock from which aliens spring"—the response "Polish" had been typed for Mrs. Wilansky. The American officials crossed it out and scrawled in "Hebrew." Patricia, proud of her Irish ancestry, was categorized as "British."

Nationality, based on documents rather than opinion, went into a different column. Here "Poland" was entered for Ida Wilansky and "Newfoundland" for Patricia. In fact, she was not an alien at all and never should have been listed as such. Her father had been born in Somerville, Massachusetts, near Boston, where her grandfather had built ships for several years. As a child born abroad to a U.S. citizen before 1934, Patricia was an American citizen herself, although born and raised in Newfoundland.[4] It was easier not to argue, however.

Having given her name as Eleanor Murphy, although baptized less stylishly as Ellen, Patricia added a final fictitious flourish to the record by describing her destination, 71 Orange Street in Brooklyn, as the home of Mrs. W.B. Bailey, a "cousin."

Caroline Bailey, the fifty-six-year-old widow of a Newfoundland police sergeant, did in fact live at 71 Orange Street in Brooklyn Heights. She and her five grown children were descended from two generations of Anglican missionaries who had gone to Newfoundland from England, undeterred by the warnings of a bishop who in 1843 described the island as a rough place where a missionary would need "a facility to adapt his speech to the lowest grade of intellect . . . and a thorough preparation for controversy with the Romanist."[5]

Undaunted, Caroline's maternal grandfather, Oliver Rouse, set sail for Newfoundland shortly after those words were written. He spent nearly the rest of his life tending to the needs of the poor—dispensing medicine, comforting families through death and starvation, educating poor children, and occasionally scolding Catholic fisherfolk for laboring on the Sabbath. Caroline had been baptized in the Church of England by her own father, Reverend John Goodacre Cragg. Like his father-in-law, he had traveled across the Atlantic to spread the Anglican gospel.

Patricia Murphy, educated by the Sisters of Mercy and raised by a father schooled by the Jesuits, was no cousin of Caroline Bailey.

Tensions between Catholics and Protestants were part of New-foundland's fabric. The island's unofficial tricolor flag had lateral green and pink stripes, said to represent the Irish and the English, separated by a white stripe. The origins of the flag are unclear, but it was flown in places like Placentia, Patricia's mostly Catholic hometown, where the white stripe was said to represent a Catholic-brokered peace. Nonetheless, the Baileys were a friendly bunch who knew Patricia from St. John's and invited her to their Brooklyn home. Here, after all, they were all just Newfoundlanders among Yankees.

At any rate, Brooklyn Heights, with a houseful of Baileys—most of Patricia's generation—was far more enticing than finding a way to Staten Island, and an elderly great-uncle, after a storm-tossed sea journey. Patricia was soon taking a cab over the Brooklyn Bridge, marveling at the views and worrying about the fare. To pass muster at port, aliens had to present fifty dollars. Classified as a noncitizen, Patricia had exceeded the requirement, bringing several hundred gleaned from her father's cancellation of a life insurance policy.[6] He'd staked the family inheritance on Patricia, viewing it as an investment. She planned to spend it carefully, but the cab ride was a necessity. Contacted from a telephone booth, Maud Bailey said steamer trucks couldn't go on something called the IRT.

Although excited by Manhattan, where there seemed to be more motor cars on a single block than existed in all of Newfoundland, Patricia found Brooklyn Heights enchanting. Here, too, were banks, buildings, and bustle on the main commercial streets, but the taxi quickly left them behind. Now it was rolling past Italianate row houses of brick, granite, and brownstone behind black iron gates. They reminded her of the Irish homes she'd glimpsed in stealthy sessions at school, flipping through Mother Aquin's society magazines. The trees and neat small yards were bare now, but flower-loving Patricia was mentally forcing bulbs.

She discovered that she enjoyed arriving in these pleasant surroundings by taxicab. What a lot of people lived here, and some of them were out in the cold air, walking their dogs. Patricia liked having people look at her as she tipped the driver for helping her with her trunks. And she decided she'd like to live here, and own a dog.

Then Mrs. Bailey and Maud were sitting her down for tea. As they chatted, Patricia noted that everyone who wanted a job here seemed to have one. In Newfoundland, the widow Bailey had inspired pity; here she seemed to enjoy considerable social status. Although her children worked, they left work each day with heads high and hands clean. Maud, formerly a poorly paid teacher in St. John's, was now a stenographer at a charitable organization. She had the afternoon off. Annie, also a steno, would be home later. Sam, the only male in the family, had an excellent accounting position at a financial company.

Sam had settled here first, followed by Mrs. Bailey and the girls, if you could still call them that, now that Maud was thirty-one. The youngest daughter, Winifred, had introduced the family to Brooklyn years earlier, when she needed a spine operation and was sent to Long Island College Hospital here on the Heights. Now Winnie had her own home in the area, married to a Welsh widower seventeen years her senior, a former lodger at Mrs. Bailey's boarding house.

Mrs. Bailey did not need lodgers here. The granddaughter and daughter of clergymen would never have stooped to that, but the death of her police-sergeant husband had left his family adrift during Newfoundland's economic crisis. Desperate to support her family, she had come to St. John's from Bonavista, a small outport town. The Protestant Baileys and the Catholic Murphys, both loosened from their small-town, middle-class moorings, had met in the island's picturesque capital city. There, Frank Murphy had sought solace in the taverns, and Winnie Bailey had found a husband, but neither family could see a future.

Now Annie was all atwitter about her upcoming cruise to the Bahamas with brother Sam. The next year, she planned a visit to Aunt Jane in Ventura County, California. Patricia was listening and resolving to see those places as well.

They were prospering socially, too. The girls let Patricia know—not in a boastful way, of course—that they were related to the Damerels of Brooklyn, whose marriages and European tours were faithfully recorded in the local newspapers. In fact, three of the Damerel boys were now at Princeton, distinguishing themselves—or so said the *Brooklyn Daily Eagle*—in the classrooms and music studios and on the polo team.[7]

As recent immigrants from an obscure corner of North America, the Baileys had not attained the lofty status of these Damerel cousins, whose ancestors had emigrated directly from England to the United States in the early nineteenth century. Indeed, older Heights residents could point out a spot on Pacific Street where a George Damerel hardware store had once stood. Mrs. Bailey might never be invited to lectures by important explorers, as the Damerel wives were. Nonetheless, she could mention the connection at one of her Daughters of the British Empire bridge parties—or when Patricia, all ears, was visiting.

It was cold and snowy for the next few days, but that was nothing to Patricia, well equipped with furs from a fox farm once owned by her brothers and seal hunts once financed by her father. The subway was running, and Patricia rejoiced in the freedom of the nickel ride to Manhattan. Other friends from Newfoundland showed her around the city, or she simply found her way.

As she later told people, she never understood why one of her friends from back home hated asking people for directions. In this, like almost everything else, Patricia was fearless. Delighted with the glamorous sections of New York, but appalled by the dinginess and cheapness of shopping areas like Fourteenth Street, Patricia was going to use every possible resource to reach her destination.

It had been a long time since she had touched a piano. The Baileys had a radio instead. Because her ostensible purpose for coming to New York was to study music and make a career of it, and because she didn't expect the Baileys to feed and house her forever, Patricia made the dreaded telephone call to Staten Island.

Soon she was being picked up at the ferry landing by her father's uncle, Frank J. Murphy, who had a motor car, a house, and little use for Manhattan, as Patricia learned during the long drive to his house. He had arrived in 1902, recruited to work on the Flatiron building at Fifth and Broadway. Newfoundlanders were known for not fearing heights; well, they feared them, all right, but not as much as they feared starvation in Newfoundland.

Frank was the brother of James Murphy, founder of James Murphy & Sons, the business that Patricia's father had inherited and lost. Frank had met failure much earlier. He and his wife, Elizabeth, brought their daughter, Margaret, to the United States when she was a young adolescent. Margaret's most vivid memory of Newfoundland was eating lobster daily because that was all they had to eat.[8]

This place looks something like Newfoundland, Patricia might have thought, as they drove for miles toward her uncle's home, past stretches of forest and farmland interrupted now and then by clusters of houses.

Arriving at 5484 Amboy Road, Patricia was incredulous. Margaret, she knew, had a dry goods business, which Patricia envisioned in a commercial district like downtown Brooklyn. There it was, in her relatives' front yard. Directly in front of their two-story house stood a one-story wooden structure with a sloped roof and a sign proclaiming, "5¢ 10¢ 25¢ Store."

The pattern repeated next door, where a sign occupying almost the entire width of a house advertised Pittsburgh Paints.

"John Spollen," explained great-uncle Frank, following Patricia's astonished eyes. "My son-in-law's brother. They're painters. He sells paint and hardware." The daughter of a merchant—but one who operated behind a tasteful sign that read, "James Murphy and Sons," with no dollar signs or product names in view, Patricia doubted she could ever invite the Baileys to visit without suffering mortification.

Once inside the house, however, her superior feelings yielded to the warmth of her welcome. Frank's wife, Elizabeth, was perhaps only putting on a brave show; she and Frank asked some pointed questions about Patricia's plans to earn a living through music. But Margaret, who'd shaken off the Irish-like accent of her parents and spoke like a New Yorker, was a revelation.

Despite its brash exterior, the store seemed full of possibilities. It gave Margaret a sense of purpose and independence that Patricia envied. Formerly a bank stenographer, Patricia's cousin had remained single until age thirty-seven. Now she had two small children, but with the store attached to the house, could keep on working. She studied Esperanto and gardening. What's more, Margaret Murphy was the first woman in Staten Island to get a driver's license.[9]

There was plenty of room in the house for Patricia, but no place for her. While Margaret was busy with her young family and her store, Patricia had little to do. Everyone told her that Staten Island was enjoying growth and prosperity, like the rest of the city and nation. A new high school had opened with a capacity for more than a thousand students. Construction had begun on two bridges, the Goethals and the Outerbridge Crossing, to connect the island to New Jersey.

But Patricia wanted only to connect with Manhattan, farther from Amboy Road than New Jersey. Lacking Margaret's driving skills, she wondered how she would get there again. The Staten Island Railroad would exhaust her time and funds, and after that, she'd need the ferry and subway. Isolated, impoverished, and dependent on the decisions of others, she shared the unenviable position of Newfoundland, Britain's beleaguered dominion.

Inevitably, Frank began to treat his grandniece like a child. When Patricia needed a new hat, he took her to the jumbled basement stores of Manhattan's Fourteenth Street, encouraging her to select a Lower East Side bargain, the kind of nondescript items worn by the downtrodden residents of this noisy, crowded district. Patricia wanted to top her bobbed hair with just the right smart cloche. She knew she'd never find it there.

Frank's encouragement to find the right hat began sounding like insistence. Contemptuous of his provincial ways and weary of being patronized, Patricia bought nothing. She endured his complaints on the journey back to Amboy Road, but she'd reached a turning point. With no definite plan in mind, she began packing.

"New York was definitely not going to mean Staten Island, Fourteenth Street, or piano exercises," she wrote, and she left the following day.

She spent the next several nights camped out on the floor of a doctor's waiting room, terrified by the hunting trophies mounted on its walls. It was a temporary favor; as a child, Patricia's mother had known the physician, but "he wanted no more part of me than did my great-uncle Frank," Patricia wrote. After a week, "I was urged politely to leave."

Patricia spent her days roaming New York, walking as much as possible to avoid transit fares. Other members of the Newfoundland diaspora introduced her to the neighborhood of Morningside Heights near Columbia University. Despite her lack of university-level schooling, she felt at home in this Ivy League atmosphere. She found a job of sorts, or at least a daily free meal, playing the piano at a restaurant where, she wrote, "young people ate, visited and relaxed."[10]

They did everything but drink there. By the time Patricia arrived in Manhattan, Prohibition had been the law of the land for eight years. Though opposed by the city's mayor and most other politicians, and only half-heartedly enforced, the federal criminalization of liquor had pushed drinking underground. Speakeasies flourished, and judges winked at federal agents who said they'd treated typists to highballs for purely investigative purposes. Nevertheless, there were costs. In the week of Patricia's arrival, a construction worker was found dead in a Staten Island rooming house, poisoned by bootleg rum. And Prohibition had destroyed New York's fine-dining restaurants. Deprived of their highly profitable bars, establishments like Delmonico's had closed their doors. Those that defied the law risked padlocking.

Patricia was familiar with the "dry" movement. Back home, the St. John's Total Abstinence and Benefit Society was a popular club with a hall for concerts and dances. It owed its origins to Catholic clergy worried about hard-drinking Newfoundlanders of Irish descent, like Patricia's barfly father. The St. John's society had not changed any laws, but it was a social force. Even as the waterfront bars thrived, the temperance movement steered some customers to places like Patricia's favorite hangout, the Blue Puttee Tea Rooms, where the most intoxicating item on the menu was a toasted coconut ice cream sundae.

In New York, cafeterias and tea rooms were Prohibition's beneficiaries. Nothing grows under tall trees, but with redwoods like Delmonico's felled, the forest floor was flourishing. In wetter times, the elite and eclectic of Columbia might have spurned the type of New York cafeteria where customers pushed trays past ladle-wielding employees and presented tickets to be punched with the price of the order, paying a cashier at the end. Though charmless—one such eatery was nicknamed "the waxworks" for its harsh lighting—many became gay cultural landmarks and magnets for bohemians, as memorialized in Paul Cadmus's painting, *Greenwich Village Cafeteria*.[11]

Seated at the piano in an alcohol-free version of a collegiate rathskeller, Patricia was expected to enhance the levity. In this, her first New York job, she failed miserably. "I couldn't play popular music," she wrote. "Chopin, Beethoven, and even my improvising was what the kids got with their lunch. With jazz sweeping the country, I was in the wrong business." The most modern tune she could manage was Sibelius's *Valse Triste*.

The pay "wasn't much," she said, consisting mostly of free meals, but she found she could earn extra by arriving early and filling in for absent workers. She befriended the evening pianist, William C. Orth, recognizing that his skills were superior to hers. Her natural sociability quickly paid off. One day she broke a heel on her way to the restaurant. With only twenty-six cents in her purse, she had no way to repair it. Orth advanced her the funds to "get me 'on my feet,'" she said.[12]

Staying on her feet financially proved harder. Even in the prosperous days before the stock market crash of October 29, 1929, her books were not always balanced. Notions of self and social status were sometimes at war with practicalities. The daughter of her hometown's most prominent merchant could not be content dishing out vegetables. Instead, she sought a job as a hostess, a position for which her temperament suited her. Employers turned her down only because she was short, she said.[13]

The name Murphy, combined with her Irish-sounding Newfoundland accent, may also have played a role. Patricia had come to America at a time of strong nativist sentiments, and laws had sharply curbed the influx of immigrants, mainly from southern and eastern Europe, but also elsewhere on the continent. Irish waitresses were fixtures at restaurant chains like Child's and Schrafft's,[14] but hostesses project an establishment's image.

Nonetheless, Patricia wanted a hostess position so badly that she practiced "escorting parties to tables in the secrecy of my furnished room." This was not quite so pathetic as it sounds: Patricia's first furnished room was quite a find. While still presenting herself as a musician, she wangled admission to the Three Arts Club, a residence for unmarried young women planning careers in music, theater, or art. Located on West Eighty-Fourth Street, not far from Central Park, the club building had a large top-floor room that doubled as art studio and lecture hall. Guest artists like Diego Rivera and Frida Kahlo came to give talks. Founded and supported by wealthy female donors, including a Vanderbilt and two Whitneys, the organization provided free tickets to concerts and shows along with housing. For evenings at the opera, the lucky residents received donations of tickets, plus second-hand evening gowns.

To win a space in this artistic sorority of about 150 members, Patricia had to present references, proof that she was single and under thirty, and a convincing case about her devotion to music. There was apparently no needs test. Among the residents were some from comfortable, middle-class families, among others constantly worried about money. Perhaps to make clear that this was not a home for the indigent, its wealthy benefactors charged what they considered moderate rent. In 1909, when the club occupied less comfortable rooms on nearby West End Avenue, residents paid seven dollars a week for room and meals.[15] Adjusting for the two decades of inflation that preceded Patricia's arrival, her weekly bill would have topped thirteen dollars, not counting additional charges such as club membership.

Hence, after just a week of "living it up," at the Three Arts, as she described it, Patricia boarded the IRT—now knowing it to be the subway—to seek cheaper digs in Brooklyn Heights. Thanks to the construction of the Clark Street tunnel, one train and one nickel took her directly from the Upper West Side of Jazz Age Manhattan to the quasi-suburban tranquility of the Heights. Furnished rooms and bed-sits priced from three to eight dollars were in plentiful supply, particularly for "ladies" and "gentlemen" who could produce the "references required."

Patricia secured cheap accommodations in Brooklyn, a half-hour by transit back to the Upper West Side, where she, at last, had found a job.

Luck arrived in a three-line classified ad reading, "Cashier—Highclass tea room needs refined young lady."[16] Patricia filled the bill at Foster's Restaurant on Broadway near West Eighty-Seventh Street, one of two operated by a Mr. and Mrs. Foster. The phrase "tea room" referred not to a beverage—New Yorkers preferred coffee—but to a genre of moderately priced restaurants. Attentive table service, soft lighting, and tasteful table settings attracted the kind of middle-class patrons preferring to eat out in places resembling their dining rooms. Unaccompanied women felt comfortable in such settings. Thanks to Prohibition and a growing female workforce, as Patricia answered the ad, one midtown block was home to two dozen tea rooms

To her delight, the job included meals and paid eighteen dollars a week. Unfortunately, however, Patricia's performance at the cash register won no more applause than her stint at the keyboard. Dinner at Foster's had a prix fixe of seventy cents, and for every dollar bill handed to her, Patricia doled out three dimes as change. Upset by the dwindling supply of dimes, the Fosters instructed her in the fine points of the nickel, a coin unknown in Newfoundland, where Patricia, in fact, had worked in her father's business. Doubts about the authenticity of her resume arose.

There were also problems with a co-worker hired for the coveted hostess position. This "Russian princess," as Patricia dubbed her, refused her time off to watch a parade of ten thousand march down Fifth Avenue in the St. Patrick's Day parade. Patricia may have missed her first St. Patrick's Day parade in New York, but she knew why some marchers carried signs protesting the portrayals of the Irish in popular entertainments. "Do not patronize plays or places which try to make a profit out of race insults," the signs said.

Patricia would never forget how the hostess at Foster's had denied her a few hours of pride on that St. Patrick's Day, nor how the woman had haughtily called her "my Irish colleen."

The restaurant proprietors began questioning her gentility. Ringing up restaurant checks at a counter stocked with sundries, Patricia urged diners to take a Tootsie Roll or a pack of Sweet Caporal cigarettes. Her efforts raised revenues but also eyebrows—in particular, those of Mr. Foster. She said he considered it "bad form" to push product so aggressively in the rarified air of his tea room.

She was fired, having "failed to enter the restaurant business at the lowest possible level,"[17] she said, or at least the lowest level she would consider. Kitchen work and serving were apparently out of the question; in her own way, Patricia was as much a snob as the Fosters and their hostess princess.

In truth, though, Patricia had had her eye on only one job: boss. She was now a recent graduate of the Ware School of Tea Room Management, a for-profit institution operated by two sisters, Jeannette and Josephine Ware, next to their restaurant on Thirty-Ninth Street. Fifteen lesson books of about twenty-five pages each, written by the Wares, comprised the core of the course, and the restaurant provided a learning lab. To keep students coming, and paying, each lesson ended with a "coming attractions" preview of the next.

Introductory units leavened business-school jargon with women's-pages fluff. A section titled "How to Have Dainty Table Covering" included photos of successful Ware graduates, such as Miss Vera Pomeroy of New Jersey, who turned her home into the Chimney Corner Tea Room. As the lessons progressed, however, there was less talk of curtain valances and more charts and formulas. Only the hardy would soldier on.

To run the gauntlet, Patricia would have learned to solicit bids from food purveyors, record goods received, route servers through the kitchen, and analyze recipes for costs per portion, among other topics. Written clearly but not condescendingly, the lessons included wage scales, staff schedules, and floor plans, and other essentials for the first-time business owner.

Leaving Jeannette Ware with a lasting impression of her apt student, Patricia passed tests with questions like:

- What would you consider the best kitchen floor covering if you have a three-year lease?

- Name two reasons why it is not usually satisfactory for an establishment serving fewer than five hundred people a day to buy uncut meat.

- What would be the monthly depreciation charge on equipment costing $3,000 with a five-year lease?[18]

"You can easily own or manage a tea room, cafeteria, or motor inn," read ads for the Ware School, whose recent graduate had just flopped as a cashier, and whose funds were dwindling.

Retreating to her rooming house on Henry Street, Patricia again scanned the classified section that had led her to the Ware School. This time, she was looking at want ads. Oddly, these started shrinking even as share prices for General Motors soared, and the Era of Wonderful Nonsense, as columnist Westbrook Pegler dubbed the twenties, carried on.

Patricia found only piecework, hand-coloring picture postcards at three dollars per hundred. With a rent of four dollars weekly, little remained for food. Not wanting to touch the sixty dollars stashed in a savings account for a last-resort ticket back home, Patricia began skipping meals. "I used all the tricks that youngsters employ when they're on their own, even munching dry raisins and then drinking a lot of water. You'd be surprised how this can fill you up."[19]

Nonetheless, she felt enlivened by the gaiety of New York, with its flappers and flagpole-sitters. Patricia was captivated by the city's dapper and controversial mayor, James J. Walker. He was a "Beau Brummel" mayor, she wrote, although Beau Brummel was an Englishman, and Jimmy Walker, famous for his chalk-striped pants and cutaway jackets, was an Irish New Yorker. While Patricia fasted, and some observers noted the lengthening of lines at Bowery soup kitchens, the mayor spent thousands refurbishing "a magic place called Central Park Casino," as fascinated Patricia called it. Its ballroom had a black-glass ceiling that reflected the dancers and a menu concocted by a French chef featuring forty sauces. Turning the old theater maxim on its head, the casino's decorator described it as a place for "businessmen who are not tired and wanted to have a good time."

The indefatigable Patricia also wanted to enjoy herself. Rather than moving to a less expensive area of the city, she remained on the Heights, where the front yard gardens were now in bloom, and flower sellers still carted their wares in horse-drawn wagons. Occasionally she'd pass up dinner to splurge on a twenty-five-cent bunch of daffodils. To Patricia, flowers were sustenance.

The news during the summer and early fall of 1929 echoed her St. Patrick's Day snub. New York's Irish-American governor, Al Smith, was the Democratic party's nominee for president. Smith, a proud Irishman always garbed in green on St. Patrick's Day, was the first Catholic to seek the presidency on a major party's tickets, and he was undergoing vicious attacks. Crude cartoons depicted fat priests pulling his strings from the Vatican; polite discussion-hall debates pondered whether any Catholic could be fit for the nation's highest office.

Smith's miserable loss to Hoover was overshadowed by Black Tuesday, but Patricia barely noticed. "The stock market crash didn't seem important to me at the time," she wrote. "Being out of a job and broke was no novelty to me." Once assured that her small savings account was safe, she continued as before.

The Great Depression was her turning point. Less than two blocks from her living quarters, in the basement of another rooming house at 114 Henry Street, three different tea rooms had opened and closed in quick succession.

Patricia considered the first two closures at 114 well-deserved failures. The first restaurant had bad food, and the owner of the second "had one of those personalities that would make people turn right around in the entrance," she wrote. However, she'd been pleased with the latest eatery to occupy the space because it served "good food at a good price—an excellent idea, I have always thought, for a restaurant."

But one evening she walked there only to find it shuttered. Unsure where else to find a decent meal for forty-five cents, she knocked insistently. She and the proprietor, John Anthony, knew each other by name. He answered the knock, informed her he was going out of business, but invited her in anyway.

Over coffee, he told her his place had been popular, with seats filled and repeat customers, but that he just couldn't charge enough to make it work. The landlord, butcher, and linen service were squeezing him with bill collection before he'd had time to make a profit.

Patricia's mind was racing. She asked Mr. Anthony how much the rent was. "Twenty-five dollars a week," he said. "Payable in advance of course."

She was thinking about her little nest egg in the bank. Mr. Anthony could read this in her face. His response, as she remembered it: "Miss Murphy, whatever are you thinking about? Don't you get mixed up in this business. It just won't pay off, no matter how hard you work. And besides, this place has got a hex on it."[20]

But she was doing some quick calculations from the Ware School's Lesson Fifteen: "How Much Rent Can I Pay?" The price seemed right, and she knew she could lift the curse with soft lights, china, and flowers. She was a novice at running a restaurant, but she knew plenty about middle-class pretensions and intolerance. Mr. Anthony served good food, but he was Italian, and she knew that descendants of northern Europeans often considered Italians dirty. Some even said that Italians made elaborate folds in restaurant napkins only to hide the dirt and stains.[21]

Within an hour, Patricia had contacted the landlord. "The wildness of my plan and my Irish ancestry must have made me very eloquent," she wrote. This particular landlord, August Behman, may also have used a theatrical casting director's eye to spot potential in Patricia. August's grandfather, like Patricia's, had operated a store in downtown Brooklyn, and his father, Lewis, had risen from grocery clerk at the family business to co-founder of Behman & Hyde, a theatrical management company that had operated vaudeville theaters in Brooklyn, Manhattan, and Pittsburgh. As a child, August had trod the boards once or twice.[22] Now the heir to millions, he had little need to do anything but collect rents from properties, including this one. It was a few doors from 146 Henry Street, where he and his wife lived when not at bridge parties, charity galas, or summering at their home on Bayport, Long Island.

Business failures, evictions, and rent strikes were growing rampant. Whether impressed by Patricia or faced with few other prospects, Behman gave her the lease. What's more, he agreed to postpone collection of her first rent payment until the end of the week.

Patricia was already doing calculations. The restaurant had thirty-six seats. If she could serve a hundred meals daily, earning a dime on each one, she'd make seventy dollars in profit each week. She would out-Foster the Fosters and, in the words of that want ad she'd answered, create a very "high-class" tea room with a "refined" staff. People wanted restaurants resembling the "English Type Living Room," featured on the women's pages of the *Staten Island Advance*. Patricia Murphy, raised in Britain's largest dominion, could create one.

But she'd provide fun, too, as only people of Irish heritage could— as Mary Powers, manager of the Blue Puttee, had done in St. John's through the sorrows of the Great War.

Using her own pen, Patricia signed the lease, most probably in green ink.

CHAPTER 4

On the Heights

Your station is your restaurant. Better still, imagine it to be your home. You are having company come in. Keep this thought uppermost in your mind, and you will always do what is courteous, thoughtful and right.

—Patricia Murphy's manual for employees, 1930

In one month, rent would be due. Before then, she had to assemble a staff, choose menus, buy equipment, convince food purveyors to extend credit, and transform a basement into a fairyland.

Like so many others, she had little hope of getting any other job. What's more, she had staked her entire savings on the Candlelight. That's what she had settled on as a name for this restaurant: the Candlelight, because she was going to replace the bare ceiling bulbs with table candles. Each table would have candles and a floral arrangement. Patricia knew what tea room patrons liked, and she was determined to provide it, even though this Candlelight had already burned her return ticket to Newfoundland.

At any rate, nothing remained there for the Murphys but gloom and peril. Her brothers, Jim and Vincent, still working as mess boys on the Norwegian ship, were engaged in a dangerous smuggling operation. The British had been slapping a huge tariff on American cigarettes, so that a pack of Players cost 25 cents in Newfoundland, where a British plant produced them, compared to 75 cents for a pack of American-made smokes. But Newfoundlanders craved the American brands, and Patricia's brothers had a scheme for providing them cheaply.

The principal task of their boat was to bring mail to the island of St. Pierre off the southwestern shore of Newfoundland. There, American brands such as Raleigh and Chesterfield were available duty-free. Jim bought ten cartons for $7.50—less than eight cents a pack—and brought them ashore strapped beneath coats to his and Vincent's chests. Even at 50 cents a pack, Newfoundlanders bought them. The Murphy brothers turned a huge profit during their thirty-six hours of free time in port, but they could see that the customs officials were getting wise to them. Out of respect to the family's former social prominence, some officials refrained from arresting them, but they warned Jim of an impending crackdown. The consequence could be jail time. The venture was abandoned.

Patricia's father had opened another store in the city of Belle Isle, a mining town where many of Frank's customers spent all the daylight hours underground. No longer busy with cigarette sales, Jim came to help during his spare time. Always alert to sharp business schemes, Jim admired the local mine owners who saved on chutes and labor by simply dumping the coal over a cliff onto a ship—one of the Newfoundland improvisations that inspired Patricia to describe her homeland as a version of the American Wild West. In Belle Isle, Jim became acquainted with an Arab shopkeeper who offered to pay him for marrying his daughter. But somehow that fell through.

A more conventional escape route had also collapsed. Patricia's sister, Lauraine, had obtained the Maybelline franchise for Newfoundland. However, an island struggling with the collapse of the cod-fishing industry and distant from world fashion centers proved a less-than-robust market for mascara.

As the year 1929 closed in frightened, fallen New York, the outlook back home was bleaker still. When Patricia's youngest sibling, Sheila, age eight, outgrew her shoes, there was no money for new ones.[1]

All hopes lay in Henry Street. "I went to all the stores in the neighborhood, putting myself in the role of a housewife planning a family meal," Patricia wrote. "I was determined to undersell her in her own home, and with wholesale buying, I knew I could do it." More likely, she had consulted one of the booklets from her course at the Ware School: Lesson 11, Menu Planning, Costs Per Portion, How Figured.

There was seating for thirty-six in the space she'd rented. It was part of the English basement of 114 Henry, a duplex townhouse sharing a side wall with 116 Henry. A shared staircase, a "stoop" in the local parlance, ascended to the two front doors of the twin buildings. To one side of the stoop, another door led to the basement of No. 114. This was the restaurant entrance. Patrons descended a few steps to the dining room, where windows offered a partial view of people passing by, mostly legs and feet.

Nonetheless, thanks to the tall stoop, it had high ceilings for a basement, and Patricia enlisted the help of an architect friend, Harry Weston, to make the most of "our cramped quarters," as she called them. "It's surprising what one can do with a basement, a staircase, and even exposed hot water pipes," she wrote. Shelves, for instance, were built next to the stairs to hold cigarettes and candies for those add-on sales she'd been forbidden to promote at Foster's restaurant.

Recruiting the right staff was critical, and with apple sellers appearing on city corners, it wasn't difficult to find willing workers. Patricia had already determined that the waitresses would be well-bred young ladies like herself; the Ware School advised against anyone "of the servant class.[2] For cooks, dishwashers, and bus boys, the school issued no so such warnings. Nevertheless, to staff her kitchen, Patricia returned to Morningside Heights. "Off I went to my Columbia University haunts to find a bus boy who could cook and college youngsters who would help out just to get meals at half price," she wrote.[3] Readers of her book undoubtedly envisioned scrubbed white youths in raccoon coats and Varsity letter sweaters.

Though just steps away from the Clark Street IRT station, Columbia's bucolic Manhattan campus was a good forty-five minutes away from the Candlelight. A young man admitted to the university's elite undergraduate school, Columbia College, then restricted to males, would have had to spend ten cents on a round-trip train ride to qualify for a half-price lunch, netting about seventeen cents for a full shift of work. Even in the depths of the Depression, few Ivy undergraduates would have jumped at the offer.

For another category of Columbia students, however, this kind of menial work was a fact of life and, as other job prospects diminished further, a sparkling lure. These were the Filipino graduate students, working their way through doctoral and master's degree programs at Columbia University by filling low-status jobs in the restaurant and hotel industries. By the late 1920s, about two thousand Filipinos lived in New York, about half of them in Brooklyn. A Filipino social center on Hicks Street, a few blocks from the Candlelight, hosted readings by Filipino poets, attended by engineering students.

Through her aborted musical engagement at the cafeteria in Morningside Heights, Patricia knew students of this sort. Racial discrimination forced many Filipinos into segregated substandard housing. Brooklyn's Filipino community, including seafarers and laborers who had come to New York after their Hawaii sugar-cane contracts expired, was centered around Sands Street, less than a mile from their Brooklyn Heights social club, yet a different world entirely. A 1928 *Brooklyn Daily Eagle* article described it as "the street of sailors, Filipinos, drug stores, sailor clothing stores and tattoo needles." Dotting the street were restaurants decorated with murals of parrots or island scenes. One specialty was *pochero manok*, a stew of chicken, beans, hot sausage, cabbage and potatoes in a base of tomatoes, onions, and garlic.[4]

Instead of this savory fare, Filipinos employed by the Candlelight would be paid in breaded veal cutlets, creamed chicken on waffles, or chopped egg and olive sandwiches. Patricia's aim was not to introduce Americans to exotic dishes, but rather to mimic the make-do, budget-stretching fare of Depression-era kitchens, supplemented by hot breads, attentive service, and a convivial atmosphere. Armed with a menu featuring three-course luncheons ranging from thirty-five to sixty cents, beverage included, and dinners priced between sixty-five and eighty-five cents, Patricia aimed to net a dime from every meal.

She was a daughter of Frank Murphy, a man who, in testimony before the Newfoundland Fisheries Enquiry Commission, remembered every penny he had charged in each of twenty years for rubber boots, pork, twine, tea, and molasses. "I can nearly tell you anything about prices," he said before proving it in hours of testimony.[5] Now his daughter Patricia calculated she could cover the rent and pocket a profit by serving one hundred meals daily.

Opening day arrived. Patricia's waitresses stood ready in the black dresses and dark stockings recommended by the Ware School. Food had been bought on credit at butcher shops and Brooklyn's Wallabout wholesale market from vendors eager in these slow times for a new account. The overeducated kitchen staff was bent over burners, and cinnamon buns—the first hot breads featured at the Candlelight—were in the oven.

Table tops presented the essential markers of refinement: flowers, candlesticks, and ash trays. Instead of a cash register, Patricia stashed a cash box behind a glass display case filled with pans decorated to look like cakes. In her book, she said she couldn't afford a cash register. In any case, the Ware School advised tea rooms to avoid the machines and their commercial associations with cafeterias. Determined to present her standard American fare as attractively as possible, with attention to garnishes and plating—"There is no excuse for heaping a plate with dull brown and white edibles," she wrote—Patricia had returned to Staten Island to borrow china from Margaret, her storekeeping cousin.

There were thirty-six set-ups, but Margaret could only provide twenty cups and saucers. If, by some miracle, all seats were occupied, the china could be juggled among tables, Patricia figured.

Her dreams about to be realized, Patricia said she was dressing "in my shabby best" upstairs when she realized with a jolt that she'd forgotten to set the tables. She rushed downstairs in a dressing gown to discover John Anthony folding napkins. The restaurant's former proprietor had come to wish her well.

An experienced waiter, Mr. Anthony was transforming the napkins into tiny upright towers. Patricia, though confident her new format would support prices higher than Mr. Anthony's, was grateful and relieved to find him arranging "every dish and piece of cutlery immaculately."

Customers, Patricia instructed her staff, must always be referred to as "guests." Once dressed, she wrote, "I adjusted my hair in the little mirror over the dresser and went out to the stairs. I heard guests at the door. I almost panicked. And then I knelt down on the stairs and prayed."

The Candlelight was in a fitting setting for prayers. Flanking the restaurant were two churches, a tall Gothic Presbyterian on its left and a Methodist-Episcopal structure bristling with turrets to its right. Both churches posted their schedule of services on small bulletin boards placed outside their doors, and Patricia had followed suit, erecting a board near the basement steps and pinning a menu to it. The new name on a hand-colored pink background—and the illustration of an ethereally slim and unmistakably fair-complexioned waitress with long skirt, apron, and stylishly bobbed hair—sent a clear message about the change of management.

Whether due to prayer, the sign board, or the proximity of the restaurant to dozens of rooming houses and three large hotels, the Candlelight was an instant hit. "The thirty-six seatings were changed more than twice over to accommodate eighty-four honored and treasured guests," and through quick rinsing and feats of legerdemain, there were tea cups for all.

Those customers brought friends. Within a month, the restaurant had turned a five-hundred-dollar profit. In her book, Patricia presented herself as hopelessly naïve about business, unable to calculate whether she was making or losing money until her architect friend, Harry Weston, sat her down for a simple bookkeeping lesson. In fact, however, by this time she had started a secondary enterprise. She was a landlady, and Weston was one of her lodgers.

The 1930 U.S. Census found them both at 65 Columbia Heights Street in part of a row of brownstones so handsome, with their balconies and corniced windows, that they captured the attention of photographer Berenice Abbott. Patricia was listed as the head of household, with four men, all older than she, as lodgers. In addition to Harry were a painter, a caterer—perhaps employed by Patricia—and another man described by a misspelled word that could be "optometrist." Giving her name as "Ellen Murphy," as on her birth documents, Patricia described herself as a dietician.

Rent in this building, where entire floors were available, some with views of the East River, was recorded as $120 per week. Presumably, she was collecting all or most of it from her lodgers. If so, they were paying the same or more than her restaurant rent.

They might also have been paying her some personal attention. In her book she mentioned "several attractive boys living in rooms above mine in the Henry Street house." She added, "After trying unsuccessfully to get me to go out with them, they would knock on my door occasionally and ask, 'Patricia, do you think you're ever going to amount to anything?'" It's possible that those "boys" were, in fact, the men lodging with her, perhaps on the same floor. One was divorced, and one was single. Two, including Harry, were married but not living with their wives. All were in their thirties and forties.

That intriguing Brooklyn episode wasn't the only one omitted from her memoir. Around this time, she was also advertising for more staff. "Waitress, experienced in exclusive restaurant," one ad read. Among Patricia's new hires was a glamorous but moody college dropout named Mildred Gillars, later to be known as the traitorous wartime propagandist, Axis Sally.[6] Born in Maine to parents from New Brunswick, Canada, Mildred shared Patricia's North Atlantic Irish heritage and convent schooling. A one-time actress then pushing thirty, Mildred—or Midge, as friends called her—waitressed between fruitless auditions. She'd previously worked in diners in Ohio, where her family lived. Nonetheless, in New York, "I dropped a lot of dishes the first day," she said.[7]

Midge, known then as a "personality girl," was not the only exasperating member of Patricia's expanding staff. Shortly after the Candlelight's launch, two young women from Newfoundland cracked the glass display case that concealed the cash drawer. Patricia wrote that she "laughed it off, but it was a terrible blow."

However, the laughter stopped as the restaurant grew, adding staff and a new tone of professionalism. Patricia's cooperative socialite-landlord knocked down walls and made alterations, allowing his thriving tenant to expand into the basement area of the adjoining building, 116 Henry, and the entire first floor of the duplex.

Within a year of its opening, the restaurant was looking for more "girls of high type," both full- and part-time to adhere to the strict rules of the twenty-six-page Candlelight employee manual, which now included charges for breakage. Though addressed to waitresses and waiters, the manual describes their roles in relation to department heads and banquet hostesses, as well as the kitchen manager, the kitchen boys, the relish girl, the salad boy, and the linen girl.

The Candlelight's signature menu item, the popover, evolved over time. The manual mentions only buns, muffins, and cinnamon rolls, warning waitresses not to ruin a dinner party by offering hot breads only to the *a la carte* customers while denying them to their *table d'hote* companions. "The relish girl will usually pass buns for you," the manual noted.

The relish girl, serving bowls of celery and radishes sculpted like roses, remained but eventually relinquished her place of honor to the popover girl. In time, a local gossip columnist would report that "the little blonde dishing out popovers at the Candlelight restaurant on the Heights is more attractive than most girls in the Broadway shows." There were waiters, too; the manual warns them to show up for work in clean collars and cuffs or pay twenty cents in exchange for them.

The Candlelight's triumph got front-page exposure in the *Brooklyn Daily Eagle* at the close of its first year of business. Two days before Christmas, two men dined on a specialty of the house, fried chicken. Apparently, they were in no rush, as the restaurant's three chicken dinners required twenty minutes of preparation, and employees were encouraged to pass this information along to customers.

After finishing this leisurely dinner, the two men approached the cashier, who was surrounded by shelves of candy and cigarettes but otherwise isolated, at her station near the door. A hand was clapped over her mouth, and $350 was robbed from the cash drawer.[8]

The newspaper said the men were unarmed and made no mention of arrests. It also reported that the crime had occurred in the early evening. With dinner barely underway and even *a la carte* orders including cinnamon buns rarely topping one dollar, the stolen sum indicated that Patricia was now doing a tremendous business.

"What had diners-out—in Brooklyn of all places, and in hard times—been given that brought them back to the Candlelight in increasing numbers and netted it a handsome profit, I asked myself," Patricia wrote. She continued, "They were given lots of good food at prices that compared favorably to the cost of meals cooked at home . . . and there were no glum faces to remind them of hard times."

Hard times had continued in Newfoundland. As if the codfish-industry collapse and the effects of the worldwide Depression were not enough, a tsunami hit the island's Burin Peninsula in 1929, killing dozens and leaving hundreds homeless. Like the Filipinos who worked at her restaurant, but better able to afford it, Patricia regularly sent remittances home. Her brother Jim recalled that his parents and five other siblings depended on her occasional fifty-dollar money orders, though his father would often drink up much of it.

In September 1930, with the Candlelight opened less than one year, Patricia brought her nineteen-year-old sister Maude to Brooklyn. Maude enrolled in the nursing program at Long Island College Hospital, just blocks from the restaurant. Maude would pursue a more practical course of studies than did her two older sisters.

By her second year in business, Patricia launched her plan to reunify the family in New York. Her restaurant wasn't the only business faring well despite the Depression. The local gas utility company, Brooklyn Union Gas, was laying pipes into previously uncharted territory in Brooklyn and Queens, adding showrooms to display home-appliance wonders such as "noiseless" gas refrigerators. The thriving utility raised wages while cutting hours for its workers. It also opened a cafeteria in its new Canarsie plant, granting the catering contract to the Candlelight.

To assist her father in his latest get-rich-quick schemes, Patricia put lobster on the utility canteen's menus, importing them from Newfoundland. The plan went awry when Brooklyn longshoremen refused to unload them. However, catering, for schools as well as the gas company, offset seasonal slumps in the restaurant business. By April of 1932, Lauraine moved to Brooklyn with the assurance of a job at the Candlelight.

The men of the family remained up north, hoping to revive their fortunes, as Patricia's mother and little sister followed Lauraine to Brooklyn for a visit spiced with a dash of commercial spying—or that's how it turned out, at least. The Candlelight had enlivened its dessert offerings by supplementing the standard baked goods with homemade peppermint ice cream and chocolate-covered sweets called bonbons.

Sheila, then ten, had probably sampled these delicacies, but Nana had gone a step further, returning to Newfoundland after five months in Brooklyn with the knowledge of how to make bonbons. Jim—who had tried seafaring, smuggling, and weekend work at his father's mining-town store—hung up his apron in the ship's mess and quit for good. From then on he would cook only bonbons, in the kitchen of the Murphy family's crowded home in St. John's.

Newfoundlanders couldn't seem to get enough of the stuff. They were particularly popular with seal hunters, who considered the tasty and lightweight confections the perfect dietary supplement for long days on the ice, a prototype of the energy bar. Frank Murphy landed a three-hundred-pound order from a grocery company, and the bonbon business flipped into high gear. Hiring two women to take charge of the cooking, Jim drummed up wholesale orders at fifteen cents per pound. The market was in Newfoundland's small towns, the outports.

Patricia's recipes seemed to have spawned an auxiliary business. This time, unlike the fake Coke and cigarette smuggling ventures, it was legitimate. Frank and Jim had secured a license to import sugar from the States.[9]

Nonetheless, the Murphy women saw more promise in Brooklyn. Lauraine joined Patricia in greeting customers at the door of the Candlelight. Nana returned with Sheila in 1933, this time for good. Patricia enrolled Sheila in Packer Collegiate, a highly regarded private school on the Heights. There were plenty of public and parochial schools in Brooklyn, but mingling with the private-school set was a form of investment. The Candlelight's party rooms were hosting wedding receptions and sorority luncheons. Such events landed in the social sections or even front pages of the *Eagle*, adding free publicity to the "hundreds of dollars spent on advertising," mentioned in the restaurant's employee manual.

Patricia was now aggressively pursuing another vocation closely related to her first: social climbing. The Candlelight had become a brand. At its door, she and Lauraine drew on their Irish Newfoundlander roots to radiate warmth and welcome: recalling visits as a child, one customer said the Murphy sisters always gave "a hug and a kiss as we came in the door." After hours, however, Patricia was vying for association with the "right people," as Hollywood movies of the era phrased it.

In the mid-1930s the periphery of Brooklyn's Prospect Park abounded with riding academies offering lessons in both basic equestrian skills and polo. On weekends, mounted police officers patrolled the park's bridal paths, ready to assist the unsteady novices showing off new jodhpurs and cravats. British aristocratic manners were aped Brooklyn-style, with names like Levine, Sabatino, and Greenberg appearing in the society columns that listed names of riders and their mounts.

Despite regularly putting in sixteen-hour days at the Candlelight, Patricia joined the horsey set every Saturday morning for a ride in the park. She also regularly exercised with a group. These habits were noted in one of the first of many business stories profiling not only the success of the Candlelight but also the remarkable nature of its founder. Thriving in less challenging economic times, another prosperous restaurant owner, Alice Foote MacDougall, had advised, "Learn to know the prominent people in your community. Interest them in your undertaking by becoming interested in theirs."[10] Patricia had no need to fake it. She was genuinely interested in high society and, as she discovered, in horses.

An old form of socializing at restaurants returned with the end of Prohibition. Although Repeal officially took effect in early 1933, months passed before the newly formed New York State Liquor Authority began processing applications for liquor licenses, carefully vetting them for signs of racketeering. In early 1934, waves of Brooklyn restaurants got the nod, some proudly listing their license numbers in newspaper ads. Patricia was among the early applicants.

Her first bar, though tiny, pumped up profits and gave patrons awaiting tables a place to sit. Moreover, the Candlelight was able to shed its "tea room" stigma. Male patronage increased, and the sorority and auxiliary-league bookings in the banquet room were supplemented by meetings of architects and courtroom employees.

Patricia's family called her "a force of nature," but her brother Jim was still resisting the pull toward Brooklyn. The bonbons seemed to promise the financial independence he craved. He was importing candy wrappers from the States, along with thousands of pounds of sugar. Then some people came to inspect the books. A duty of $7.50 was now required for every one hundred pounds of sugar imported. The new expense, a consequence of the United States National Recovery Administration—the same relief effort that had aided Patricia—was about to ruin Jim.

This happened in early April of 1934. On the day before Easter, Jim brought his hard-luck stories to all small-town stores owing him money. He collected thirty-five dollars. He gave some to his family and bought a boat ticket to New York.

Patricia's youngest brothers, Shannon and Vincent, joined the others, while their father remained a partial holdout. When Patricia expanded her bar into a lounge in 1936, opening-night customers were invited to write their names on the cocktail glasses in frosted effect. They were seated on stools upholstered in seal fur and served at a bar with a façade of the same fur, imported from Frank Murphy.

That same year, Lauraine became engaged to a young engineer, a Candlelight Restaurant customer named O. Telfair Smith, who lived a few doors from the restaurant. The newspaper engagement announcement listed her parents as "Mr. and Mrs. Frederick Francis Murphy of 114 Henry Street and St. John's, Newfoundland." Frank came down frequently, while keeping one foot up north, but Nana was with Patricia for good.

As the twenties progressed, Patricia hired African American chefs, but Filipinos comprised much of her kitchen and serving staff. A regular customer at the time noted that it would have been difficult for them to find other work. It also might have grown more expensive to hire white workers. Competition, for labor and in pricing, was increasing. Repeal revived the restaurant trade on the Heights, where three hotels surrounded the Candlelight—the St. George, the Margaret, and the Bossert—each with multiple dining rooms. Patricia deployed armies of workers into the hotels. To gain entry they claimed to be guests before pulling out hand-colored flyers from hidden pockets.

Price, not atmosphere, became paramount. When one hotel offered to supplement fixed-price dinners with ten-cent shrimp or oyster cocktails, Patricia's regular customers deserted. With its tiny kitchen unsuitable for the mass preparation of oysters—enormously popular at the time—the Candlelight confronted nearly empty dining rooms.

It recovered. But Patricia was sick of Brooklyn. The fixation of the locals on low prices and unadventurous menu items—"how many things can you do with potatoes?" she wrote—had taken a toll. Hemmed in by two churches, she felt she was under religious surveillance. Her summer garden, where servers ladled out daiquiris from a punch bowl, had closed temporarily. A minister on one side of her had complained of noise from the outdoor fountain, while the other pretentiously demanded finger bowls with his dinner, never noticing she substituted sherbet cups.

Brooklyn "wasn't the big time," Patricia wrote, and, "I never derived any real satisfaction from a ferocious amount of work." Her unpublished manuscript continued, "There was nothing broadening about being a success in a provincial and highly prejudiced district," and the Brooklyn experience "almost made me hate the restaurant business."

The word "provincial" survived in the published book, while "prejudiced" did not. Patricia almost certainly meant the prejudices she'd personally experienced, particularly against her gender. She would not leave them behind as she expanded beyond the borough.

As New York excitedly anticipated the 1939 World's Fair, Patricia thought she saw a way out. Three years before the opening of the fair, restaurateurs were calling in favors and pulling strings, vying for a concession. Exposure at the fair could bring a restaurant national or even world fame. For Patricia, it would have been a life-changer.

Her letter of application for "at least one" concession was attached to a letter from a person acquainted with Charles Green, secretary of the World's Fair, which in 1936 had already set up an office in the Empire State Building. "Dear Charlie," began the letter from Frank R. McGregor of the Advertising Club of New York. He described Patricia as his friend and the Candlelight as a restaurant "which has been known all over New York during these last seven years." The term "tea room" appears nowhere in this letter, which also trumpets Patricia's operation of "industrial cafeterias for large companies, including Brooklyn Union Gas."

McGregor wrote, "Anything you can do to assist her in getting a good concession will, I'm sure, pay you big dividends in satisfaction when you see what a fine job she does with it."[11]

She never got the chance. Her letter was apparently ignored. Establishments owned by men, including The Brasserie, were chosen.

From Brooklyn Heights, where the hotel rooftops offered spectacular views of Manhattan, Patricia hatched another plan of attack. She would make her mark on the Midtown restaurant scene, but not by waiting for the approval of "Charlie," or any other man. Instead, she would take over another woman's tea room, gird it with armor, and do battle.

CHAPTER 5

Remodeling

If ladies are in the party, draw out chairs to enable them to rise
more easily.

—Patricia Murphy's manual for employees, 1930

"I could scarcely have made it harder for myself," Patricia wrote of her
first foray into Manhattan. But her choices were limited. Spurning the
Upper West Side, scene of her own regrettable restaurant experiences,
she homed in on Midtown East. Convinced that the future lay in the
area around Park Avenue and Fifty-Seventh Street—"the new center of
doings," as she described it—she found a desirable spot and contacted
the broker representing it.

"I marched in prepared to do business, elevating my five feet as far
as I could in high heels," she recalled.

The response, she said, was "barely restrained laughter." The broker
said he'd agreed to meet with her only because he thought "Pat Murphy" was a man. Confronted instead with a "small excitable woman,"
Patricia continued, "he didn't have to spell it out." Landlords were wary
of business failures, the area around Park and Fifty-Seventh was highly
competitive, and as she wrote, she was blackballed by gender.[1]

Patricia said she managed to control her "fury," but others heard
about it. Her decorator friend, Jack Lynas, whose skills had familiarized
him with the restaurant scene, came to the rescue. A woman named
Betty Barclay wanted to sell her tea room at 33 East Sixtieth Street in
the classy Lenox Hill section between Madison and Park.

The space was long and narrow, and the location was a side street,
but Patricia grabbed it. Lynas was amazed she could afford it. She put
him to work painting the walls with red-and-white stripes. With the

nation still recovering from the Depression, modernism was displacing nostalgia as the restaurant décor of choice. "It's new; it's smart; it's ultra-modern," said the ad copy advertising Patricia's new cocktail lounge in Brooklyn, and she wanted the same forward-looking feel in Manhattan.

There would be no liquor, however. Even after Repeal, alcohol remained controversial. Eleanor Roosevelt was serving only wine in the White House, and Patricia's landlords wanted nothing stronger than chilled grapefruit juice.

She was disappointed. It might be hard to attract male custom-ers, and she knew the same sexism that had denied her a prime loca-tion could doom her with the "dainty" label. Heavily dependent on the patronage of women, this eatery was doing mediocre business. Patricia had hoped to bring in more of the area's many working women while balancing them with males.

Even the frilly Schrafft's chain, synonymous with the ladies-who-lunch crowd, had liquor licenses for many locations, for heaven's sake. Applying in 1934 for permission to serve alcohol, the chain had cited "widespread demand" and the need to follow "new trends."[2]

Then there was the matter of a name for Patricia's new place. It would by no means become a second Candlelight Tea Room, though in Brooklyn, where several "candlelight rooms" had cropped up in vari-ous restaurants, she sometimes still used that long form. By 1938, "tea room" was becoming a curse, associated with "matrons," a word that even Patricia, for all her professed championing of women, used as a derogative. She described Betty Barclay, who had leased several Man-hattan properties by the time Patricia met her, as "one of those ladies whom you would expect to find running a tea room" and scoffed at her numbers: about eighty-five lunches and sixty dinners served per day.[3]

Nonetheless, Patricia said she was awed by the prices Barclay charged—considerably higher than Brooklynites would bear. Assured that even without a bar, "an energetic and ambitious proprietor might possibly do a 300-dollar-a-day business, I was sold," she added. It would have taken tons of eighty-five-cent dinners and forty-five-cent lunches to equal that in Brooklyn, where her restaurant and catering operations had reached full capacity.

She was in, but so insecure about her social debut, at age thirty-three, in Manhattan's Silk Stocking District that she requested permis-sion to use the former owner's name. She modified it, however, to "The

Barclay," shedding all associations with the lavender-and-lace tea room crowd, but risking confusion, or legal problems, with a Manhattan hotel of the same name.

Now that she owned a small chain, Patricia had new green-and-white matchbooks made. The inside cover listed the addresses of her two places: "The Barclay" in Manhattan and "The Candlelight" in Brooklyn. The cover headlined them as "Patricia Murphy's Restaurants," and that's how customers spoke of them. Like Macy's or St. Patrick's, they were simply Patricia Murphy's.

Her restaurants were far apart, but not so far to prevent Patricia from benefiting from the economy of scale. Even while adjusting the menus to local demands—seventy-five-cent lamb chops, a luxury item in Brooklyn, were a Manhattan staple—she was power-buying in quantity. Both her locations sought private-function and industrial-canteen business: three white matches mixed among the green ones in her matchbooks bore the legends, "Luncheon," "Dinner," "Catering."

Still, there were geographical challenges in managing restaurants divided by eight miles of heavy city traffic, with the East River Drive still under construction. Patricia wrote of driving madly across town in a blue roadster with vegetables piled high in the rumble seat. That was probably untrue. Even if Patricia knew how to drive—and no one remembers having seen her do it—she preferred to let others chauffeur her.

She was also letting others take a hand at steering her business, placing her trust in managers recruited from outside her large family. Incorporated separately—the new location was owned by the Candlelight Sixtieth Street Corp.—the restaurants remained an important stream of family income, supporting Nana and ensuring that Sheila could eventually go to college. Frank, still playing the part of paterfamilias long distance, could travel back and forth to New York. The Murphys had security, which was rare in the thirties.

Strangely, however, none of them were working at the restaurants. In her brief stint as a single woman in Brooklyn, Lauraine had been a tremendous help with hostess duties, which as detailed by Patricia in her employees' manual, involved far more than guiding customers to tables. The hostess oversaw the servers, arranging work schedules, assessing their work, and handling customer complaints. But Lonnie and Telfair had a baby now. They'd bought a house on Long Island near Telfair's engineering job, and Sheila had gone to live with them. The little sister once forced to wear outgrown shoes now lived in an attractive area of Manhasset developed by the Metropolitan Museum.

The Murphys no longer lived in Brooklyn. Patricia rented one of the apartments above her Manhattan restaurant, which had shed the Barclay name and was now officially a Patricia Murphy's Candlelight. Her unmarried siblings and Nana had moved from their rooming houses on the Heights to a large apartment in the Jackson Heights section of Queens. Maude, finished with nursing school, had a job in a hospital. Shannon and Vincent were clerks at a delicatessen.

Jim, with his experience as a ship's cook, could have been a big help in a restaurant. Instead, he seemed to have declared his independence from Patricia. Arriving in the spring, he took a job as a door-to-door vacuum cleaner salesman, gaining entrance into homes because, as he put it, "I had a baby face." Weighing 107 pounds himself, he hefted the fifty-pound appliance into living rooms where there were few rugs on which to demonstrate it: they'd been sent out for summer storage.

Living next to the Candlelight at the Hotel St. George, he worked for his oldest sister briefly, grabbing the evening papers each night to plot an escape. Sipping coffee while he circled want ads—"I would be awake all night, in Newfoundland we only had tea," he said—he found a job at the Hotel McAlpin in Manhattan, first as a cashier and then in the accounting office.[4]

Nonetheless, Patricia told a restaurant reviewer that she had been "aided by two sisters and three brothers" in expanding across the East River. Like a doll displayed in a glass dome, Sheila was insulated from kitchen grease. The other siblings were at times available to lend a hand, albeit reluctantly, in Jim's case. In return, the Murphys could again enjoy the comforts of middle-class life. Although located inside the city limits, Jackson Heights, along with Brooklyn Heights, was known as one of the city's first suburbs, or at least a quasi-suburb. Nana could enjoy the landscaped courtyard in the center of the six-story brick structure with elevators and intercoms, a taste of nature enhanced by modern conveniences, known as a garden apartment building.[5]

There were plenty of flowers at Patricia Murphy's on East Sixtieth Street, where Nana's first-born had bloomed into a full-blown socialite, perhaps too full-blown to reveal her real age to those outside the family. Recounting how Jack Lynas, perspiring over his decorating tasks, sent her for the occasional "tall cool drink" at a liquor-licensed restaurant near her own, she said she encountered difficulties. The neighboring restaurateur didn't like her taking drinks off the premises, and, she added, "they claimed I was too young."

That anecdote, obviously apocryphal, may have revealed Patricia's shame as she turned thirty-three with two Candlelights but no husband. Conflicted, like her new Manhattan restaurant—its faux-antique mirror frames reflecting the past while Lynas's bold wall stripes marched toward the future—Patricia cheered on a new generation of women while coveting the social position of their critics. "As for the secretaries and salesgirls who started patronizing Sixtieth Street, I couldn't have been more delighted to see them, both from a practical standpoint, as they constituted a huge new group of restaurant goers, and because of my deep feeling of kinship for them. You can imagine my indignation when some of the matrons and dowagers who lived in nearby hotels came to me and objected strenuously to my allowing 'riff-raff' to patronize the premises."[6]

In fact, Patricia was enchanted by the nearby hotels, particularly the beaux-arts Pierre with its opulent ballroom. Her identification with working women did not exclude aspirations to fit in with the "dowagers"; it is possible to have poor and rich kin. Most matrons or dowagers have acquired wealth through marriage; strictly defined, the terms refer to matrimony and widowhood. Not yet old enough to settle into those roles, yet more mature than many of the working "girls," lunching at her new eatery, Patricia could please both groups with her revamped menu, at least.

It was a bar, after all, that kicked the Sixtieth Street restaurant to a new popularity level—a salad bar. Patricia used the term to describe a high counter displaying dishes prepared by a "salad designer," a culinary worker recruited from New York's Filipino community, on which she'd continued to depend as she expanded. Office and retail workers could quickly eyeball the offerings, select a dish, and enjoy it at a cloth-covered table amid the flowers, doilies, and geometric wall designs.

Presentation was everything, or rather everything besides serving speed—of paramount importance to workers who, thanks to the salad bar, could enjoy a respite at Patricia Murphy's yet clock back on time after lunch. For some it was an occasional splurge; soda fountain counters, cafeterias, and the Automat also angled for the wage earners' lunch money, some by offering twenty-cent specials.

However, only at Patricia Murphy's did customers get unlimited popovers. Patricia mentioned them in every ad, linking them even more closely to her name than she had in Brooklyn. During Prohibition, candies, gum, and ice cream gained popularity as substitutes for alcohol. The popovers at Patricia Murphy's survived Repeal. Salted rather than sweet, and served with apple butter and creamy cottage cheese, they may have seemed almost healthful to Depression-era customers. As in Brooklyn, popover girls dressed in uniform, and uniformly white, offered apparently limitless quantities of them.

And why not? Analyzed by the price-per-portion formula taught at the Ware School of Tea Room Management, popovers were champs. Wheat was cheap, and the filling was air.

Eighty-five cents bought a salad, beverage, and dessert along with the popovers or other breads. Patricia Murphy's salads were "the glamour girls of the salad world, scoring a pin-up rating," raved food writer Clementine Paddleford in the *New York Herald Tribune*. She described generous scoops of salmon salad or cottage cheese cradled in "huge half-head of lettuce with enormous leaves, crisp curling at the edges," adding that, for fifteen cents extra, there were crabmeat salads with almost a cupful of the meat. Except for the bargain cottage cheese and fruit salads, all were "doused with French dressing," she added approvingly.[7]

Patricia was soon soaring past Betty Barclay's numbers while maintaining her predecessor's relatively relaxed hours—closed on Sundays and in the summer, a luxury she'd never been able to afford in Brooklyn. Not long before, she'd been a charity case at the women-only Three Arts Club. Now she could afford to move in the same circles as the women listed in the Social Register, who donated to such causes.

Hence, while still proudly celebrating St. Patrick's Day at her restaurants and continuing to print menus and matchbooks in green ink, Patricia took steps toward anglicizing her image. That left the question of her family, but in New York—where high society's Four Hundred included both the old and more recently rich—or at least newish-rich persons of the male gender—she hoped such matters could be finessed. Establishing the U.S. citizenship to which she'd been born continued to be a problem, requiring her to carry her father's birth documents while traveling, but ailing Newfoundland was still British. Just to be sure, Patricia had taken to describing herself as Welsh-Irish through her mother, Mary Griffiths Murphy, whose maiden surname was common in Wales, though her devout Catholicism was not.

A year after her Manhattan opening, Patricia became engaged to an investment banker named Edwin Schuyler Robinson. A member of the Bankers and Lake Placid Clubs, at age thirty-nine he was already living the life to which Patricia aspired. A vice president and director of a Wall Street financial firm, he made ocean voyages to Britain and wintered at the Castle Harbour resort in Bermuda. There was a fly in the ointment, however: at the time Patricia met him, there was a Mrs. E.S. Robinson, who had accompanied him on these trips.

Like Patricia, Mrs. Robinson enjoyed horseback riding. The former Doris Williams, who had immigrated to Brooklyn from England as a young girl, holds the reins in a 1932 photograph that ran in the *Eagle*. The Brooklyn paper took an interest in the couple, who lived in the Bay Ridge section of Robinson's native borough. The photo was taken in February, but Doris is squinting into the bright Nassau sun.[8]

Patricia looked forward to taking the reins from Doris and taking Manhattan by storm. The last two months of 1939 were a whirlwind of activity. On November 13, four days after Doris obtained a New Jersey divorce from Robinson on the grounds of abandonment, Lauraine and Telfair hosted a meal at the Hotel St. Regis. Patricia's father was in New York for the occasion, and he and Nana toasted Patricia and her beau, to be married three weeks hence. The *Trib* reported, "Miss Murphy Engaged to Schuyler Robinson; Troth to Grandson of Count Told at Dinner Party."[9]

It seemed that Patricia had acquired not just a fiancé but also aristocratic bloodlines. Robinson's maternal grandfather, the announcement said, had been the Count Godfrey Schultze von Altman of Switzerland before becoming an American citizen and marrying a descendant of Betsy Ross.

At best, this pedigree was incomplete. Robinson's mother, born in Germany but raised in Brooklyn, was the former Sarah Schulze (spelled, unlike the cited Count's, with no *t*). Her father, Godfrey Schulze, was a bookkeeper. In 1880 he told a census taker that he and his parents had been born in Prussia. Whether real or imagined, a Swiss connection was preferable to a Prussian one in America after the Great War.

Better yet in these nativist times was the claim of Robinson's kinship with Betsy Ross. It is possible that Godfrey's American-born wife, Josephine Cuyler Schulz, was descended from the legendary flag-maker. If so, it was one of the few flashes of authenticity in the *Trib* piece, which like other engagement announcements, was likely based on information provided by the bride-to-be. Like her ship documents, it embellished her given name, Ellen, calling her "Eleanor Patricia Murphy." Her parents, renting in Jackson Heights, Queens, were said to be "of Brooklyn and Newfoundland." To earn a certificate, Patricia had played piano for an examiner sent to Newfoundland from England. The announcement inverted the trip, stating that Patricia attended St. Michael's "and Trinity College, London, England, where she studied music."

Announcing the engagement in Brooklyn, the *Eagle* identified her as the owner of two Candlelight restaurants. The *Trib* did her more favors, referring to thirty-four-year-old Patricia as a "Brooklyn girl" without mentioning her work. The boom in female employment fueled Patricia's Sixtieth Street restaurant, but her own career was a social hindrance. The Social Register had dropped women for working in fields like show business, and Patricia, not yet listed in the Blue Book, desperately hoped to be.

Unable to travel back in time and emerge as a New York debutante, she did manage to describe her father as an importer-exporter, descended from a Boston family of ship owners. Frank's father, James, born in Newfoundland, had indeed fished out of Boston in his own vessel before founding the family store in Placentia. Frank owned two schooners, likely inherited from his father, and spent four winters at sea, skippering herring boats.[10] Patricia's maritime heritage was genuine, and references to her grandfather as "Captain James Murphy" were earned: he had overseen crews of Irish-born sailors. Missing in the account, however, was Patricia's Irish background.

Sanitized of ethnicity and restored to girlhood, Patricia was ready to marry and play society hostess. A week after being toasted at the St. Regis, Robinson rented a single-family townhouse at 56 East Eightieth Street. There was ample room for a live-in maid and butler, who would assist at parties.

Accompanying two of the engagement notices was a somewhat spartan portrait of Patricia credited to the Bachrach studio.[11] Her large eyes gaze slightly to the left under tight dark curls. She wears a collarless top unadorned by jewelry.

Her wedding photo took things to the opposite extreme. In fact, the engagement portrait, juxtaposed with the nuptial one, might have been before-and-after images in a magazine makeover feature. For the wedding, Patricia sat for society photographer, Ira L. Hill, whose stylized, retouched photos had made him a Park Avenue and Hollywood favorite. By the late thirties, Hill—known for his scandalous personal life—was delegating routine work to studio assistants. But he himself photographed Patricia, with whom he shared a business philosophy about appearances.

Explaining the paintings, hangings, and music at his Fifth Avenue studio, Hill said, "I induce the mood most propitious to beauty." Patricia posed in her wedding garb, the dress barely visible beneath the heavy lapels of her fox jacket. Her shoulders, made massive by the fur, are swiveled right as she looks directly into the camera. A remarkable hat consists of two pieces: a cap covers the top of her head while a pleat-covered saucer balances almost vertically against her forehead. Known as a draped cloche, the hat nearly conceals Patricia's wide brow, focusing attention on her paperweight eyes—or at least one of them. A shadow cast by the hat nearly obscures the other eye. Her face seems heavily made-up, probably with Hill's retouching pencil.

Holding brown Lady Slipper orchids, as she had in the portrait, the societally retouched Patricia married Robinson before a lush display of chrysanthemums and snapdragons in the townhouse that would become their home. A large reception followed a private ceremony performed by a minister of the Church of Divine Science named Emmet Fox, whose weekly services at the New York Hippodrome regularly filled all 5,000-plus seats.

Patricia's three sisters were bridesmaids, and her three brothers joined two of Robinson's friends as ushers. His best man, Walter Bryant Pierce, was best of all. Formerly married to a railroad heiress, he was a longtime member of the smart set, and his second wife, a Frenchwoman, was similarly well connected. Surrounded by family and important people, joined in marriage by Fox, and photographed by Hill, Patricia was at the top of her game.

She felt she was already flying even before she and her new husband left for their honeymoon. They kept the destination secret while letting everyone know they'd get there by plane.

On the following day, there would be write-ups of the wedding in the *Times*, *Trib*, and *Eagle*. But the best gift had arrived the day before: an inch-high mention in a society magazine called *The Spur*, a reference to the equestrian arts pictured in its cover illustration. There it was, the Murphy-Robinson marriage, on the same page as a calendar of the season's debuts and near news about the Vanderbilts and Mellons.

Just ten years earlier, hungry and confused, Patricia "had continued her musical studies in New York" with a disastrous piano gig at an Upper West Side cafeteria. A souvenir from that nightmare appeared at her dream wedding. Music accompanied the posh reception, provided by a harpist, a Hungarian trio, and William C. Orth, the hash-house pianist who had lent her money to fix her broken heel.

Patricia never failed to reward loyalty. But of course, there was the other side of the coin.

CHAPTER 6

War

When you are not busy, stand at your station at attention.

—Patricia Murphy's manual for employees, 1930

Within a few months of the wedding, both Patricia and her husband had changed jobs. In February, the business section of the *Times* reported that "E. Schuyler Robinson, formerly vice president of D.M.S. Hegarty & Co. is with W.B. Pierce & Co." The groom had gone into business with his best man.

Pierce had been involved in more than one partnership himself, both professionally and personally. Six years before taking Robinson in with him, he had left one Wall Street brokerage to form another. More remarkably, he and his current wife, Paula, had begun a sensational affair while still married to their first spouses. Embarrassed by this obvious expression of female desire, Paula's first husband had blamed it all on Pierce, publicly accusing the broker of exerting Svengali-like "extraordinary influence" to alienate her affections.[1]

If Pierce possessed superhuman persuasive powers, they probably weren't needed to draw Robinson to his firm. Robinson's old boss, Daniel Hegarty, had hired a new man around the time of Patricia's wedding, possibly as preparation for Robinson's departure. The doors at Wall Street brokerages constantly revolved.

Patricia's new job—homemaker—was a far more drastic change. Six months after her wedding, the U.S. Census reported that she hadn't worked "for wages or profit" in the last week of March 1940 and was engaged only in "home housework."

"I tried my hand very briefly as hostess of my own home," she wrote later. She had not, however, given up ownership of the two restaurants.

But a wife's job was often understood as a husband's failure, and the Robinsons' butler, who spoke to the census taker, reflected their anxiety to conform to social norms. The butler gave Patricia's age as thirty-one, eight years younger than her husband. In truth, she was well into her thirties and just five years his junior. However, the butler probably didn't know the truth; the same fib appears on the couple's marriage license application.[2]

Whether innocently or by calculation, the butler gave Robinson's first name as "Robert"—it's Edwin on his birth certificate—perhaps indicating he was called "Rob." The servant also described his employer's Hamburg-born mother as a New York native,[3] possibly because he'd never met her. At any rate, with war raging in Europe, the birthplace of Robinson's mother was best forgotten, like the Prussian origins of his grandfather, the "Swiss count."

Even with the United States officially neutral, the rumble of war had reached Brooklyn. The Navy Yard there, already hiring thousands of civilians, was expanding. Three shifts toiled at the yard six days a week, and the personnel office was scrambling to fill vacancies.

Society was taking note, as well. The second Mrs. Pierce, born Paule-Jeanne Lauthier in Perpignan, helped organize two benefits for refugees fleeing Occupied France. One featured a fashion show with outfits modeled by debutantes of the season, including her daughter.[4]

Still fed up with demanding and parsimonious patrons, Patricia considered switching to cotton importing and exporting. But times were changing. Even in Brooklyn, more people had fuller pockets. They were starting to dine out more and complain less.

As for her marriage, "the relationship was doomed from the start," she wrote. When close friends or relatives visited her from Newfoundland, she gave them the royal tour of New York and her restaurants, plus an earful about Robinson. He had married her for her money, she said. It was she who paid the rent on the townhouse, she wrote, even if his name was on the lease. She also told her siblings and parents that Robinson was an alcoholic.

In the manuscript of her autobiography, she wrote that "in my youth and inexperience I married an equally young and irresponsible man who represented himself as a Wall Street broker."[5] Both were in their thirties, hardly children, and Robinson had been married before. The words "represented himself as" were deleted before publication; Robinson was indeed a broker, not merely posing as one. However, misrepresentation was grounds for divorce, and Patricia was exploring her options. At any rate, he had misrepresented his love for her.

Patricia was more pleased with someone else in whom she'd placed her trust. Mary Catherine Rogers, a hostess at the Brooklyn Candlelight, had become indispensable. When not throwing parties at her doll's house on East Eightieth Street, Patricia kept close tabs on both of her places. Nana was taking a hand in managing Brooklyn while Mollie, as people called young Miss Rogers, was charming the customers and scrutinizing the books.

Given the razor-thin profit margins in Brooklyn, waste and employee theft were monitored with vigilance. Portions not sold had better remain on the server's steam table, and, as the employees' manual cautioned, "If each is careful not to waste the butter on your station by letting it become soft and untidy, many pounds of butter will be saved." The hostess oversaw and graded the servers. Mollie did so well that Patricia named her treasurer of Candlelight, Inc.

Patricia and Mollie had an ice cream connection. Even in her first week of business, when she had no idea how to pay for it, Patricia made sure ice cream was on her menu. Like popovers, this was an item not easily available at home, particularly in the era of ice boxes. She wrote, "I remember chasing after the ice cream man for half a block to pay him his bill. I couldn't catch him, and it was just as well. It was for $29, and I didn't have that much after ten days in business." That ice cream man may well have been Mollie's father, an Irish-born immigrant who had come to Brooklyn via Scotland, where Mollie was born.

Working for Patricia, Mollie reported an annual income of $1,500 in 1939, just a few hundred dollars less than the earnings of her father, by then an ice cream pasteurizer. Mollie's sister, Grace, was one of the high school girls employed by Patricia as a junior hostess.

Patricia also shared the riches with her parents. Frank still had one foot in Newfoundland, rebounding since the outbreak of war in Europe. In September 1940, the United States struck a destroyers-for-bases deal with Britain involving leases for American military bases, paid not in cash but in ships. Several of the new U.S. bases were in strategically important Newfoundland, including one at Argentia, near Patricia's hometown of Placentia. Yankee dollars flowed in, lifting all boats in Newfoundland.

Brooklyn was also buoyant, as the Navy Yard won a ten-million-dollar government contract for further expansion. With President Roosevelt's support, it began preparations for immense new dry docks and the construction of super-battleships. The Yard's expansion demolished the Wallabout wholesale market, a teeming micro-metropolis of fruit, vegetable, and live poultry vendors that had been Patricia's first business academy.

At the Wallabout, "I got fine food at a very good price and . . . they often gave me great bunches of celery or lettuce, taking pity on the harassed small girl who some stall keepers thought might be collecting for Sisters of Charity." So Patricia wrote, although probably she sent others out to haggle. By mid-1941, all 250 vendors had relocated to Canarsie, close to the Brooklyn Union Gas cafeteria, where she had served lobster lunches.[6] The gas company was now one of many customers served by Candlelight Catering Company, incorporated separately from her restaurants and headquartered in Manhattan.

Patricia could afford to send her parents to the classy Sedgefield Inn near Greensboro, North Carolina, a rambling Tudor-style resort with an eighteen-hole golf course. In November of 1941, the *Eagle* society page listed area couples who had registered at the inn. Frank and Nana were among them.

Less than three weeks later, the Japanese attacked Pearl Harbor. Patricia's not-so-young husband was a shade too old to be drafted. For her brothers, it was only a matter of time.

In the meantime, there was plenty of merriment at the restaurants between occasional blackout drills that doused the lights on Times Square and sent reluctant New Yorkers into shelters after they'd finished marveling at the moon. Patricia no longer fretted about the preponderance of women at her Manhattan place. Instead, she put up special hat shelves for the various branches of the service—not vital for a foldable sailor hat or G.I. garrison cap, but Patricia was always partial to officers. Anyone in uniform was escorted to the front of the line, especially important at her Manhattan location, where she still had no bar or other area for waiting diners.

Liquor or no, like every other midtown Manhattan restaurant in wartime, Patricia Murphy's Candlelight was jammed. Farm boys, laborers, and clerks were on leave or waiting to be shipped out, and The Candlelight was a short hop from girlie shows and nightclubs.

As for Patricia's regular working-girl customers, they could ask for higher pay or easily find it elsewhere. New York's factories had sprung back to life, supplying tons of military supplies for ships docked at its piers. Suddenly flush with cash, workers spent much of it on dining and entertainment. After all, with all metal requisitioned by the army, no amount of dough could buy a Ford or a fridge.

Civilian food shortages and price controls brought Patricia challenges as well as customers. "Anyone in the restaurant business will tell you that the confusion and red tape that came with the setting up of the O.P.A. and rationing could scarcely have been worse," she wrote, referring to the federal Office of Price Administration. "At times one was penalized for honest mistakes." As for the "constant offers from the black market to secure provisions underhandedly," she said it took courage to resist.[7]

The hiring binge continued at the Navy Yard in Brooklyn, but given all the rationing headaches, Patricia decided to open it only for dinner, when she could fill its dining rooms and cocktail lounge. Luncheon had become lunch, and even women were eating it from steel pails: the yard eventually began hiring women to work right alongside the men. Gals in slacks were welding and wiring aircraft carriers.[8]

War arrived on her family's doorstep in the form of a draft notice for Shannon. Youngest of the Murphy sons, Francis Frederick Murphy—his legal first and middle names were the reverse of his father's—Shannon was enlisted in Lower Manhattan and shipped out. Less than two years earlier, he had boarded the Fort Townshend with his father and brother Jim, bound to Newfoundland to visit friends and family. Now he was headed for an uncertain future.

Jim, the oldest of the boys, stayed ashore, where he was enjoying life. After his years among sailors who had disgusted him with their vulgarity, he had found good times and pleasant companions. For several years, he had been dating Monica McDonough, a former co-worker at the Hotel McAlpin. A native of Wellsville, a small town in upstate New York, Monica had been educated at an elite institution for girls, the Bennett School.

Monica hit it off with Jim's sister Maude, and he spent much of his free time with the two women and their friends. When his romance with Monica became a water-cooler topic in the hotel accounting office, he found a new job with the firm that looked over the hotel's books.

Then Jim received his greetings from the Selective Service, sending him to an enlistment station on Governor's Island in the Hudson. All the posters, newsreels, and music aimed at marketing the war had not worked their magic on Jim. Experienced in business, he could see through the hype. He didn't want to go.

There was a possible way out, thanks to his Newfoundland upbringing. At age six, Jim had broken his arm in a way that pushed the bones out of alignment. At the time, his father's business was thriving, and the family probably could have consulted an orthopedist in St. John's. However, instead of having his bones set, Jim was told to carry a bag weighted with sand. The home remedy failed, leaving Jim with a deformed left arm.

The words didn't come. "I had intended to say, 'Hey, look at this arm,' but at the physical, I didn't say a word about it. You get in with the guys, and you don't want to be rejected," he later recalled.

He was assigned a bunk bed for the night. Then, "I'm up in the bunk at 3 in the morning," Jim said. "They throw shoes and clothes at you. They give you a duffel bag full of stuff . . . there are guys on either side giving you inoculations."

Monica and Jim's family had assembled at Governor's Island to say goodbye. Jim's first hours as a soldier lacked gravitas. "I get out on the stoop," he recalled, using New York vernacular for the stairway of the enlistment center. "I swing the duffel bag over my shoulder, it goes twirling around, and I fell down the stairs in front of Monica, Lauraine, Maude, Vincent—four or five people. Very embarrassing," Jim continued.

If Patricia was there, he didn't remember.

Still in New York, he was given an aptitude test. One section involved the identification of tools and their uses. Jim knew them all. "In Newfoundland, if you wanted something done, you had to do it yourself," he later reflected. The hotel accountant learned he'd be trained as a mechanic.

Jim requested a three-day leave, claiming that he was the sole support of his parents and needed to take care of things. In this intriguing lie, the oldest Murphy son switched roles with the oldest Murphy daughter. The answer was no, but ever the confident salesman, Jim asked to speak to the officer in charge.

It was wartime, when lives were lost or saved by a tap on the shoulder or a duck of the head toward a cigarette lighter. In Jim's case, the fateful moment was the meeting with the major. "You say your name is Murphy," the officer said, glancing at a document that listed Jim's birthplace. "You must have gone to St. Bartholomew's," he said. Jim had; that was his high school.

Jim returned from his leave to find that his artillery outfit had shipped out to North Africa. There were Allied victories there in late 1942, but his outfit was completely wiped out. His Newfoundland origins had deformed his arm but had rescued him from peril.

Soon New York receded into the distance, but Jim departed on a train, not a ship. He and his fellow soldiers awoke in southern Florida, where he spent his days drilling on the beach, encountering no greater danger than sunburn. From there, he went to an Army Air Force airfield in Lincoln, Nebraska, for training as a mechanic.

He and Monica had been writing back and forth. Jim urged her to come to Lincoln and marry him. "She already had three years invested in me," he said, recollecting his sales pitch. She agreed, and came out. The real tough sale was to the church. "The bishop for all of Nebraska was there, and he was against G.I.'s getting married," Jim recalled. "We had to get our birth certificates from Newfoundland. They put a lot of red tape in our way. I said I could get married at a justice of a peace."

Jim prevailed: the banns were read at a Catholic church in Lincoln, and the outlook brightened. A distant cousin of the McDonoughs recognized Monica's name and took the young couple under his wing, treating them to dinner and finding an apartment where they could live.

Rooms were booked at the Cornhusker Hotel for the G.I. wedding's New York guests. Lauraine, whose husband was in the Navy, came with her young son, Owen. Vincent, still a civilian, was there. As for Patricia, whom Monica privately described as "a piece of work," she was matron of honor.

Patricia put her pastry chefs to work and had the wedding cake flown in. Monica never had a chance to select her own. She and Jim were tiny plastic figures on her successful sister-in-law's confection.

A few months later, Vincent was drafted into the army. Jim completed his training in Nebraska, where Monica was working at the army PX store and far out-earning his soldier's pay. When the army asked Jim where he'd like to be stationed, "All the guys in my outfit wanted to go back to New York. I put down California because the war was in the Atlantic Ocean, the real killing would be in Europe. I wanted to see California anyhow."

He was assigned to Lockheed in Burbank. Monica joined him shortly afterward. At a pre-arranged time, they reunited at Hollywood and Vine and celebrated with wine and chips. Their movie-worthy romance continued with Jim's three-week leave, which they spent hiking through the snow in Squaw Valley.

Monica was hired by Lockheed, eventually becoming a department head and "making really good money." When Jim was sent farther inland to Santa Ana, the couple saw each other only when he had free time and could hitch a ride. Discovering that she was pregnant, Monica quit her job, much to Lockheed's perplexed disappointment. She would not give her reason for leaving; pregnancy was not openly discussed. She did tell Jim about it in a letter, but the letter went astray. His mail was often misdirected to another James Murphy in the service.

When he failed to mention the pregnancy in his next letter to Monica, she was infuriated. "I didn't get anything for Christmas that year," he said. But he did get a pay bonus for their first child, born in early September of 1943.[9]

A month earlier, Patricia had made another journey across the United States. This time it was not for a wedding. She went to Reno to divorce Robinson on the grounds of mental cruelty. The couple had not been living together since late 1942.

Relieved to be done with it, Patricia wrote, "There was not enough affection, understanding or companionship to give the break-up any of the dignity of tragedy."

No longer required to pose as the "house homemaker" of the 1940 census, Patricia moved back to Brooklyn. Hard work prevented her from dwelling on her mistake, she wrote. There was plenty to do.

Restaurants were forced to scramble for staff. Patricia's Filipino workers were not subject to conscription, but could enlist; many Filipino Americans did so in solidarity with the compatriots defending their homeland. Those who remained won new respect from white Americans after Bataan and Corregidor. In Manhattan, the department store company Abraham & Strauss sponsored a radio talk by the president of the Filipino Women's Club of New York on "The Customs and Cooking of Our Allies."

New York had a long way to go toward racial equality. One of Patricia's competitors in Brooklyn Heights was a restaurant called Mammy's

Pantry. Its ads featured an Aunt Jemima–type illustration of an African American cook. In 1938, a black journalist, Theodore "Ted" Poston, and his wife, Miriam, sued the owner of the Montague Street restaurant under the Civil Rights Act. Their suit alleged that the owner, Christine K. Heineman, had said, "I'm a Southern lady, and I won't serve you." They lost in a Manhattan court.[10]

Then, in early 1942, a play by William Saroyan set in a fictional New York restaurant opened on Broadway. Among its characters were two Filipino dishwashers, including one who spoke passionately about the plight of Filipinos in America, including discrimination in employment. The play was a critical flop and closed within a week.[11]

However temporarily, the war opened some doors for restaurant workers. Short-handed in Brooklyn, Patricia advertised for waitresses who were fast and experienced, not "high type," as she had demanded in 1930. She also placed an ad for "Dishwashers (Colored)." According to the ads, waitresses could expect about seven times a dishwasher's wages.[12]

If throwing herself into work helped Patricia, so did the presence of Sir Barton, her canine companion. She rented an apartment in a charming brick building at 14 Cranberry Street, not far from the Brooklyn Candlelight. Eventually, she rented the adjacent apartment, too, so Sir Barton could have the run of both yards.

Her parents also returned to Brooklyn, renting close to the restaurant at 1 Clark Street. Lonely in her Long Island suburb with Telfair gone, Lauraine also came back to Brooklyn Heights. She and her son took up residence on Grace Court, a picturesque cul-de-sac, and as soon as Owen was old enough, he had a steady job walking Sir Barton.[13]

The sisters visited back and forth. Lauraine was at Patricia's apartment when a freak earthquake shook Brooklyn in August of 1944. Pictures fell, and Lauraine fell off a chair. "I was petrified," Patricia told the *Eagle*. "I thought there had been a terrible accident in the subway." Others thought the quake was an enemy bombardment.[14]

The war never reached New York or Jim, now a staff sergeant in California with two children. After the Allied victory in Europe, plans were made to send his outfit to India, along with others that hadn't seen action, but then the Japanese surrendered.

CHAPTER 7

Love

When face to face, your personality counts.

—Patricia Murphy's manual for employees, 1930

Things returned to normal, but a different normal. The upscale Manhattan home furnishings store W&J Sloane wasn't designing interiors for ships anymore. The company put away the citation bestowed by a vice admiral and concentrated on other matters, such as providing floor-to-ceiling flower racks for the front windows of the East Sixtieth Street Candlelight.

Still lacking a liquor license, and with the swarms of servicemen gone from Manhattan, Patricia was nonetheless doing fine. Meat shortages continued through much of 1946, but that didn't affect the Candlelight's big draws, salad and popovers. There was no shortage of table-top flora, for which the Candlelight relied on vendors such as the small New York chain My Florist. Patricia was capturing enough of the postwar prosperity to lease an alcove next to the dining room to seat peak-time overflow.

For now, she kept advertising in the *Christian Science Monitor*, using "no liquor" as a draw for the abstemious. However, she worried that the market had shifted. Male customers wanted a drink, and she wanted them.

The flowers were essential. Like popovers, they were part of Patricia's signature. During the war, every restaurant was full, but now you needed something to set you apart from the competition. Always looking for ways to cut costs, Patricia wished she could switch from My Florist to My Home-Grown Flowers. Gardening had always interested her, but she had no time or space to indulge it. She left such things to Nana, who could coax flowers from even the rocky soil of Newfoundland.

The Brooklyn Candlelight was in good hands. Vincent had been managing it since his army discharge, assisted by the able Mollie Rogers. The two had taken a romantic interest in one another. One of Mollie's younger brothers, John, was assuming responsibilities, too.

With the war over, lunch was again served daily in Brooklyn. Obsessed as always with clientele gender balance, Patricia announced the lunch reopening in an *Eagle* feature that got the message. "Although from outside appearances this noted restaurant may look like a tea room, just watch the hordes of men going in," said the report, also mentioning that Sweet 16 parties and "women's club festivities" were welcome for just a dollar per person.

Restaurants were no longer the only place to spend spare cash. Returning G.I.s were using their veterans' benefits to attend school, buy homes, or start businesses. Patricia, however, continued with her largely Filipino staff. The Rescission Act of 1946 had singled out Filipinos for exclusion from the G.I. bill. Filipino Americans who had enlisted with the promise of benefits returned to find their options still limited.

Not every G.I. had come home, of course. Shannon, the first of Patricia's brothers to be drafted, had survived the war physically but not mentally. Battle fatigue, as the effects of combat were called, had led to his confinement in the psychiatric ward of a Veterans Administration hospital. Such things were not spoken of, and the Murphy family rarely mentioned it even among themselves.[1]

These days, a lot of federal spending was bypassing New York and going south and west. Jim had decided to stay in California after his discharge, along with Monica and their two small sons. He was keeping books again, this time for a big produce company. So, when Frank went back to Newfoundland for a visit one year after the war's end, he went accompanied by the only son available to him, Vincent.

His daughters were all in Patricia's orbit, in one way or another. Lauraine still lived near the Brooklyn Candlelight. Her husband, back from the navy, had resumed the long commute to his engineering job in Long Island, while their son attended Brooklyn Friends, a private school. Maude had a role at the Candlelight in Manhattan.

Single again but still bent on social acceptance in Manhattan, Patricia decided to stake her claim to the Upper East Side. No longer would she be a tenant on East Sixtieth. The "original cash-and-carry girl,"[2] as she called herself because of her supposed reluctance to borrow, was going to take out a mortgage and buy the building.

Her Sixtieth Street Candlelight Corp. secured a bank mortgage for $26,000 on No. 33.[3] The cash-and-carry girl was taking on substantial debt. She could finally escape the confines of her original submarine-like space and open an additional dining room upstairs, on what had once been the parlor floor of the building.

Soon after this 1947 purchase, an *Eagle* gossip columnist wrote that Patricia and Vincent planned to drive to California, where Patricia would give the car to another brother, Jim, and return to New York by train.[4] The weather was cold, the Manhattan restaurant was under construction, and Nana, Lonnie, and the Rogers siblings could keep an eye on Brooklyn. Moreover, Patricia wished to have a talk with Jim about opportunities in her expanding empire. She was alone, and family was important.

Jim may have been unaware of the *Eagle* gossip item. If he had, he would have resented its portrayal of Patricia as philanthropist and him as a charity case. Any job pitches she made apparently failed; she and Vincent returned alone. Jim may have taken them to a California landmark that impressed him tremendously, not with soaring redwoods or sparkling beaches, but rather with its balance sheet.

Knott's Berry Place, as it was called then, was near Santa Ana, where Jim had been stationed during the war. Even during the worst gas shortages, city dwellers drove out to see its replicated ghost town, smoking volcano, and "pitchur gallery," sprawled out on more than a hundred acres of land. Jim saw these attractions for what they truly were: distractions to induce people to wait for hours for a restaurant seat.[5]

The Knott family's restaurant often served ten thousand people a day in its six dining rooms. Families made a day of it, sometimes too absorbed in shopping for berries or gawking at a mining-town relic to hear their table announced on the loudspeaker. During the war, the place was said to take in half a million dollars per year, and now it was more popular than ever.

Jim thought the concept would work in New York, obviously not in the city, but in the suburbs. Preoccupied with her Manhattan plans, Patricia's mind was working on a different track.

Jim and Monica's two small boys were adorable. The car was bestowed on the family, and its acceptance indicated that Jim's bookkeeping job wasn't paying all that much. Still, he wasn't ready to give up on California. Working for his big-shot big sister probably held little appeal for Jim, nor did the prospect of moving back to Manhattan, Brooklyn, or even Queens. Families like his were leaving the cities.

Patricia and Vincent took the train home to Brooklyn, where the *Eagle* had printed another gossip item, more intriguing than the one about their trip. A columnist, Lew Sheaffer, wrote,

Well, waddaya know! Mildred E. Gillars, "Axis Sally," worked at the boro's Candlelight Restaurant as a waitress from 1930 to '33. She was a real looker then, popular but "temperamental."[6]

Ordinarily eager to see her name in print, Patricia kept it well away from this item. The government had arrested Mildred for making propaganda broadcasts in Germany for the Nazis, aimed at lowering the Allied soldiers' morale. Arrested in Berlin in 1946, Gillars had been charged with treason and was awaiting trial.

Patricia's doings provided regular fodder for Sheaffer's columns, and he was a cheerleader for her restaurants. If she was the source of the "temperamental" descriptor, placed conspicuously within quotation marks, that was the last she had to say on the matter, anonymously or otherwise. Other news organizations either failed to notice the item or let it drop, perhaps because Patricia declined to confirm it.

However, the *Eagle*, in which Patricia regularly advertised, did not run a correction or denial. At trial, Gillars said she had worked as a waitress in New York without naming any establishments.

No one wanted to dwell on the past anyway. Soon the *Eagle* was noting that Vincent was now officially the manager of the Brooklyn Candlelight while Patricia devoted her "time and talents" to the one in Manhattan. Diners were filling the bottom two floors of No. 33, but room for expansion there was limited. The building was tall and slender. Like many of the area's townhouses, it had been built for one family before the retail invasion.

Among the noted former residents was Michael J. Meehan, at No. 35, attached to the east wall of Patricia's building. Like Patricia, he had immigrated—in his case, from England—with nothing, and then made a rapid New York ascent. Starting as a Broadway ticket seller, he had become a broker, earning a fortune in the late 1920s by special-izing in RCA stock. Known for hosting parties in vast hotel ballrooms, he was forced to quit the New York Stock Exchange amid charges of stock manipulations. Meehan was long gone from No. 35. With a façade stripped of its original Italianate stone carvings—now considered old fashioned—the space was filled with furnished rooms.

Patricia wanted the deed. Borrowing another $32,000,[7] she became a developer. The two buildings were combined into a single lot, 33–35 East Sixtieth, a combined building with space for further restaurant expansion on the first floor.

No longer would Patricia make money purely from the restaurant businesses. Some of those furnished rooms in the second building could be rented as commercial space. Her catering business now had an office, and she was making money without selling meals.

Patricia ran her final "no liquor" ad in February 1947. Frank had a new customer for his seal skins. As in Brooklyn, she used the fur to cover the seats in her new cocktail lounge.

She had not expected the seal skins to become a memorial to her father, but in the summer of that year, Frederick Francis Murphy died of a stroke in St. John's, where he had long maintained a residence. The only American-born member of the Murphy family was buried in Newfoundland, the only place where he felt of use and at home. The obituary in the *Eagle* described him as a member of the fur and fish exporting firm of James Murphy & Sons, Ltd. That was the name of the company founded by Frank's father, defunct since 1925. The Brooklyn paper described Frank as the father of Candlelight owner Patricia Murphy, adding that his firm "took a leading part some 50 or 60 years ago in popularizing sealskin furs in New York City."

If New York had, in fact, ever been seized by a seal skin trend, it had ended. Patricia's Manhattan restaurant had "an unusual little bar," Robert W. Dana wrote in his 1948 book, *Where to Eat in New York.* However, upholstery was beside the point. Patricia "decided it would put her out of business if she couldn't serve liquor," wrote Dana, adding, "She has drinks now, but the popover is still king."

Aged forty-three, Patricia was surely not annoyed to read Dana's description of her as "an ambitious young lady." He said she had opened her Manhattan restaurant "aided by three brothers and two sisters." That information could have come only from Patricia: she credited all her siblings with her success, even Shannon, now so ill.[8]

Sheila was a special case, not included in the list of restaurant helpers. The only Murphy sister to marry young—Maude was still single—

Sheila was now Mrs. John G. Fox of Pittsburgh. Thanks to Patricia's financial support, she had graduated from Wellesley with unsoiled hands.

Patricia's love for her family and her soaring business were not enough. She spread the word that she was looking for romance, and friends found her a blind date for New Year's Eve of 1947. They described him as a distinguished naval architect.

Captain James Eugene Kiernan, six years older and about a foot taller than Patricia, had been a superintendent at the Brooklyn Navy Yard throughout the war. While the yard was fueling her business in Brooklyn Heights, he was more likely to be dining at the officer's club.

Patricia's blind date came with an impressive resume. A decorated veteran of World War I, Kiernan had been a technical adviser to the governor general of the Philippines. Stateside, he was no stranger to society. Between the wars, he and his late wife, Helen, had entertained at their Q Street home in Washington, where the *Washington Post* once featured a photo of Helen on its main social page under the caption, "Navy Hostess."

In other words, he had the pedigree Patricia had looked for in her first husband, with the added benefit of not having to make any of it up. What's more, he was genuinely available. Helen had died in October, and their two daughters were grown. One, Geraldine, had met her future husband at an officers' club reception hosted by her father.

The ruddy-faced captain, James "Rosie" Kiernan, shared Patricia's passion for throwing parties. This was an important commonality.

But, as Patricia wrote, "There was no blinding light or clash of cymbals" when the two met. The weather was lousy on the final night of 1947. Friends had arranged for the captain to escort Patricia to a Manhattan party, but those plans were abandoned. A five-day snowstorm had paralyzed traffic in New York. Temperatures rose on New Year's Eve, but cars remained buried, and sleet added to the woes.

However, the subways were running. Patricia's friends brought the party to her house instead, bringing the captain as well. She took little notice of him, busying herself with chilling champagne bottles in the snow outside her back door. Noticing she could use some help, Rosie went out and gave her a hand.

That impressed her, but what to do with "this Navy character" soon became a problem. Their mutual friends began planning for a party

Patricia gave each January at the Plaza Hotel, and because "the man in uniform looked sort of out of things," she invited him.

As Patricia told it, her intention was only to play cupid, or as she put it, Samaritan. She said she found him a date for the Plaza—a young, gorgeous doctor's daughter—whom he dumped in favor of her. However it actually happened, the two middle-aged people soon found themselves spending every day together. Rosie lived in Brooklyn and would drive Patricia to Manhattan, or in other ways make himself useful.

Patricia's new beau had few cultural pretensions despite, or perhaps because of, his impressive credentials. One of five children raised in Brooklyn by Irish-born parents, "he didn't care for any of the rather sophisticated activities I had engaged in since really discovering Manhattan," wrote Patricia, who instead found herself accompanying Rosie at prize fights and hockey games.

A violator of gender roles herself—particularly now that her business had scaled up beyond tea-room dimensions—Patricia celebrated others who challenged gender stereotypes. For the success of her Brooklyn launch and the discovery of a Manhattan location that could be leased to a woman, she credited Jack Lynas. The owner of an eponymous Brooklyn Heights shop advertising "interesting artifacts, bric-a-brac & antiques," Lynas during World War I had illustrated patriotic postcards. The cards were of the kind that Patricia hand-colored after being fired from her restaurant jobs, suggesting it was Lynas who found her the coloring work. Since decorating Patricia's two establishments, he'd created a chartreuse-and-burgundy interior for another Brooklyn restaurant, the Morillon.[9]

Another of Patricia's gender-role-defying associates was a woman who had graduated from Columbia's school of architecture and studied at the Bauhaus Institute in Berlin. Before the war, she had been a partner in the Chicago architectural firm Rodgers and Priestley, founded by close associates of Ludwig Mies van der Rohe. This exceptional but underappreciated woman was Nathalie Swan Rahv, wife of Philip Rahv, editor of the left-leaning literary journal *Partisan Review*. Patricia hired her as the architect in charge of the Sixtieth Street remodeling.

The broadmindedness exhibited in Patricia's choice of architect did not extend to her taste in men. Patricia's first marriage to the desk-bound Robinson had been a disaster. She associated maleness with uniforms and tools. Dressing, as Nana did, in furs and orchids, she liked to take the arm of a man who was all sharp shoulders and brass buttons. Captain J.E. Kiernan, still on active duty when they met, fit the profile completely.

Moreover, this designer of ships took an ardent interest in tinkering with the mechanical innards of her restaurants, adjusting the air conditioners and refrigerators that had always intimidated Patricia. Who cared if he preferred boxing over ballet?

Perhaps striking a balance of cultural tastes, they attended an ice show at Madison Square Garden at the wintry start of 1948. Starring the celebrity figure skater Sonja Henie, the *Hollywood Ice Revue* combined athleticism with hula routines and broad slapstick. Patricia wrote that Rosie had proposed to her on February 13, during an intermission at the Metropolitan Opera House, and she had happily accepted. Subsequently, she said, he had formalized the engagement at the ice show. As the company of skaters formed a line and cracked "the whip," Patricia excitedly grabbed Rosie's arm, and he slipped his Annapolis class ring on her finger.[10]

The proposal, as well as the ring, may have been offered amid the plebeian din of the Garden, not the rare air of the Met; the ice show closed on February 10, three days before Patricia's version of the engagement date. Either way, the mature couple's courtship had proceeded at figure-skating velocity.

Having agreed to marry, they returned home to Brooklyn and Nana, who read the news on their faces and was enormously pleased. At age forty-three, the owner of two thriving restaurants and two Upper East Side buildings, Patricia still needed her mother's approval.

Nana had enthusiastically supported her during the Robinson divorce, encouraging her to expedite the matter in Reno rather than face the delays and difficulties of New York's onerous divorce laws. Patricia had also had her first marriage annulled by the Catholic Church. No obstacles prevented Patricia and Rosie from applying for their marriage license on July 7. This time, Patricia would be married by a Roman Catholic priest, not a celebrity Protestant minister, in Manhattan's St. Francis of Assisi Church.[11]

Rain came down as Patricia and Rosie emerged from the church, surrounded by umbrella-toting relatives. A family snapshot shows Rosie in his uniform standing next to a smiling Patricia. More relaxed and slender than she usually appeared in photos, she wears a smart-looking dark dress. It is short-sleeved and wartime short, ending slightly below the knee. She has apparently resisted the voluminous skirts and sculpted bodices of Dior's New Look. Decorating her wide-brimmed hat are a few simple ribbons; her gloves extend just slightly past her wrist.

Much thinner and far more relaxed than usual in photos, Patricia has removed her fur stole on this July day and is absent-mindedly holding it in one hand. Next to her, Nana, with fake flowers weighing down her hat and real ones pinned to her heavy fur scarf, looks positively Victorian.

No longer the dolled-up, retouched, melancholy "Brooklyn girl" of the photo announcing her first marriage, Patricia could finally be herself. Her second marriage license, unlike her first, listed her true birthdate. She had no secrets from Rosie, and he had no compunctions about taking a supportive, supporting role in her career. His daughters were grown and married; his accomplishments during and between two world wars spoke for themselves.

A few days before their wedding, Rosie had published a paper in a marine engineering journal on a method to determine a ship's stability at sea. It was based on Navy-funded research he had been doing at the Stevens Institute of Technology in Hoboken, New Jersey. As Rosie stood with his new wife outside the door of St. Francis Assisi Church—notable for having conducted special 3 p.m. masses throughout the war for service personnel only—he was ready for his next step. After spending his youth at Annapolis and his entire adult life in the Navy, Captain James E. Kiernan had retired from the service, stating that it was for reasons of disability. He had someone with whom to enjoy his retirement.

In a patriotic gesture, Rosie had just mailed a check to the Navy for $12,000. It was the amount he'd received for his ship-stabilization research. Married to Patricia, he didn't need it.

Patricia wrote that Rosie became "an ideal partner in my Candlelight career," looking after the machinery, allowing her to discard her polite public demeanor and "blow off steam," and taking care of "annoying personnel problems." However, he did not become her business partner in the legal sense. She remained the sole shareholder of her corporations.

The two may not have enjoyed the same type of cultural events, but they both liked spending. Patricia wrote that her business, not his military pension, sustained their lifestyle. Rosie would complain loudly about prices at restaurants other than Patricia's, but that didn't get in the way of their lavish traveling and entertaining.

In 1949, Patricia's Sixtieth Street Candlelight Corp. submitted plans to the city building agency for $5,000 in alterations to the multiple-dwelling structure at 35 East Sixtieth Street. The architect on record was J.E. Kiernan, more familiar with designing hulls than habitats. However, that building did not require the artistry of Bauhaus-trained Nathalie Rahv. It was just a cash cow.

Although attracted to Rosie for his down-to-earth ways and quick to ridicule his sartorial choices—ear muffs in the winter, floppy hats in summer—Patricia must have sensed he shared her taste for the good life. In March of 1949, Newfoundland became part of Canada. Had he been alive, Patricia's father would surely have had his opinions on the matter.

Patricia, though always concerned for her homeland, was far away from its frigid winters. She and Rosie had joined other high-rollers at the exclusive Jupiter Club on Hobe Sound, Florida. It was a dress-down playground for millionaires.

They were ready to play. But first Patricia needed to make more money.

CHAPTER 8

Schism in the Suburbs

Be honest and loyal to the Candlelight's ideals and standards.

—Patricia Murphy's manual for employees, 1930

Five years after the end of World War II, Patricia's brother Jim walked along the tree-lined streets of Brooklyn Heights. From time to time he put his hand in a pants pocket and pulled out a pin, the type of pin tailors used for alterations, which he tossed on the sidewalk. It was hard work, avoiding the glances of passersby, who might comment on this odd behavior or even retrieve a pin for him, thinking he had dropped it accidentally. Nothing that Jim did happened accidentally.[1]

He was back in New York after an eight-year absence. No longer the skinny army private who had tumbled down the steps of the induction center, Jim was now thirty-seven. He had finally succumbed to Patricia's entreaties and come back East, leaving the perfect California weather and the not-so-perfect bookkeeping job at the produce company. It would be good for his two sons to grow up near their cousins and grandmother, provided they didn't need to live in the city, which was even dirtier and noisier than Jim remembered it.

So, they packed up when Jim got the call. A third Candlelight Restaurant was about to open on Long Island, and Jim was to be general manager. Patricia was in pursuit of the newly prosperous postwar consumers who were fleeing the city and flooding the suburbs. She had found an ideal site, a building that had served as a golf course clubhouse in the North Shore community of Manhasset until the course was carved into residential lots. It was a "big, spraddly place," resembling "a giant ranch house of the West," according to the *New York Herald Tribune*. And Patricia had giant plans for it.

87

She again employed Nathalie Rahv as the architect. If the leftist politics of Nathalie's husband, Philip, made others uncomfortable in the postwar climate, they did not disturb Patricia. She gave Rahv a free hand and an enormous canvas. The echoing rooms of the former country club—including one with a stage for community events—were to be transformed into strikingly attractive spaces for dining and conversation.

Repeating a collaboration begun in the Sixtieth Street Candlelight, Rahv worked with former theatrical lighting designer Richard Kelly. Patricia allowed Nathalie and Dick to rewire the entire place, in and out. Downlights, recessed lights, and dimmers—a recent lighting innovation—sculpted out shadowless areas of luminescence. Each plant box had a Slimlight, and lamps concealed in the roof shone on the dormer windows. Dick created chandeliers of brass-shaded lamps and wagon wheels to bring the eyes down from the main dining room's towering gable ceiling; Nathalie latticed the bleak walls of the former theater with yellow battens to surround the Garden Room with stripes and squares. Fluorescent fixtures made the metallic threads in drapes seem to dance in the Coral Room.

Each of three dining rooms became a smart, modern setting for Patricia's place settings and her napkins, still folded as Mr. Anthony had taught her on the Brooklyn Candlelight's opening day. Sconces, flowers, fireplaces, and candelabra blended with vinyl, Masonite, and pale plastic upholstery to revere the past while reveling in the present.[2]

Surrounding most of the building were a vast garden, greenhouses, and chairs on flagstone paths, lit by lamp-filled trenches and floodlights. An asphalt parking lot sprawled unapologetically in front of the restaurant. Motorists could drive right up to the bay windows. Patricia boldly rejected the longstanding rustic-restaurant tradition of forcing drivers to sneak around to the rear.

The car was king in burgeoning suburbia. Twenty years before Murphy opened her restaurant, Manhasset's population had numbered five thousand. That figured had tripled since the war's end. The area where Consuelo Vanderbilt once had a grand estate now attracted families headed by businessmen and professionals. Moms chauffeured kids to piano lessons and orthodontist's appointments; dads commuted to Manhattan, only twenty-eight minutes away on the Long Island Railroad.

Nevertheless, at the dawn of the fifties, the place was practically a fine-dining desert. When Patricia leased the former clubhouse in late 1949, she succeeded an Elk's Club that had hosted parties but eventually folded. Burger joints and drugstore soda fountains abounded, but "glamorous dining," as Patricia described the Candlelight experience, was offered at only a handful of establishments, such as The Riviera in Port Washington and The Swan in Roslyn. There were also department store restaurants on Miracle Mile, the long line of retail establishments that marched along Northern Boulevard toward the Candlelight. But Patricia viewed Miracle Mile more as an enhancement than a competitor. Many an urban-dweller wary of moving to the "sticks" was relieved to see names like Lord & Taylor in Manhasset.

Patricia had picked a winning combination once again. The location was ideal, and the gardens would entice people to wait for tables. Better yet, they could spend money at the gift shop, another important feature. Patricia may have been inspired by Jim's praise for the restaurant at Knott's Berry Farm, which snared diners with tourist attractions. If that was true, Patricia never said so. She never discussed any ideas about the business with Jim. She treated her brother like any other employee.

That treatment could vary. For the most part, Patricia's employees seemed content. They affectionately called her "Mama," and many of her Filipino waiters from the city followed her out to Long Island to join the thirty-server staff. Then again, there was the morning of opening day when Patricia, in a fit of nerves, turned to her architect, Nathalie, and screamed, "This has all been a horrible mistake!"[3]

It wasn't, of course. The three hundred seats filled up in no time, with twice that number regretfully turned away for lack of capacity. Jim suspected his sister would expand the building, but without consulting him. Put in charge of three dining room captains, he yearned for much more.

So, he quit. He had brought his family across the country so he could manage the Manhasset Candlelight, but in its first weeks, he walked off the job. "There were two dominant personalities, James and Patricia," Jim's grandson, Paul, said. "They didn't take orders from anyone."[4]

Jim went to the Brooklyn Candlelight to tell Vincent, who as usual was on duty as manager, distressing his younger brother by unburdening himself within earshot of several "old-line customers," as they called the regulars.

Vincent calmed Jim down, took him aside, and showed him a letter typed on engraved stationery. Although meant for and addressed to Patricia, it had been opened by Vincent, who recognized it as business correspondence. He had intercepted it with perfect timing.

The letter was from Koppel & Koppel, a real estate firm. The Koppels were offering a vacant property to Patricia. It was so perfect that Jim, who had been driving all over Long Island for weeks, could barely believe it. The location was prime. The place had been built for a restaurant and was currently in use as one. That would save a fortune on remodeling and buying equipment.

Wary of rentals, the Koppels were asking $1,500 a month. They were far more reasonable about prices for purchase, and Jim knew he could talk them down further; it was the kind of deal making he had done daily at his California purchasing job. He and Monica had saved $3,000 from the army pay bonuses they'd received for having kids: sixty bucks a month extra for their first son, fifty for the second. Moreover, Monica's sister, Eileen, was willing to kick in $1,500 as an interest-free loan.

But he needed more to negotiate for the property. Hence, after sowing pins over a ten-block area of Brooklyn Heights, Jim headed to Lauraine's apartment on Grace Court, intending to retrace the same route alongside her. The walk with Lauraine was going to be a hunt for more capital.

He spent the briefest time possible at Lauraine's home before feigning an itch for some exercise. It was a good time to lure her outside; she and her husband, Telfair, were preparing to move, and the place was in mild disarray. She readily agreed to Jim's suggestion of a walk down Hicks Street, to avoid Henry Street and the Candlelight.

It was a rare day off for Lauraine, and she didn't even want to look at a restaurant, much less the Candlelight. Like Jim, she'd been recruited as a manager for Patricia's new place on Long Island. Jim's defection had only created more work for her. She used to pity Telfair for having to commute to his engineering job on Long Island. Now she had joined him, going East against the stream of westbound suburbanites. It was time to move back to Long Island.

Just a few blocks into their stroll, Jim interrupted Lauraine to look at the ground. He widened his eyes in surprise. "Look!" he said. "A pin!"

"That means good luck," said Lauraine, as Jim had predicted. Superstitions were part of the family's Irish Catholic heritage, and Jim was relying on them. He wanted Lonnie to believe in a bright future because it wouldn't happen unless she and Telfair kicked in something like $9,000.[5]

"Another pin!" Lonnie exclaimed a few minutes later. That was the last either of them spotted, so absorbed were they in their conversation. They walked past the Georgian buildings and Italianate brownstones of Brooklyn Heights, and Lauraine warmed to Jim's idea. She and Telfair would own a 25 percent share of the new restaurant corporation, with Maude, Jim, and Vincent sharing the rest. Jim was relieved that Maude had finally married. Jim knew she was eager to ditch restaurant work. As for the nursing training she'd begun in Newfoundland and continued at Brooklyn's Long Island College Hospital, she had abandoned it. Maude liked to buy nice things, and Patricia paid better than the hospitals.

Jim only hoped he could squeeze enough value out of his sisters to get a new place started. As a young girl, Lauraine had charmed the Brooklyn customers—notably Telfair—but she was older now and less likely to rein in her sharp tongue. Jim's wife doubted these two sisters-in-law would contribute much to the new enterprise, but even as Jim plotted against his oldest sister, he was protective of these other two.

Vincent would kick in some cash while remaining a very silent partner. Vincent didn't want word getting back to Patricia about his possible involvement in mutiny. He had married Mollie Rogers, long-time hostess and manager at the Brooklyn Candlelight, now mother to their fast-growing crew of young boys. More cautious than Jim, Vincent didn't want to jeopardize his relationship with Patricia. He wanted to stay on her payroll.

Lauraine wasn't concerned about loyalty. As it turned out, Jim had approached her at a good time. She was incensed that Patricia kept insisting that she and Telfair live in an apartment attached to the Manhasset restaurant. Now closed on Mondays, the Manhasset restaurant would soon be open every day, and Patricia wanted Lauraine on the premises.[6]

Patricia wouldn't even have known about Manhasset had it not been for Lauraine and Telfair. Before the war, when the place was practically rural, he and Lauraine lived there with Owen and Sheila. Until he joined the service and Lauraine moved back to Brooklyn to work for Patricia, they had owned a house on Ryder Road, named for the painter Albert Pinkham Ryder. All the streets in the Munsey Park area had artists' names; the Metropolitan Museum was the developer.

The Metropolitan also owned the building that housed the newest Candlelight. For all its excellence as a museum, the Met was a flop as a landlord. The golf and Elks clubs had barely made rent. Now a realty company was in charge, and when Patricia Murphy signed the lease, the news made the business pages of *The New York Times*.[7]

The new tenant already seemed like a solid one. Clementine Paddleford of the *Trib* had given the Manhasset Candlelight a glowing review, writing how its three hundred seats had quickly filled up on opening day, with six hundred people turned away. The reviewer noted the abundant light in the Terrace Room, which, with its enormous windows and a fireplace chimney extending to the rafters, resembled a Western ski lodge. In these pre-foodie days, Paddleford rapidly summed up the prime rib and Southern fried chicken offerings as "all-American country cooking, nothing complicated or fadified about Patricia Murphy's cuisine." Far more space was devoted to the now-familiar tale of Patricia's rags-to-riches ascent and a description of the Manhasset grounds, where adjoining the restaurant would soon be a bake shop selling takeout, including Patricia Murphy's packaged casseroles for the new TV-dinner generation.[8]

There was also a standalone gift shop, Patricia's version of her father's general store in its glory days. In addition to knickknacks and jewelry, she sold Patricia Murphy–branded candies and condiments, as well as a line of fragrances, including Green Orchid perfume in a jewel-top bottle. Before quitting, Jim brought his two small sons to the restaurant one day. Aunt Patricia gave them each five dollars—on condition that they spend it in the gift shop, which had absolutely nothing for children.

Another Murphy child played a pivotal role in Lauraine's decision. Owen, twelve years old when the Candlelight opened in Manhasset, probably couldn't even remember his toddler years on Long Island. His parents were eager to resume their suburban dream, but in a house, not in an apartment over a parking lot. In defiance of Patricia's desires, Telfair and Lauraine had already placed a down payment on a home in Oyster Bay.

"My mother had no intention of living over the store," Owen said many years later.

Lauraine didn't need any more pins. Eyes narrowed below her large forehead, she told her brother about an incident that now seemed to galvanize her decision. She had taken Owen out to Manhasset recently.

Hungry, but hesitant to bother his working mother, he found some turkey in a restaurant refrigerator. Along came Rosie, or the Captain, as Owen was instructed to refer to Patricia's husband.

There is no way to know exactly what happened. In later life, Owen had no recollection of the event, but he clearly remembered what others had told him. They said the Captain had instructed the boy that taking turkey from the restaurant fridge was the same as stealing. "And then he slugged me," Owen said.[9]

It is possible that Captain James Kiernan had used corporal punishment to teach his nephew a lesson. The story raises questions, however. Kiernan, who had commanded many men during his long naval career and, with his first wife, raised two daughters, surely knew how to exert authority without using his fists. Moreover, Jim apparently did not pass this story on to his children and grandchildren. A grandson of Jim, Paul Murphy, said he had never heard it.[10]

While there is no way to check whether the episode unfolded precisely as Owen was told, it indicates that Lauraine's family felt mistreated, even abused, by Patricia and her husband.

Privately, Jim thought that Telfair Smith, Lauraine's spouse, and Joe Kearns, the husband Maude had found late in life, were going to let life pass without grabbing the brass ring. "They were unimaginative guys who went strictly by the book and never made a decent living," Jim said. Worried that his sisters would never be well provided for, he started a restaurant.

Like the tale of the Captain and the slugfest, Jim's fraternal concern might have undergone some rearview magnification. Joe, like Telfair, was an engineer. Jim scoffed at their annual salaries, which he estimated for his grandson as $7,000 each. However, either because he had a working wife, or because he was the sole heir of parents who had died before his marriage, Telfair was the man Jim needed.

If Lauraine had qualms about the new restaurant's location—less than five miles from Patricia's, it would be angling for the same customers—Jim assuaged them. He told her what he thought they should name their new place: The Lauraine. Patricia wouldn't be the only Murphy sister with her name up in lights. Nana would see *that*. The younger sister would finally get her attention. Lauraine reassured Jim that she and Telfair were in.

By the end of their walk around the Heights, Jim was out of pins, but he had the nine grand he needed. It was a lot of money, all they had in the world.

&

In May 1950, the Manhasset Candlelight was one month old. Patricia and Rosie were living in the spacious apartment, spurned by Lauraine, that Nathalie Rahv had crafted into the restaurant building. Patricia's cocktail of choice was a Manhattan, named for the place she and Rosie had planned to enjoy while her siblings—well compensated, of course— watched the store. It was supposed to be Florida in the winter, Manhattan's Pierre Hotel in the fall and spring, with plenty of traveling in between.

Still, better not to have any Judases on her staff. She was on top of the world, she repeatedly told herself. The Manhasset Candlelight was a juggernaut, fueled by the *Trib*'s glowing review, which jammed the place on weekends, as urban-dwellers escaped the city's noise and congestion to indulge in the craze for country dining. Gas was cheap, and even before construction of the Long Island Expressway, the Northern State Parkway made it an easy drive. Under headings like "Gracious Country Dining" or "Dining Out in the Country," newspapers grouped dozens of small ads for suburban restaurants. In the *Times* and the *Trib*, the Red Barn and Silvermine Tavern invited diners to Connecticut, while the Princeton Inn and Molly Pitcher beckoned from New Jersey.

There were even plenty of bookings for weekday lunches. The book clubs, political groups, and charitable organizations energized by suburban women needed meeting places. After lunch, it was convenient to shop for cut flowers in the greenhouse, a whole baked ice cream pie or some upside-down pineapple squares in the bake shop, and scarves or letter-openers in the gift shop.

Somebody had been using a letter-opener in Brooklyn, Patricia told Rosie as they downed their cocktails. Patricia had bumped into one of the Koppels at a party. He'd said he had been so pleased to settle on a price for Elizabeth Flynn's in Great Neck with the other Murphys. How silly of him to think that Patricia might want it; she was obviously on to much bigger things in Manhasset. But it was a nice starter place for her kid brother and sisters.

Patricia never connected Vincent with the purloined letter. Everybody loved Stish—Vincent's childish mispronunciation of his name had stuck—and he had been a rock through all this. Patricia could never have run her trio of restaurants without Vincent holding down the fort in Brooklyn. Restaurant competition in the borough was intense, but Stish kept the Candlelight up to Patricia's exacting standards. The restaurant had outlived one of the two churches that used to flank it. A liquor store now stood in part of the space formerly occupied by the First Methodist Church, and preachers no longer complained about the Candlelight's garden, where the booze flowed freely every summer. Mollie's younger brother, John Rogers, was now Vincent's right-hand man.

Patricia planned to sell off the city restaurants while maintaining ownership of the combined building on Sixtieth Street, where rents and catering would continue to bring in money. She didn't own the Brooklyn building, but she had a long-term lease and could sell the business, name and all.

For both city locations, she could afford to wait for the right price. They were still running smoothly and profitably. There had been a small embarrassment at the Sixtieth Street location when she was sued for mislabeling blue cheese dressing as Roquefort. Some pest representing a French cheese association ran around Manhattan filing suits like this all the time. It was the kind of thing that wouldn't happen in suburbia.

Patricia and Rosie customarily supplemented their cocktail glass set-ups with a refill carafe. At a time like this, Patricia's hand might have shaken as she refreshed Rosie's drink. She had been in a terrible state these days, ever since those three had stabbed her in the back, but sleepless nights and headaches could not prevent her from running calculations through her head. Jim, Maude, and Lauraine had bought their location for a pittance. Her cigarette holder perched on an ashtray, its smoldering contents no longer capable of calming her.

It had all started with the tragedy of another businesswoman, Elizabeth Flynn. Patricia knew her competition, and she had not been surprised to see Flynn's name over a restaurant on Middle Neck Road in Great Neck. The sign had already come down, she was told. In its place was a board proclaiming, "Lauraine."

In life, Elizabeth Flynn had started out as a Bonwit Teller buyer. Then, like Patricia, Flynn had established a chain of successful New York City restaurants during the Depression. In 1931, she made headlines by leasing a four-story building for her third midtown eatery and announcing plans to compete with the adjacent Waldorf Astoria.[11] More recently, an Elizabeth Flynn restaurant had appeared in Jackson Heights, the leafy Queens neighborhood once home to the Murphy family.

Like Patricia, Flynn had planned to conquer the suburbs. But the day after her Great Neck restaurant opened, she swallowed a drug overdose and died.[12]

What a marvelous stroke of luck for Jim that a career woman so like his oldest sister had killed herself! Elizabeth's husband, no businessman, had tried to run the place himself after her demise, swiftly plunging into bankruptcy. Koppel & Koppel, eager to find a buyer, had accepted $25,000 for the property, where Elizabeth Flynn had already tastefully decorated the dining room and cocktail lounge.

The brokers had handed over the keys for only $10,000 down, with the rest in $300 monthly payments. "I knew it was a steal," Jim said later.

That wasn't the only steal. He was planning to copy most of Patricia's menu, with exactly the same descriptor—"old fashioned good and plenty"—that Patricia ran in newspaper ads. Patricia knew this, as she had told her staff to pump her food vendors for information. "The Lauraine," as the temporary sign on the Great Neck restaurant read, was not yet open for business, but her brother was stocking the refrigerators and pantry.

They could call their place whatever they wanted, but Patricia knew that Lauraine and Maude were just along for the ride, and the money. A more authentic name would have been "The James."

She raised her glass and cast a conspiratorial glance at Rosie. "To us," she said. It was her favorite toast these days. Only Rosie shared her complete and utter outrage. Her head was buzzing with anger. Great Neck was *her* market.

Great Neck couples had been eagerly booking wedding receptions at the new Candlelight. Just west of Manhasset on a nearly identical peninsula jutting into Long Island Sound, Great Neck was practically Manhasset's conjoined twin, though less high-toned and far more welcoming to Jews. Great Neck, already filling up with Jewish and Gentile arrivistes in the 1920s, had been F. Scott Fitzgerald's inspiration for West Egg in *The Great Gatsby*.[13] A year after the novel's 1925 publication, the editor of *The Great Neck News*, saw a theatrical adaption of it and wrote, "There are characters aplenty . . . that live in the fanciful 'West Egg' of the book and play who would be recognized on Middle Neck Road." That road was now part of the Lauraine restaurant's address.

In Fitzgerald's work, the strivers of West Egg yearned for the status of old-money East Egg, a stand-in for the Port Washington peninsula on which Manhasset stands. A generation later, as Patricia Murphy's Candlelight Restaurant moved into the old golf clubhouse, the great estates of both peninsulas had given way to single-family homes. Still, Manhasset continued to arouse envy in less "restricted" Great Neck. In 1950, Manhasset had better-financed schools than Great Neck, and it had the big-name stores of Miracle Mile.

Manhasset's superior status was cold comfort for Patricia, who knew her three traitorous siblings had secured a splendid location with 135 seats, a cocktail bar, and enough room for dancing. The circular building on Middle Neck Road, with glass walls nearly all around, didn't meet Patricia's standards for elegance. It suggested an invasive species from Miami, where Elizabeth Flynn had opened her first tea room. However, Great Neck liked that look, and Elizabeth knew it because—though Patricia never said as much during Elizabeth's lifetime—she had the same sharp instincts as Patricia herself.

The kitchen was, of course, well outfitted. Still, Jim et al. had found it necessary to add one more piece of equipment. This was the part Patricia simply could not believe when her sources told her. They had a special oven for popovers. They were actually going to steal Patricia's signature dish. They were even looking to hire popover girls and relish girls.

In a fairy tale, a powerful character—whether good or evil—might have made a drastic pronouncement like, "Your child will be mine," or "All spinning wheels must be destroyed."

The rented apartment where Patricia was swilling cocktails had a living room with built-in shelves, floor-to-ceiling drapes, and a wall-sized mirror, but no moat or throne. Still, Patricia believed in her special powers. Together with Rosie, former designer of battleships and commander of a destroyer, she concocted a strategy.

Early the next morning, as Rosie brought Patricia coffee and toast spread with Royal Queen Bee Jelly—convinced of its energy-boosting powers, she devoured vats of this popular dietary supplement—her plan took shape.

The Royal Queen Bee of Long Island would tell all her tradespeople and suppliers that anyone doing business with her siblings' place in Great Neck could forget about doing business with her.

∾

It seemed to make no difference, at least at first. The Lauraine Murphy restaurant was an instant hit when it opened its doors in June 1950, less than two months after the opening of the Candlelight in Manhasset.

The first small newspaper ads for the restaurant dubbed it simply "Lauraine," but the Murphy surname soon materialized after it. Long Island residents referred to the business as "Lauraine Murphy's," just as they called the Candlelight restaurant in Manhasset simply "Patricia Murphy's."

The new restaurant's name appeared on the Great Neck building in letters resembling a woman's handwriting. The signs on Patricia Murphy's Candlelight restaurants also used a script typeface. Patricia's signature was a key part of the brand she had built for twenty years, more recently extended into the merchandise sold at her Manhasset gift shop.

Jim and his two sisters knew how to remix Patricia's formula. The Murphy name was known to the many Great Neck residents who had seen signs or ads for the two Patricia Murphy's eateries in the city, as well as the new one neighboring their town. There were enough customers eager for familiar meals at moderate prices, plus the attention of smiling popover girls, to fill both Long Island restaurants.

This was an era of blatant copying, a time when American stores like Macy's advertised their "line-for-line copies" of Balenciaga and Chanel originals at deep discounts. Jim, Lauraine, and Maude, like the stores knocking off Paris designs, could not match Patricia's originality. But they could beat her on price.

Patricia had planned on ratcheting up prices in Manhasset, calculating that North Shore suburbanites might even like to make a show of their free spending. World events stood in her way. Shortly after she opened her restaurant, the United States became involved in the Korean War, and Americans plunged into a panic of buying and hoarding food. Soon food prices were soaring, and price controls were back. Nearly all dinners at Patricia's three Candlelights were priced below two dollars, including appetizer or soup, beverage, dessert, and unlimited popovers.

The one exception was the sirloin dinner at $2.95. Lunches topped out at $1.10.

Wartime's Office of Price Administration had changed into Truman's Office of Price Stabilization. Just below the list of seventeen dessert selections, including deep-dish blueberry pie and raspberry jello, was the message, "All prices are our O.P.S. ceiling prices or lower. A list showing our ceiling prices for each item is available for your inspection. NOTE: Meal time is cocktail time."

Of course, Jim and Company charged nearly the same in Great Neck: they were subject to the same government regulations, they bought from Patricia's vendors, and their menu was practically identical. Cocktails at Lauraine Murphy's were somewhat cheaper—fifty cents for a martini. Patricia Murphy's in Manhasset was asking sixty cents.

Whether because of the food, the format, or the bargain booze, Lauraine Murphy's opening month was a smash. The only problem was overhead. The Murphy siblings had taken over a going operation, albeit a failing one, with a kitchen and wait staff. Jim, tougher on labor than Patricia, grew alarmed at the payroll costs—$1,500 for their first week in business. He laid off nearly all the employees and told Maude and Lauraine to roll up their sleeves and pick up the slack. Jim's wife—formerly Monica McDonough, a valued Lockheed department head in wartime—temporarily abandoned her post as stay-at-home mom. Jim recruited her to prepare menus and handle the payroll, now reduced to $300 weekly. They found a babysitter, freeing Monica to work a seven-day week.

Proceeds for the first month were $11,000, and $4,500 of that was profit. "We were ecstatic," Jim said.

The mood didn't last long. Summer is typically a hard time for restaurants, and there was a polio outbreak that July. Great Neck residents deserted the area and fled to the Catskill resorts, Jim later recalled. "Our business dropped down to nothing," while Maude and Lauraine, whose habits he often deplored, "went all over spending a lot of money," he added. At the end of September, the restaurant's surplus had dipped down to $10,000.

Then came a storm of historical, if not Biblical, proportions—"the hand of God," Jim remembered thinking at the time. One might even have believed that the wrath of his oldest sister had blown it over from Manhasset, except that it raged there, too, and over the whole of Long Island.

The U.S. Weather Bureau had just started to name hurricanes, using women's names only. However, this one, which slammed into Long Island on November 21, 1950—five days before Thanksgiving—was nameless. In the many newspaper articles reporting the deaths, injuries, and homelessness it caused, it was called simply, "the storm."

The winds began blowing on a Saturday morning. Around 4 a.m. on Sunday, the phone rang at Jim's rented house in Roslyn. The police told him that some of the windows of the restaurant had blown out. In heavy winds, he drove five miles west on Northern Boulevard, detouring around debris and fallen trees. The art deco restaurant had sixty feet of ten-foot-high curved glass, most of which now lay shattered on the sidewalk.

As Jim watched the remaining windows fly out, he thought, "This is the crushing blow." He and his family "were used to, and even expected, bad luck." He thought it might be "God knocking the hell out of us." If he saw a possible punitive connection between his travails and his affront to Patricia, he made no mention of that when recounting these events to his grandson.

By morning, the storm had stopped, but about 75,000 homes had lost power all over Long Island. Early reports counted two deaths, five injuries, and thousands left homeless. As ambulance sirens shrieked through the streets, Jim and the restaurant employees who had shown up for work blocked off the sidewalk where the glass had shattered. Then they began the hunt for plywood to board up the windows, competing with hordes of shopkeepers and homeowners looking for the same thing.

Jim contacted a local carpenter he knew, another native of Newfoundland, and together they searched all over Long Island for plywood. At 11 a.m., as Lauraine Murphy's was being boarded up, a woman stepped over the jagged glass bordering a naked window, took a seat at the one table that the storm had left upright, and ordered lunch. Recalling this later, Jim could find no explanation other than, "The storm discombobulated people."

The restaurant had no electricity, but the gas in the kitchen was working. Some food was brought to the solitary customer. Lauraine Murphy's was not yet in shape to re-open, but the premature customer set Jim and his crew into high gear; they had to get ready. Working all day and through the night, they covered the windows with plywood and tar paper and arranged the drapes over the patches. The interior looked dark but presentable. Then three days after the storm, the lights suddenly popped on.

Jim flung the door open, and Great Neck streamed in. Power was still off in most of the nearby homes, and storm-weary Long Islanders needed a place to eat, and to gather. Jim, who had not seen a bed for forty-eight hours, returned home and spent hours trying to fall asleep. "I kept stopping and starting, like I was falling into a pit," he said.

As it happened, he and his siblings were emerging from one, for good. From that day forward, they did not have to worry about money. In the storm's aftermath, Lauraine Murphy's became a North Shore institution. Business thrived, and high school and college students clamored for part-time jobs at Lauraine Murphy's as busboys or popover girls, filling out applications both there and at Patricia Murphy's.

By St. Patrick's Day 1951, Lauraine Murphy's repaid its loans, including the $9,000 owed to Telfair and Lauraine and the smaller amount borrowed from Jim's sister-in-law. Jim, Lauraine, and Maude had all bought houses. In the following year, Maude and her husband, Joe, took Nana on a grand tour of Europe, hiring chauffeurs and drivers to take them all over the continent.

Patricia's dire warnings to her food purveyors and linen suppliers were thwarted. Companies wishing to do business with both Patricia Murphy's and Lauraine Murphy's simply made their Great Neck deliveries in unmarked vans.[14]

The queen's powers were limited. Muzzled by her relationship with Nana, who surely would have agonized if Patricia had phoned a newspaper and made the family split public, Patricia used the only ammunition remaining. She placed a large display ad in the *Great Neck News*, stating that "Patricia Murphy who conducts" three restaurants in Manhasset, Manhattan, and Brooklyn (exact names and addresses given) "has no connection with any restaurant established in Great Neck."

More significantly, she hurled a thunderbolt that left permanent damage. Refusing to speak to Jim, Lauraine, Maude, or their children, Patricia—who marked every festive day with a restaurant celebration—forever diminished the holidays for all of them. Never again would her family gather together.

Nana, still living in the Brooklyn Heights apartment she had shared with Frank, was forced to see her children separately. Sheila remained close with Patricia while working out ways to see the other siblings.

As for affable Vincent, converting Patricia's paychecks into shares of Lauraine Murphy's, he managed to feign distress at the opening of the competitive restaurant while maintaining close ties with his confederates. When they were curious about innovations at Patricia's restaurant, Vincent filled them in.

Disgusted with Long Island, Patricia soon had her sights trained elsewhere. She would bring Vincent with her, of course. Thank God there was *someone* in her family she could trust besides Nana and Sheila.

CHAPTER 9

The Crown Jewel

A good meal and perfect service may be ruined by too much heat or closeness of the air. Air freshness is necessary to an enjoyable meal.

—Patricia Murphy's manual for employees, 1930

A year after opening the Candlelight in Manhasset, Patricia and Rosie were contacted by *Interiors*, an artistically produced magazine for the residential design trade. The trade book, known for its generous use of fine photography, wanted to shoot not only the restaurant, but also their apartment. Their target audience, after all, was not restaurant builders, but rather decorators, architects, and industrial designers working on homes.

Patricia, of course, agreed. It was free publicity for the restaurant, which would also be photographed. It would also be a poke in Lauraine's eye for spurning the apartment. There was no need for the magazine to know that she and Rosie were there only by necessity. In Patricia's narrative, the Captain had offered her the gift of a country house, which she declined in favor of a country restaurant.

"It gives her a busboy's holiday," was the subtitle of the eight-page magazine article headed, "Mrs. Kiernan's Country Home." In the body of the piece she was "Miss Murphy," a "small, dainty, vigorous woman" madly dashing between her restaurants with little time to rest. Nonetheless, the large front hall of the apartment had been converted into a dining room for private entertaining. Ceremonial kimono sashes, or obis, hung full-length on the seventy-three-foot walls of the room, part of the building's former theater, and a large Korean chest stood near a wall. These treasures had been collected by the Captain during his service in Asia.

The largest of eleven black-and-white photos showcased the living room's smoked mirror, occupying an entire wall. It also showed a wall cabinet holding Chinese jade and porcelain, as well as Patricia's European silver teapots. In every room, architect Nathalie Rahv had artfully blended the Captain's swords and screens with Patricia's French antique chairs and Fortuny fabrics.

Nathalie and Patricia had also found a balance. As *Interiors* reported, "Although Mrs. Rahv's forte is not French antiques and Mrs. Kiernan dislikes anything new, they had already worked together once and their lines of agreement were presumably drawn." That was true, and two years after the *Interiors* article came out, Patricia would enlist Nathalie's aid a third time in her escape from Long Island.[1]

She had planned to be a sort of philanthropist for her family in Manhasset. Now the plan to bring them together had split them apart. Ironically, it was also producing enough cash to buy her and Rosie a ticket out. She was bored with her first three restaurants and sick of the Long Island hurricanes, which had flooded the Manhasset Candlelight several times.

Her head was buzzing with plans for remodeling the enormous estate she and Rosie had bought in the Port Sewall section of Stuart, Florida. The estate was vast, on twenty-eight acres of land, including a lagoon and private island. The neighbors were intrigued by the way she was redoing the house in colonial style, unusual for Florida. That was a real country home, not this apartment with floor-length shantung curtains drawn each night to hide the "black countryside," as the *Interiors* article put it.

Two years after the *Interiors* piece ran, General Electric featured Richard Kelly's ingenious restaurant and garden lighting in its own magazine, *Light*. The article read a bit like the explanation of a magic trick: drawings of conduits and lamps concealed in roof gutters and planters accompanied gorgeous photography of dining rooms and landscaping.[2]

GE was mesmerized by the tall, thin pipes that Kelly had sunk into Patricia's garden, with perforated cone-shaped shades concealing floodlights. Some of these spindly modernist mushrooms shone over an enormous floral clock. Metal hands told the time above the legend, "Patricia Murphy's Restaurant, Manhasset, L.I." spelled in white flowers against a red or pink background, depending on the season.

In just four years, the restaurant and the clock had become Manhasset landmarks, as if they had always been there. Measured by the clock, it was a short time, but several other indicators signaled it was now time to go.

In a photo of Patricia taken for the GE piece, she is dressed almost like a stereotypical housewife of the 1950s. Seated with Rosie on a love seat, her hands folded on her lap, she wears sensible, chunky heels and a sleeveless dress so unadorned that it could be mistaken for a housecoat. Rosie constantly showered her with expensive jewelry, she said, and here she wears a ring, earrings, and several bracelets—all failing to defeat the ordinariness of her clothing. Her chin-length hair, dark in the black-and-white photo, is pulled back in a nondescript style. The GE photographer seems to have interrupted her on a work day.

That was possible because the work had become incessant, as well as joyless. There was the stress of checking on three restaurants, and Manhasset's constant frustrations. She had doubled the number of dining rooms to six, including a new Gold Room that sat 250. But there was always a juggling act between expanding and maintaining parking. The garden, too, seemed limited, and Patricia was increasingly interested in horticulture. The Manhasset greenhouse was full of flowers for the restaurant, plus her collection of orchids and rare plants. She needed more space to leave her mark on the gardening world, to cultivate and win prizes.

To create a single restaurant that would surpass the income of three, she would need several million dollars. Her brand and her businesses were now worth that much.

In the spring of 1953, Patricia started to slip out of Manhasset, so quietly that the public never even noticed, which was part of the plan. As Long Island diners waited hours for a table on Mother's Day, Patricia formed the Westchester Candlelight Corporation. As president, she signed a twenty-one-year lease on land owned by a Queens-based company formed by Bernard Oakin and Samuel Rose, developers who planned to build a shopping center in northeastern Yonkers.[3]

She had agreed to pay $40,000 a year for eight acres in a residential area of Yonkers, a large city with a whiff of urban decay arising from its declining manufacturing base, but also a thriving middle class. It was located on a main thoroughfare, known both as Central Park Avenue and Route 100, traversed by 2.5 million vehicles annually. Just north of the intersection of that route and Tuckahoe Road, it was but thirty minutes from Times Square. Even better, the highest-income families in Westchester lived within a half-mile radius of it, or so its developers claimed. The area around the restaurant was laced with parkways and expressways, and a planned extension of the New York Thruway would ensure its future in the era of the Interstate.

Patricia alone signed the lease, though it listed both her and James E. Kiernan as Westchester Candlelight's majority shareholders and directors. In truth, she was the sole owner of all its capital stock, as with her other restaurant corporations. Never forgetting the day an Upper East Side commercial real estate broker had laughed her out of his office, she may have listed Rosie on the lease to assuage her male landlords.

The developers did, however, accept Patricia's nontraditional choice of architect, even contributing $2,000 toward Nathalie Rahv's fee. Despite Patricia's loss of faith in Nathalie's design moments before the Manhasset opening, the two had teamed up again for this, their most ambitious project. Mrs. Rahv, as the lease named her, was to guide the building of a restaurant with eight hundred to one thousand seats, extensive landscaping, and a parking area, in compliance with all codes and in accordance with Patricia's exacting standards. The developers set a deadline of one year for the project's completion.

The floral clock in Manhasset became a stopwatch. The Westchester site would require extensive excavation, including the construction of an artificial lake near the restaurant. There was to be parking for five hundred cars in airport-scale lots at the front and rear. But before the earthmovers rolled in, Patricia and Nathalie flew to New Orleans for inspiration. Patricia wanted to put a high-volume, moderately priced restaurant in a French colonial structure suggesting luxury and languor. Nathalie would share Patricia's vision, then apply her modernist filter.

New Orleans' French Quarter had more enticements for Mrs. Rahv and Mrs. Kiernan, traveling without their husbands, than just its unique architecture. The district was famous for drink, as well as food, and Patricia was a tippler. As for Nathalie, she and her literary husband, Philip—now on the verge of divorce—were famous for drinking guests under the table at their Greenwich Village soirees. In his poem "Man and Wife," Robert Lowell wrote a line recalling how he once "outdrank the Rahvs" in their Greenwich Village apartment.[4] Literary critic Diana Trilling said Nathalie had confessed to feeling miserable amid the *Partisan Review* crowd and requiring several stiff drinks to suffer through their parties.[5] Dorothea Straus, the wife of publisher Roger W. Straus Jr., described her as a tall, graceful "American Valkyrie," a bit "stout and florid" in middle age, and prone to indulging in "regal drunkenness."[6]

Several people who had regularly attended the Rahvs' soirees or stayed with them overnight were unkind to Nathalie in print. Her former Vassar classmate, Mary McCarthy—an ex-lover of Philip, who had introduced him to Nathalie—demoted the architect to a bland clothing designer in *The Oasis*, a roman a clef about left-wing intellectuals. In that novelette, McCarthy explained the Rahvs' marriage as little more than the attraction of a Jewish outsider male to a blue-blooded Protestant woman.

Nathalie was, indeed, a former debutante born to wealth and prestige. Her father, Joseph Rockwell Swan, a one-time Yale football coach, was an investment banker in a firm that eventually became Smith Barney. Her mother had helped found Junior League of New York. Philip's friends dismissed Nathalie as just a source of funds for Philip's important work—a "perpetual Guggenheim," said the philosopher William Barrett.

Her untalkative nature drew criticism. She *sags*, Lowell complained in a letter to another poet, Elizabeth Bishop[7]. Around the time of the Westchester Candlelight's construction, McCarthy described Nathalie, then in her early thirties, as looking "ancient" and unhappy, with "grey and coarse" skin "like material woven in a prison."[8]

Yet her profession, so unusual for a woman of that time, escaped notice. No one mentioned her former partnership in a Chicago architectural firm associated with Mies van der Rohe—abandoned because Philip wanted to live in New York. The writer and cultural critic Dwight Macdonald dismissed her as "completely un-intellectual and un-literary."[9]

Nathalie's alleged silences and pallor did not dampen the New Orleans trip. Society-minded Patricia appreciated Nathalie's social-register status, but she hired her for her qualifications. The two modern-day Valkyries, tall and short, soaked up the French Quarter's offerings, probably in more ways than one.

Upon their return to New York, sketches and plans were submitted to the landlords, as agreed upon, and excavation began within the prescribed two-month window. A two-story building was erected, fronted by five iron-railed balconies on each floor. The gently sloped roof had two chimneys to accommodate the building's fireplaces, and the restaurant was reflected in the artificial lake, built to mirror its entire width. Patricia billed it as the largest restaurant in the East of the United States, and nobody publicly challenged that assertion.

The land was sculpted into gentle hills, and gardens and trees were planted at a cost of $170,000. As in Manhasset, Patricia planned to change the flowers with the season. No longer limited to a mere 1,500 feet of garden path, as she was in Long Island, she'd have 50,000 tulips in spring, 5,000 chrysanthemums in fall, and a vast rose garden, of course. She loved roses almost as much as orchids. She desperately needed greenhouses, as well as a standalone gift shop, but all kinds of idiotic obstacles were standing in her way. Her developer landlords wanted to build a shopping center nearby, using the Candlelight as lure for prospective tenants. Anticipating objections from a florist and a home furnishings business, they had amended Patricia's lease to prohibit her from selling cut flowers and furniture.

That did not figure into her plan to sell cut orchids, just the kind of thing people would buy from her in quantity. The Manhasset greenhouse held her treasured collection, which she would eventually transfer to Westchester, and she was also working with hybridizers in Florida, where orchid laths were being built on her estate. Orchids were the third stroke of her signature, after popovers and candles.

Other problems were more daunting. Four months after she signed her lease, the Yonkers Common Council passed sweeping zoning changes meant to encourage businesses to move into the area while placating civic groups worried about density and pollution. In September of 1953, a contentious three-hour public hearing concluded with a vote by the city council to approve 127 changes to the city's quarter-century-old zoning ordinances. The land Patricia had leased was restricted to residential use, allowing only low-density apartment buildings. Previously, it had been zoned "business-apartment," permitting commercial use.

The zoning overhaul was trumpeted on the front page of the city's newspaper, the _Herald Statesman_.[10] Eyes wide open, Patricia and Nathalie laid the foundations of the restaurant in October, a month before the changes would take effect. Prior to finding this site, Patricia had considered a less expensive Westchester location with a building already in place, but zoning issues had scared her off. Now she refused to retreat from the obstacles awaiting her. The restaurant might be grandfathered in, but she would require variances to build a gift shop, a greenhouse, and an incinerator, all part of her original plan. Overnight, variances had become difficult to obtain. Previously requiring approval by the Zoning Board of Appeals, they now were also subject to a vote by the Common Council. Still, she forged ahead.

Unable or unwilling to concede points to area homeowners fearful of development, Patricia described them as "narrow-minded," the word she had previously applied to Brooklynites. She could not fathom their ingratitude for her enterprise in "beautifying a formerly barren and forbidding area," as she wrote.[11] (In truth, part of her property had previously been occupied by Bronxville Nurseries, perhaps demonstrating its fertility rather than barrenness; that company, however, had not always paid taxes.)[12] She resented the people of Yonkers for their doubts, their failure to see that her Xanadu would sharply raise their property values.

The real ingrates, of course, were Jim, Lauraine, and Maude. She'd heard they were hunting for a second restaurant site in her own Manhasset backyard. There could soon be a Lauraine Murphy's across the street from Patricia Murphy's. They were riding on her coat tails, benefiting from her reluctance to publish further disclaimers of association with them.

Patricia was weary of trying to conceal the family feud, not only for Nana's sake but to safeguard her image: the Manhasset restaurant represented grace and elegance, not spite and anger. The North Shore of Long Island was a small world, where many of Patricia's popover girls and seasonal busboys were high school or college kids who worked at the supposed "sister restaurant" when the Candlelight had nothing for them. Vincent and John Rogers had more contact with the staff, but when Patricia dropped in, there was always some bright-eyed kid eager to mention knowing her treacherous siblings. Women lunching at the Candlelight did the same. How tiresome to summon a responding smile!

Luckily, a man from Stamford, Connecticut, seemed serious about buying Manhasset. He was Patricia's accountant, Michael Tavlin. It was important to sell to the right buyers, who would adhere to Patricia's exacting standards if they were to continue using the Candlelight name. Tavlin lacked restaurant experience, but he had teamed up with Meyer Zimmerman, a Stamford neighbor who'd operated suburban eateries. Working directly with Patricia without a broker, they were negotiating price, including the right to use her name. She appeared to have a buyer in Brooklyn, too.

In the summer, Patricia had sold the restaurant on Sixtieth Street while maintaining ownership of the expanded building it occupied. The apartment in Manhasset may have earned praise from *Interiors*, but on the lease for the Yonkers property, Patricia listed 33 East Sixtieth Street as her personal address. A notary began writing "Nassau County" as Patricia's home on the lease, then struck it out. The county that had spawned Lauraine Murphy's would never be home to Patricia.

Indeed, in negotiating with Tavlin and Zimmerman, she'd agreed not to open any restaurants in either Nassau or Queens County. In return, they'd agreed not to sell even one share of stock in the Manhasset Candlelight to members of her family. She wasn't going to watch Jim move in and replant "Patricia" with "Lauraine" on the floral clock.

By spring of 1954, plans for the dining rooms in Westchester were taking shape. Nathalie again worked with Richard Kelly, who in the meantime had lit the Desert Inn in Las Vegas and judged a Museum of Modern Art lamp-design competition alongside Marcel Breuer. Kelly began making regular trips to Westchester from his Manhattan office, meeting with Patricia to show her sketches of custom light fixtures, and talking to Nathalie about the bulldozing he'd require for an electrical cable.[13]

At night, the restaurant would appear to motorists like a glowing glass brick—Nathalie's stark exposure of structural elements having overthrown Patricia's French-Colonial concept. Instead of a glaring neon sign, motorists would see the restaurant's floodlit asbestos roof and inviting luminous windows. Its glimmering reflection in the dark lake would be visible from the highway.

The interior lighting would also be remarkable. Sunken practically into the landscape, the first-floor Garden Room had an air-conditioning duct running its length. Dick and Nathalie had transformed the duct into a sleek cantilevered shelf for plants and uplights. As in Manhasset, old and new complemented one another in the Westchester Candlelight, as did American and Asian elements. A heavy Chinese table holding massive floral arrangements separated the cocktail lounge from a dining room. In the Venetian-themed Crystal Room, poles covered with Naugahyde supported a tent-like striped fabric ceiling. In the Gold Room, an Asian scene handscreened onto wallpaper by Albert Van Luit managed to look right with office-type Chairmaster chairs upholstered in sand-colored vinyl.[14]

Dick worked with local factories to create European-style chandeliers holding slender candle-like lamps for the Crystal Room, first showing various samples of the artificial candles to Patricia for her approval.

In the Gold Room, he devised fixtures, twelve feet in diameter, resembling enormous bouquets of Asian flower blossoms and leaves. Sprayed gold, the metal foliage artfully concealed lamps and light diffusers.

Patricia wanted special lights for the wall of her bar, upholstered, as usual, in her late father's seal skins. Her celebrated lighting designer had among his carefully organized files an article from *Women's Day* titled "Anyone Can Make a Lamp Out of ANYTHING." Written by Marguerite Dodd, author of books on housekeeping and cooking, it encouraged budget-conscious readers to grab some wire and sockets and convert old siphon bottles and curtain rods into home lighting. Working on a similar principle, MoMA's lamp-design judge turned cookie tins into a lamp for the wall of Patricia's bar.

For lighting the rose garden, the azalea hill, and the terraced areas with seasonally changing plantings, Dick consulted repeatedly with Victor E. Carlson, Patricia's horticulturist. She relied on Carlson almost as much as on John Rogers and Vincent.[15]

But even after purchasing a home in Hartsdale, a half-hour north of the Yonkers Candlelight, Vincent was secretly continuing to hedge his bets with a continued investment in Lauraine Murphy, Inc. Justifying Patricia's fears, Jim had found a prime location at 1445 Northern Boulevard in Manhasset, less than a mile from the Candlelight there. It was a Louis Sherry restaurant, one of the newest in a chain once famous for its ice cream and candies. The building was only a few years old, but the owner, who also worked for a major hotel business, had left it in the care of his middle-aged girlfriend.

The asking price was $100,000. That was not unreasonable, considering the building's beautiful decor, the new equipment, and the location in the heart of the famous Miracle Mile shopping district. With the Long Island Expressway still in the planning stages, there were perpetual traffic jams on Northern Boulevard, New York's Route 25A. Louis Sherry was serving breakfast and high tea. Jim wanted to cancel breakfast, make some money from lunch and tea, but focus on dinner and drinks. Motorists could park their cars in the restaurant's lot and have a meal while waiting for the traffic to lighten.

Jim's offer was $50,000. It was refused, but he didn't raise it. He could see that the girlfriend left in charge didn't know how to order. She worked like the tea room owners of decades past who were unable to meet the demands of the postwar era. "A piece of meat came into the kitchen, and she says to the chef, 'Be careful. That has to last for three or four days,'" Jim recalled, adding, "There was no way you could run a business like that. What if you got busy? The place was empty."

Jim went to Florida on vacation and returned to find his offer accepted. His first act after closing the deal was to fire the entire Louis Sherry staff except for the baker.[16] "In April of 1954, ads announced the opening of a second Lauraine Murphy's restaurant, within spitting distance of Patricia Murphy's. Some of the ads brazenly described Lauraine Murphy's as the "home of the famous popover."[17]

Still, Vincent and Mollie made plans to bring up their kids in Westchester. The two Lauraine Murphy's together did not approach the scale of Patricia's restaurants. Their Great Neck place had about 135 seats, and the former Louis Sherry restaurant added only 100. Jim was planning to expand into an adjacent linen store, with a banquet room upstairs, but contractors had discovered some problems that would make construction costly.

Vincent would not consider uprooting his family until all that was resolved. Jim's estimate of the expansion costs had ballooned to $135,000 from $35,000. Known for being tight-fisted, Jim also planned to buy several chandeliers for his new dining rooms. The cost, $5,000 each, was staggering, but as Vincent gushed over Patricia's décor, sibling rivalry triumphed over parsimony.

Beneath her own museum-quality chandeliers, Patricia reviewed the new staff in Westchester as she prepared for her fourth restaurant opening. Some were Filipinos who had worked for her previously, or knew someone who did. Among them was Gabriel Burgos, her chef. A recent graduate of St. John's University, Gabriel planned menus of cheese soup, stuffed shrimp, roasts, swordfish, and fried chicken, supplemented by hot breads, trays of relishes, pies, cakes, and sundaes—familiar foods in generous portions.

Supplementing workers transplanted from her other restaurants were eager new hires. Yonkers had so far failed to replace its former rug mills and factories with new industries, and the local people were hungry for jobs. For part-time and seasonal work, there was a large pool of housewives and students.

Breaking slightly with tradition, Patricia had the napkins folded upright, but not quite the way Mr. Anthony had taught her. The Great Depression, even the war, seemed so long ago. In Westchester, where the shopping centers touted "suburban style," Patricia's linen napkins relaxed. Instead of resembling towers, they lay casually on the table, forming low peaks at the fold line.

As the grand restaurant in Westchester opened its doors, buyers for the three others had been found. Patricia's accountants in Manhasset, Tavlin and Zimmerman, had sweetened their bid to $700,000. There were still some matters to resolve regarding Patricia's continued need for the Long Island greenhouse, but the deal was almost done. The city restaurants had also been sold. All were still named the Candlelight and were known colloquially as Patricia Murphy's. In Manhasset, Tavlin and Zimmerman wanted to maintain the official name as Patricia Murphy's Candlelight.

On September 24, the waiters in Westchester stood ready in their red uniforms. Popover girls revealed the piping-hot goodies below the hinged lids of their picnic baskets, the type used to transport Toto in *The Wizard of Oz*. This was Yonkers in Technicolor. The gilded-brick fireplace of the Gold Room blazed with warmth. Exotic plants, described as looking "cannibalistic," co-existed with seal fur in the fabulousness of the cocktail lounge. The elaborate autumnal table decorations included some of the thousands of chrysanthemums planted on the grounds.

No hex was cast by the new method of folding napkins. Built against the wishes of its residential neighbors, Patricia Murphy's Candlelight Restaurant regularly filled all one thousand of its seats several times daily. The servers were trained to be attentive and polite while discouraging dawdling over meals. Bonuses were awarded to the dining room staff with the highest turnover.

Price controls on food had ceased at the end of the Korean War, and there was enough wealth in Westchester to charge $4.25 for full dinners at the high end, sirloin or filet mignon. The affluent county quickly embraced its largest restaurant, which offered ever-changing garden displays, table decorations, and staff costumes. Queues formed for tables, flash bulbs popped, sacks of crumbs were flung to ducks, and on a typical Sunday, 20,000 popovers were consumed. By the time a Christmas crèche with real sheep was installed on the grounds, Patricia Murphy's Candlelight Restaurant had hosted annual meetings or dinner parties for a bank, a realty board, the Ancient Order of Hibernians, the B'nai B'rith, and the Urban League.

Relations remained cordial between Patricia and the buyers of her restaurant in Manhasset, where she still housed her orchids and rare plants. They shared the costs of display ads for "Patricia Murphy

Candlelight Restaurants," listing the Yonkers and Long Island addresses under the banner "Two Great Country Restaurants." The menus, the matchboxes, even the meal checks promoted both. To the Long Island public, Zimmerman and Tavlin had transitioned into Patricia Murphy.

That lingering after-image, the illusion that Patricia remained in Manhasset after the sale, was reinforced by an Associated Press wire story printed in papers across the nation in January of 1955. Written by Cynthia Lowery, it was headed, "Happy Housewife Feeds 4,000 Every Day." One newspaper, in Jackson, Mississippi, added parenthetically, "With Hubby's Help."

After quickly recapping Patricia's rags-to-riches story and reporting the recent sale of the two city restaurants, the AP piece stated that she served between one million and 1.5 million diners annually. "With her husband, James E. Kiernan, Patricia operates two huge and thriving restaurants—one in Manhasset, Long Island, the other in suburban Westchester County," the piece said, adding, "The Kiernans work from 10 a.m. to midnight each day, commuting between their restaurants."[18]

The million-meals-a-year statistic was the newest wrinkle in Patricia's legend, now that the old ones—about the sixty-dollar investment and the juggling of twenty teacups among thirty-six customers—had turned a bit stale, at least in Greater New York. It was all fresh, however, to those reading about Patricia Murphy for the first time in the *Corpus Christi Caller-Times* or the *Lansing State Journal*.

The Westchester Candlelight had opened just three months before the AP piece ran. Hence, it would have been difficult for Patricia to produce the million-meal statistic from what was now her only location. Nevertheless, she seemed eager to identify herself with Manhasset, if for no other reason than that the operation of one restaurant, albeit an enormous one, seemed too simple. Patricia liked to be thought of as overworked and overachieving.

She and Rosie were hardly working fourteen-hour days. They were at times commuting between Manhasset and Yonkers, but only because the sales agreement with Tavlin and Zimmerman had acknowledged Patricia as the sole owner of the plants in the Long Island greenhouse. It had also given her the right to continue using the greenhouse for one year, with the assistance of the Manhasset gardening staff, free of charge.

That agreement became more valuable than Patricia had expected. A month after the AP piece appeared, Nathalie Rahv appeared before the Zoning Board of Appeals. Pointing out that the restaurant's foundations had been laid before the city passed hundreds of ordinance changes, she argued that the construction of a greenhouse and other planned additions to the Candlelight should not require waivers. Her argument was rejected.[19]

Now there were mountains of red tape separating Patricia from her greenhouse. Tavlin and Zimmerman were growing impatient with her frequent visits to Manhasset and her demands on their gardening staff. Still, she had achieved her goal of winning some horticultural certificates and ribbons.

The commutes she didn't discuss with the AP writer were her frequent trips to Florida. She and Rosie had become regulars on Eastern Airlines. In Yonkers, they lived in a modest house at 1750 Central Park Avenue, a few hundred yards from the Candlelight. Their real home was their estate in the Port Sewall section of Stuart, where no zoning interfered with Patricia's greenhouses and orchid laths. When the metalwork on the main orchid house was finished, it would resemble a Victorian gazebo, with iron cupids standing guard.

When Rosie first saw the property's lagoon and island, it reminded him of sailing into Kinsale on Ireland's West Coast. Hence, they called the site Kinsale, and the guests who attended their lavish parties there learned to pronounce it with the accent on "sale"—appropriately enough, as the sales of her first three restaurants and the income from her fabulous fourth kept it going. The estate was located thirty-five miles north of Palm Beach, where Patricia and her captain had made an entrance into society, associating with people like the second Mrs. Raymond Royce Kent, a brewery heiress who entertained bullfighters, polo players, and movie stars.

For the AP story, designed for mass consumption, Patricia remained silent on her love of luxury, choosing instead to portray herself as a harried housewife, working long days and commuting, perhaps in a station wagon, with her husband at her side.

In the same year, a different side of Patricia was presented in *Investor's Reader*, a publication of Merrill, Lynch, Fenner & Beane, which, despite its name, presented itself as a "news and educational publication about business and financial matters" not to be consulted for stock tips. A half-dozen women were on its staff, but its stories were mostly about men; the issue focusing on Patricia in a section called "Management" included longer pieces about the male presidents of Chrysler and

Pfizer. The profile of Patricia, titled "Charms in the Kitchen," stressed her femininity, describing her as "petite and piquant" and noting that employees called her "mama." Her profit margins, however, were praised without reference to gender. At 15 to 17 percent, "they are the envy of many a restaurant owner," said the report.[20]

As in the AP interview, Patricia again emphasized her hard work and twelve-hour days. But with *Investor's Reader* she also talked business, estimating that food comprised 45 percent of her costs, forcing her to carefully monitor other spending. Always an unreliable source, Patricia said she had started her first restaurant at age eighteen. That mistruth made this interview consistent with others previously published while guarding her brand against the tarnish of age: her name had proved itself highly valuable, and she wanted to keep it that way.

Patricia used the Merrill Lynch magazine as a platform to speak about women's rights. Earlier in her career, "she found banks highly skeptical about underwriting a woman's business ventures," the magazine reported. For the first time in print, she boasted of her wealth, saying, "I have made a few million all right."

The piece names Captain James E. Kiernan as her husband, with no mention of his business role or lack of one. Above the text is a photo of the couple. No longer the dowdy matron of the General Electric magazine photo taken in Manhasset, Patricia occupies a seal-skin seat in her Westchester bar. Surrounded by foliage, she is smiling at her husband across a dark, reflective tabletop. The two appear immaculately tailored—he in suit and tie, she in a smart checked jacket—yet relaxed. Her manicured hands lay close to his on the table; her cigarette, in a holder, burns in a tray near cocktail glasses and a modernist candlestick. Her short dark hair, professionally curled, is pulled back from her temples and forehead, offering a clear view of her jeweled earrings. She looks far more put-together than in the GE photo.

Investor's Reader said its photo showed Patricia and the captain "enjoying a restaurateur's holiday," but added, "Murphy occasionally finds time to leave her candles and kitchen to escape to her Florida home and raise orchids." She was also finding time to flaunt her millions.

James Murphy & Sons store in Placentia, Newfoundland, ca. 1920.
Photograph courtesy of Paul Murphy.

Brooklyn Candlelight cocktail lounge, ca 1936. Photograph by Warren B. Sievers, courtesy of Paul Murphy.

James F. Murphy, Patricia's brother-turned-rival-restaurateur. Photograph by Mayfair Photographers, courtesy of Paul Murphy.

Patricia marries Capt. James E. Kiernan, 1948. Her mother is on the right.
Photograph courtesy of Paul Murphy.

Ample parking in front of the Manhasset Candlelight, 1951. Photograph courtesy of the Library of Congress, Prints and Photographs Division, Gottscho-Schleisner Collection.

The Crystal Room at the Candlelight in Yonkers, 1954. Photograph courtesy of the Library of Congress, Prints and Photographs Division, Gottscho-Schleisner Collection.

Patricia experimented with different looks. Here she appears in a 1959 ad for her Jewel Gift Shop in Yonkers. Retouched photograph from an advertisement, courtesy of the Barnard College Archives and Special Collections.

Patricia poses at the controls of her plane, *Miss Tango*, which she never really piloted. Photograph courtesy of the Photography Collection, Harry Ransom Center, University of Texas at Austin.

Patricia posing for the book cover of her 1961 autobiography, *Glow of Candlelight*, and the cover portrait. Photograph and illustration by Jon Whitcomb. Photograph courtesy of The Ohio State University Billy Ireland Cartoon Library & Museum and the estate of Jon Whitcomb. Illustration courtesy of the estate of Jon Whitcomb.

Patricia (r) at the Candlelight in Fort Lauderdale. Photograph by Gene Hyde, courtesy of the Fort Lauderdale Historical Society.

Patricia in Fort Lauderdale with her young nieces and Sheila's husband, John G. Fox III. Photograph by Gene Hyde, courtesy of the Fort Lauderdale Historical Society.

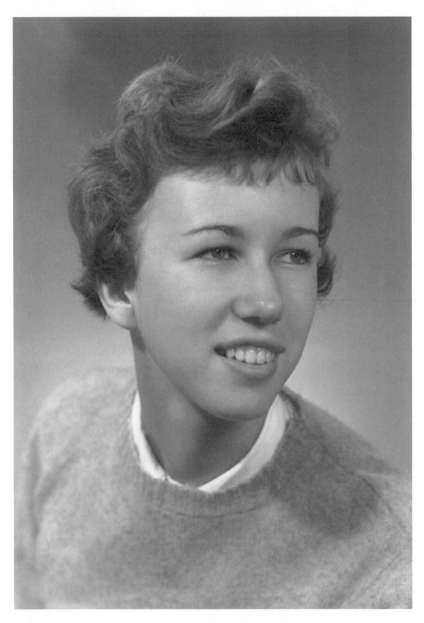

Sheila, the only sibling who remained in Patricia's life after the feud. Photograph by Gene Hyde, courtesy of the Fort Lauderdale Historical Society.

CHAPTER 10

Revenge

Should there be any mistake, we can easily trace the one to blame.

—Patricia Murphy's manual for employees, 1930

A constant stream of visitors came to marvel at Kinsale. The garden clubs exclaimed over the rare specimens in the orchid house, the birds of paradise, and the oleanders, but what they loved best was relaxing on the patios under the shade trees that cooled the enormous shingled white house. Party guests loved the swimming pool and its elaborate cabana, a replacement for one left in tatters by some fun-loving members of the Kinsale crowd. The new cabana had a glassed-in formal living room with a concealed bar.

As many as 675 guests could be accommodated at one time. Themed parties with costumes were held, such as the all-day Victorian party and the St. Patrick's Day celebrations with green ice.

In the words of a Palm Beach gossip columnist: "When this famous gourmet entertains, what with the superb victuals and viands she produces and the magnificent setting which is the site of her home, guests are not likely to soon forget the experience."[1]

In February of 1956, Michael Tavlin was summoned to this Floridian paradise. He may have suspected that Patricia was not asking him to dance. The two Patricia Murphy's Candlelight Restaurants of Yonkers and Manhasset no longer engaged in joint advertising. Patricia had ended that after Tavlin and Zimmerman raised questions, or reminded her of the one-year deadline, regarding her use of the Manhasset garden and greenhouse. The dual addresses and the plural form of the word "restaurant" had disappeared from menu covers, ads, and the like.

Tavlin's invitation to Kinsale could not be related to the "hothouse," as he and Zimmerman called it. Patricia finally had her greenhouse in Westchester after months of battle with Yonkers officials. Initially, they had closed ranks against her. Following Nathalie's failure to have all Candlelight expansion considered under the old zoning rules, the Candlelight lost a second plea, for an incinerator. Vincent, identified as the Candlelight's manager, told the Zoning Board of Appeals that the Candlelight produced twenty-five to thirty cans of garbage daily. The $600 monthly cost of having it hauled away could be eliminated with one $6,000 incinerator, he said. Nathalie also spoke, maintaining that the incinerator would be odorless and smokeless.

Owners of homes and property were unmoved. They argued through lawyers that a variance for one incinerator might eventually produce a string of them along Central Avenue (the local abbreviation for Central Park Avenue). They spoke of "smoke" and "nuisance." Permission was denied.

Patricia wasn't about to make the same mistakes in applying for the greenhouse. For this she staged a small-scale soap opera. Vincent, Nathalie, and pocketbook issues were left at home. Rosie filed an application for the greenhouse permit. Meanwhile, Patricia put out the word that the Captain had been about to buy her a fur coat, but she asked for a greenhouse instead.

In this romantic context, the couple appeared before the zoning board to assuage fears about creating a nuisance. The retired decorated naval captain explained that gardening was Patricia's "hobby" and that she had never sold a flower or plant. Both claims were somewhat disingenuous. More than a hobby, horticulture served Patricia's commercial interests: gardening prizes and elaborately landscaped grounds promoted the Candlelight. Moreover, Patricia had every intention of selling her customers cut orchids. However, it was true that the greenhouse would not operate as a nursery open to the public.

Completing the charm offensive, Patricia showed off her horticultural certificates and ribbons, "not to mention my best feminine wiles," she added. The zoning board unanimously approved a variance for the greenhouse and, soon after, so did the Common Council.[2]

Patricia had asked the Yonkers authorities for swift action, noting that her valuable orchid collection would soon need to be moved from its temporary housing. Now she was hosting Michael Tavlin, the man who had created that urgency—the would-be evictor of her collection.

She made him a surprising offer. She wanted to buy back the Manhasset Candlelight.[3]

The restaurant had continued to be immensely popular, and Tavlin, chiefly responsible for running it, had proven his mettle as a restaurateur and was fast becoming wealthy. Far from being eager to shed this restaurant, he was hoping to buy others in the suburbs. It's said that everything has a price, but Patricia and her former accountant could not reach an agreement on one for the Candlelight. He said he would consult with his partner, Zimmerman.

Tavlin left Patricia "quite irate," according to the account he gave Zimmerman, who concurred with his decision.

There would be no sale by Munsey Candlelight, the corporation that Tavlin and Zimmerman had formed. The business name referred to the area of Manhasset where the restaurant was located, and where the newspaper publisher Frank Munsey had owned six hundred acres before bequeathing them to the Metropolitan Museum. In the early twentieth century, half that acreage had been Sherryland, the enormous estate belonging to French confectioner and restaurateur Louis Sherry, with a mansion built to resemble a Versailles palace.

Estates like that, mostly gone by the 1950s, had typically taken top honors at the important flower shows that Patricia planned on entering. She was assembling a nearly estate-scale horticultural operation of staff, plants, and equipment in the North and the South. The plan was to transport plants between the two ends of the East Coast, amazing northerners with oleander and Hawaiian ginger while stunning southerners with lilacs and laurels usually confined to temperate zones. Novelty on her restaurant grounds would draw customers, and blue ribbons would get her name in the papers.

Tavlin and Zimmerman might name their corporation after a former estate owner, but they had stood in the way of Patricia's own estate-making. They had their own ideas about why Patricia wanted to buy back Manhasset when she appeared to be doing fine with just Westchester. To outsiders, however, the proposal may have seemed mystifying. Patricia had repeatedly presented herself in interviews as a driven, hands-on manager madly rushing between distant restaurants as her loving husband urged rest.

Contrary to this carefully crafted myth, Captain Kiernan took an active part in pursuing the Manhasset buyback. One month after the initial rebuff, Tavlin was invited to meet with him as well as Patricia.[4]

The couple were in Washington, DC, where Rosie had once lived and entertained. Rosie knew the capital and its inhabitants; the meeting would be on his turf.

Although nettled by Tavlin's intransigence, Patricia was excited about visiting the nation's capital, where her husband's connections had led to a special investment opportunity. She was about to buy a piece of a spectacular action movie based on the life of naval hero John Paul Jones. The project, to be filmed in Spain, had the blessing of recently retired Fleet Admiral Chester W. Nimitz, who would personally advise it. The film's producer, Samuel Bronston, was working with C.D. Jackson, a former speechwriter and special adviser to President Dwight D. Eisenhower, to finance the picture by bundling investments by people outside of Hollywood—people like Patricia.

The long-dead John Paul Jones was Patricia's kind of man. She may have enjoyed the company of artistic people like the architect Nathalie Rahv of the *Partisan Review* set and the decorator and illustrator Jack Lynas, but her romantic imagination was populated by ship captains and airplane pilots. Her second husband was a case in point, and her frequent flying between New York and Florida, when not on Eastern Airlines, had acquainted her with charter pilots whom she admired. Her investment in the John Paul Jones film came with a guarantee of an invitation to the set. The film had not yet been cast, but Henry Fonda and Paul Newman were being talked about for the leading role. At any rate, it seemed like a sound investment. Because of the low costs of filming in Spain, the producer projected the cost of his spectacular epic blockbuster—the genre of the moment—at just two million dollars.

Sam Bronston, the producer, was also the type of person who won Patricia's approval. Born in East Europe and raised in France, he did not fly a plane or command a ship, but he was determined to establish a Hollywood-in-Madrid. Like Patricia, he charmed people with his personal elegance, and he had a novel and audacious business plan.[5]

To a Washington whirling with these plans came Michael Tavlin. Patricia's former personal accountant was no John Paul Jones, nor even a Sam Bronston. He and Meyer Zimmerman were copycats, like her brother Jim, skilled only at replicating her format.

Tavlin came to the meeting with Patricia and Rosie prepared to once again negotiate. However, the parties remained far apart. Patricia threatened to open another Candlelight in Long Island, this time in

Suffolk County, if Tavlin and Zimmerman continued their obstinacy. In purchasing the Candlelight, Tavlin and Zimmerman had asked Patricia to agree not to compete in Nassau or Queens Counties. They had placed no restrictions on Suffolk, less developed and harder to reach from New York City. Suffolk didn't worry them.

Again, the meeting concluded with no deal and an irate Patricia.

Only fourteen months earlier, she had eagerly rid herself of the Manhasset restaurant and fled Nassau County, the battleground of her family feud. Now she was desperate to retake the Candlelight, even with Jim, Lauraine, and Maude operating their new Lauraine Murphy's right down the road. It was a business of change. In the heyday of Sherryland, who would have predicted that a tastefully decorated Louis Sherry restaurant would fail miserably and be sold to Jim at a bargain-basement price?

Whatever her reasons for wishing a return to Manhasset, Patricia sought no further meetings with Tavlin. Like John Paul Jones, she had not yet begun to fight. Shortly after the Washington confrontation, a new item debuted on her menus. On the back cover, beneath the large words, "Patricia Murphy's Candlelight Restaurant," a legend appeared:— *the only restaurant personally owned and operated by Patricia Murphy*

It was a short line of type, very like the wording Patricia had added to her Long Island display ads shortly after the Lauraine restaurant had become Lauraine Murphy's. That was a small-scale battle, however, not waged on menus or even in major newspapers. In fact, Patricia seemed to have abandoned it quickly, either because it had little effect on Jim's success in Great Neck and eventually Manhasset, or because it upset her mother.

Not everyone reads the back cover of a menu carefully. However, among the thousands of customers seated daily at the Yonkers Candlelight, at least some did—some who knew there was also a Patricia Murphy's Candlelight Restaurant in Long Island. It didn't take long for the news to travel twenty-five miles to Manhasset.

Tavlin and Zimmerman were alarmed. Customers who had thought Patricia was always there, though unseen, like a spiritual presence, were asking questions. The machinery of the business transaction was poking out from behind the flowers. They went to court seeking an injunction against her, claiming she was causing "irreparable damage" and "loss of patronage" to her restaurant by making their use of her name—for which they'd paid $200,000—appear illegitimate and improper.

Denied a temporary injunction after a special-term court hearing, Tavlin and Zimmerman persisted. In August 1956, the case went before an appellate division of the New York Supreme Court. Defending Patricia, her lawyer accused Tavlin and Zimmerman of "vainly trying to create" a "misleading impression on the dining public that Patricia Murphy, the person, is still the owner of the Manhasset restaurant, and still lending her outstanding skills and ability to its operation."

The words on the menu constituted a public service, the defense contended. Patricia said that after selling the Manhasset place,

> . . . I received one or two complaints a day about the operations in the Manhasset restaurant . . . In addition to the complaints, numerous people informed me that when they asked about me at the Manhasset restaurant they were informed that I am still managing it but was away on vacation and would return soon. When the complaints became too numerous, I placed on the menu of the Westchester restaurant the legend 'The only restaurant personally owned and operated by Patricia Murphy.' This I had the right to do legally since the contract actually or impliedly does not prohibit it; and morally, since it is the absolute truth."

Zimmerman scoffed at Patricia's professed concern for enlightening the public. He pointed out that during the time of the alleged complaints, the two restaurants were engaged in joint promotion and advertising. He said,

> I submit that the defendant should not be permitted to blow hot and cold on this issue; to jointly promote these restaurants and find no deception in such joint promotion when it suits her purpose, and to claim to be the unmasker of deception when it does not.

Arguing that Patricia was motivated by spite, not truth, he pointed to the timeline of events:

> The reason for this discontinuance [of joint advertising] . . . had nothing to do with food or complaints or anything of

the sort. It had to do with a dispute which Mrs. Kiernan and myself had concerning the flowers which were growing in the hothouse in Manhasset. Albeit this is trivia, but it was just such trivia as this which initially caused bad feelings between plaintiff and defendant.

Patricia had acted out of "pique" and "ill will," Zimmerman said, concluding, "She must not be permitted, simply because she is angry, to destroy the goodwill for which she received so much." The lines on the menu "must be stopped before our entire investment is jeopardized," he said.

Patricia's response to this doomsday prediction was to cite the articles in the *New York Herald Tribune* and *Investor's Reader* that mentioned the Manhasset sale. She also presented a *New York Times* article, fresh off the presses. Her female Horatio Alger story was enshrined in the newspaper of record under the heading, "Once Hungry, She Serves a Million Meals a Year." The *Times* reported that the "five-foot girl with more energy than even Brooklyn could contain" had sold all her eateries except her Yonkers establishment. "Here she 'takes it easy' looking after 300 employees and several acres of prize-winning plants," it continued.

"The legend on the menu is certainly insignificant compared to this publicity," Patricia said.

The publicity defense proved persuasive. The appellate division's panel of seven unanimously upheld the previous ruling, which had concluded, "To state on her menus that which had already been well publicized, apparently without objection . . . does not warrant the granting of an injunction."

Tavlin and Zimmerman pursued the case no further. Patricia was free to continue printing the legend on her menus. She had reaped more than the usual benefits of hiring publicists, including Kay Vincent, the former *Trib* fashion editor.

The menus, however, soon became so busy with illustrations that the legend was barely noticeable. The simple dark green menu with white lettering, Exhibit II in the court appeal, gave way to a collage of color photos. Lengthy captions described the restaurant's spring gardens with its 50,000 tulips, the fall chrysanthemums, and the Christmas decorations in the Crystal Room. Also pictured were staff members dressed in holiday themes, including a bewigged George Washington escorting his Martha—probably a popover girl pressed into First-Lady service.

The lake and the orchid collection were also pictured on the new menu covers, from which the word "Yonkers" had been banished. The menu attached to Meyer Zimmerman's affidavit had listed the restaurant's address as "Yonkers, Westchester, Central Avenue (Route 100) just north of Tuckahoe Road." The new menus abbreviated this to "Central Park Avenue, Westchester New York," supplemented by a phone number.

The Candlelight's disassociation with its Yonkers address provoked a letter to the editor of the *Herald Statesman* that criticized other businesses and a local business for the same practice. The vague address didn't prevent tour buses from finding the restaurant, and their increasing numbers were clogging the parking lot. Patricia needed to expand. Apart from the stigma attached to nearly all cities at a time of suburban expansion, she had personal reasons to spurn connection with Yonkers. She anticipated further combat with a city that had continually obstructed her.

She was pleased with the Yonkers labor force, however. "Everybody pulled together, even though we had a motley crew always—Filipinos, local Westchester kids, even an Arab in the kitchen," she wrote in her autobiography.[6] (The published version replaced "motley" with the more neutral "assorted.") The Arab was James Sayegh, a Lebanese Christian who arrived in Yonkers in 1956, bringing his family over about eighteen months later. Hired as a busboy, he eventually became executive chef of the Candlelight's catering division. One of his sons, Nader James Sayegh, described Patricia as "very generous," noting that she hosted special Christmas celebrations for the employees and their families. To support his large family, the busboy-turned-chef sometimes worked a second job to supplement his pay of approximately ninety cents an hour, his son said—the price of a cocktail. However, he eventually bought a four-family house, and his son cannot remember any complaints about how Patricia treated him.

"Patricia Murphy's was very important in his life," said Nader James Sayegh. "The whole family liked the fact that he was working there," continued the son. It was one of the area's "classiest businesses," he added, remembering Patricia as well dressed, or in his words, "always decked out."[7]

Another Yonkers local, a recent graduate of Fordham University, was also plucked from the busboys' ranks and placed on a swift management trajectory. This was Gregory D. Camillucci, an able managerial assistant to Vincent and John Rogers. Young Greg fell into the category of Patricia's masculine ideal: he was about to enter the Air Force, where he would train to be a pilot. To send him off in style—and encourage his return to the Candlelight—Patricia paid for Greg and a friend to tour Europe in the summer of 1956.

As for the county in general, Westchester's wealth was feeding Patricia's. New dishes were slightly more adventurous than in the past. Some were flown up from Florida, like filet of Pompano with toasted almonds. Prices flew somewhat higher, too. A filet mignon or whole-lobster dinner now cost $4.50, including an appetizer, salad, two vegetables, and dessert. Whiskey sours had crept up to eighty cents, and some could afford ten dollars for a bottle of Piper Heidsieck.

Patricia was establishing herself in Westchester society. Instead of airing brash radio commercials, she persuaded a local AM station to come to the Candlelight and broadcast fifteen-minute programs called "Patricia Murphy's Luncheon Guest." These WNRC segments included interviews with leaders of the Bronxville Junior League about their charitable projects and children's theater. One featured a league board member named Robin Chandler, previously on the staff of NBC's "Today" show and married to the actor Jeffrey Lynn.[8]

Bronxville was classy. The Kennedys had lived there for a while. When building the Candlelight, "we thought we were in Bronxville," Patricia claimed. Her lease, though, always made plain she was in the City of Yonkers, which—flush from her court triumph—she again prepared to meet in combat.

This time, if her strategy worked, she wouldn't have to lift a finger. Others would do the fighting for her.

CHAPTER 11

Spinning to a Stop

Take the bitter with the sweet; it is good grace.

—Patricia Murphy's manual for employees, 1930

Patricia often boasted that her husband bought her lavish gifts despite warnings from his alarmed brother, John. But as she boarded a train in Washington, dripping in fur, emeralds, and gold lamé, the Yonkers restaurant was financing her finery. Rosie's annual salary while on active duty was $7,500—"a ridiculously inadequate sum for a captain in this country's service,"[1] Patricia wrote, "that would not have gone far at Kinsale," not to mention their other spending.

They were coming from a cocktail party, part of the festivities marking Eisenhower's second inauguration. They'd also been to an inaugural ball. A year had passed since they'd invested in the John Paul Jones film. Projected costs had doubled to four million dollars, but some major corporations had climbed aboard the cinematic *Bonhomme Richard*. Now that Pierre du Pont III was backing Sam Bronston, there was less need for modest-scale investors. Patricia seemed to have gotten in at the right time.

Movies were never a sure thing, and neither were horses, but Patricia was betting on one of those, too. She now owned a show horse, another so-called gift from her husband. Her determination to view the St. Patrick's Day on Fifth Avenue had escalated into trips to Ireland, where her heavyweight hunter, Treaty Stone, competed. When Patricia crossed the Atlantic, "she always went first class," said her protégé, Greg Camillucci, adding that her vessel of choice was the Queen Elizabeth.

Camillucci also remembered her numerous steamer trunks. As the train waited in Washington, she had porters load them into her first-class train compartment. Rosie got off to check something about their tickets. Minutes passed, but Rosie failed to return. Patricia panicked, had the trunks pulled off, and searched for him in the station. With mink on her back but not a coin in her purse—Rosie always took charge of cash and tickets—Patricia was stranded.

A call from the stationmaster's office revealed that Rosie had reboarded before the train pulled out. Realizing Patricia's mistake, he had gotten off at the next station in northern Virginia and was waiting for her. "It was the only time we were ever separated," she said.

She soon reunited with him, taking with her trunks stuffed with gowns and baubles, the new uniforms of her rising social position—made possible, she wrote, because her business had "profited mightily." There was no cash register in the Westchester Candlelight. Payments were tucked into drawers of a lacquered Chinese desk, lest the crass noise of moneymaking pollute the tasteful atmosphere. But even as additional safes were installed in the office to accommodate the contents of those drawers, the restaurant had yet to reach its full potential.

She needed variances to add a new wing for banquets and parties, expand parking, and finally build her gift shop. The gift shop would be a standalone store featuring gifts from around the world. She'd order merchandise for the shop on buying trips that could qualify for tax write-offs. Retailing had already proven a success at the greenhouse. Despite the Captain's assurances to Yonkers officials that Patricia had no intention of selling flowers, she was doing a tremendous business in cut orchids. The newest menu item at the Candlelight was a fresh corsage, listed over the soups and appetizers. Priced as low as $1.50, it was the perfect gift for one's dinner companion.

As planned, sales of the cut flowers were paying the wages of Patricia's "greenhouse boys," as she called them, growing in number as new Saran-covered extensions sprouted from the octagonal orchid house at Kinsale. Patricia's "hobby," as Rosie had described it to the zoning appeals board, was supporting her weather-defying floral displays in Westchester. Much as Birnham Wood came to Dunsinane, bromeliads and bird-of-paradise flowers would march to the chilly North.

Sometimes Patricia reserved an entire train compartment for plants, companions for her and Rosie on their rail travels. No flowers accompanied them as they departed from the second inauguration of the nation's Republican president. Three months earlier, the Westchester Candlelight had hosted a four-hundred-person rally organized by the Yonkers Democratic Women's Organization in support of New York Mayor Robert F. Wagner, Jr.'s unsuccessful campaign for the U.S. Senate. That was business. Equally comfortable with Rosie's allegiance to the navy and Nathalie Rahv's leftist connections, Patricia had no firm political affiliation.

Voters in Yonkers were somewhat fluid. Republican Mayor Kristen Kristensen, a man born and raised in Norway, had been elected to a fourth term, while Democrats dominated in the Common Council by a 9–3 margin over Republicans.[2] Patricia would need the approval of the mayor and council to build on more acreage, and this time she had powerful new allies. Some powerful developers wanted the area around the Candlelight rezoned from residential-only to commercial and residential.

Two owners of large swaths of land along Central Avenue had joined forces to confront the city. They were petitioning for ordinance changes that would allow millions of dollars of commercial development close to Patricia's restaurant. A combination office park and shopping center was planned near Roosevelt High School. To the rear of the Candlelight, a one-hundred-room hotel was envisioned. They were talking to Patricia about having her run it.

Patricia was not at all sure she wanted to operate a business owned by others, but it didn't hurt to lead them on. Some heavy-hitters were pushing for the zoning changes. Chief proponent for the retail-office complex was C. Van Ness Wood, head of Eastern Shopping Centers, Inc., based in Yonkers but with visions stretching far beyond that city's limits. A spinoff of Grand Union, Eastern Shopping Centers had already won zoning changes in Vestal Hills, New York, where it was breaking ground for a huge shopping plaza. Other sites in New York, as well as New Jersey and Florida, were lined up in its crosshairs.[3]

Involved only in the smaller development proposal, Patricia could ride the coattails of the larger one. The projected cost for the hotel was one million dollars, compared to $2.4 million for the office and retail proposal. However, the two petitions would go before the Common Council together, jointly represented by an attorney who had formerly headed the Yonkers planning board. Patricia would benefit from Eastern Shopping Center's capital and clout.

Public hearings and the vote weren't likely to be scheduled before the summer. In the meantime, Patricia was willing to discuss terms for managing the hotel. The developer, it seemed, preferred a motel, which would require yet another ordinance change. It was like a game of Monopoly, except that there were no pieces to represent a gift shop, parking lot, or restaurant wing—the things Patricia truly wanted to put on her square.

Meanwhile, the train took her and her captain south to Kinsale, where she truly felt alive. Patricia was "always a faraway figure, you might not see her for months," said Greg Camillucci, the busboy she had anointed for management. Her absences, however, made the business what it was. The guests at Kinsale could simply enjoy viewing baskets of orchids while floating on their backs in the pool, but Patricia and her horticultural staff grew the flowers that heightened her social profile and drew customers to her tables. "She was amazing in her ability to bring people in, especially women, because of her tremendous expertise in botanicals," Camillucci said.

The summer of 1957 was an especially busy time at Kinsale, where workers were busily completing work on the interior of the house. The finished rooms were to be photographed by Samuel H. Gottscho and William H. Schleisner, the esteemed architectural photographers whose work had illustrated the magazine articles about Patricia's restaurants in *Interiors* and *Light*.

While she was away, Vincent and John Rogers kept things humming at the restaurant. There had been an unpleasant rumor, however. The only time the Candlelight closed was on Christmas Day, and Patricia had an inkling that her treacherous siblings had celebrated the holiday by taking an unauthorized tour of her restaurant. The only way they could have achieved this was under Vincent's supervision. Jim, Lauraine, Maude—and naturally, Nana and Sheila—had of course visited Vincent and Mollie in Hartsdale. But other than Patricia's mother and youngest sister, none was welcome at the restaurant.

Owen Smith, Lauraine's son, said Vincent had shown them the Candlelight during one of Patricia's absences, and they had been quite impressed. Vincent was even more impressed by his Long Island siblings. The Lauraine Murphy in Manhasset was doing well after expansion, and they had sold the original one in Great Neck at a good price. There was money in the bank to finance the purchase of another property if the right opportunity arose. Vincent's secret investment in their business had turned out well.[4]

It would be secret no longer. In March of 1957, Vincent and Mollie bought a four-bedroom Tudor house with a sunken living room, not in

Westchester but rather in Long Island. They were leaving Hartsdale and moving to Plandome Manor, close to Lauraine Murphy's. Vincent would work with Jim, his shipmate from those desperate days in Newfoundland of toiling on a boat in the rough North Atlantic. Patricia's youngest brother would be a partner in a restaurant business, not just a manager.

One can only imagine Patricia's reaction when she realized that Vincent and Mollie had deceived her for seven years, and that everyone else in her family must have known about it.

But there was nothing she could do about it. She couldn't print a damaging legend on her menu or add an insinuating line to an advertisement. She could only rely more heavily on John Rogers, who despite being Mollie's brother and Vincent's brother-in-law, wasn't likely to bolt to Long Island. Like Vincent, John had many children to provide for. Patricia was going to make it clear he would be rewarded for loyalty. If all went well with expansion, she might even give him some shares in the business.

Everyone got along with "Stish," the family nickname that still stuck to amiable Vincent. Patricia couldn't count on anyone but Rosie to side with her. Nana and Sheila, tired of the disputes, only wanted peace. Patricia felt increasingly drawn to Rosie's family. She was talking to fragrance experts in Switzerland about developing floral-scented perfumes to sell at the restaurant. They would start with orchid names, but she was also thinking of naming one fragrance "Regina Rose," after her niece by marriage. John Kiernan, Regina's father, annoyed her with his lectures about extravagant spending, but a scold was better than a snake in the grass. In naming her fragrances, she'd avoid the stink of her own siblings.

Patricia soon had other matters to preoccupy her. Opponents of the zoning change petitions began preparing for a hearing on June 11, when the Common Council was scheduled to vote on them. The *Herald Statesman* followed the issue closely, repeatedly describing the location of the proposed multi-million-dollar developments as "two properties west of Central Park Avenue near Patricia Murphy's Candlelight Restaurant and Roosevelt High School." Her name was linked to a project that was far from universally popular.

She did not attend the hearing, where Arthur J. Doran, attorney for the two developers, deployed weapons honed during his years as the chief city planner. Neighboring property owners had been enlisted to speak in favor of the development. One landowner spoke of failed attempts to build garden apartments in the residential-only zone because "Central Park Avenue was irretrievably a business street," where banks wouldn't finance the construction of apartment buildings. Other speakers pointed to the tax revenue bound to result from the proposal. C. Van Ness Wood, the shopping center builder, appealed to the aspirations of the Yonkers crowd, aware of their inferiority to Bronxville and Scarsdale. Space in the proposed office park would be rented to "prominent businesses," Wood said, and the shops would be "of the better class."

These arguments did not deter strenuous objections from other neighbors, who said the development was "spot zoning," antithetical to the principles of city planning, and "would start a cancer growing." As for the secondary project, Doran announced that his clients were negotiating with Patricia Murphy to manage the proposed motel. He expected Patricia's name to lend cache, but his listeners heard only "motel." Incensed homeowners protested that a motel had no place near a high school.[5]

An architectural drawing of three split-level buildings, labeled "Candlelight Hotel" was produced. Patricia's brand was plastered over a hot-sheet motel, as opponents saw it.

The vote was tabled for two weeks later. In the meantime, the *Herald Statesman* printed the architectural rendering with a caption pointing out the Candlelight designation. The implication was that discussions with Patricia had gone far past the negotiating phase.

The local PTA and the citywide council of PTAs had representatives at that meeting. A half-dozen other parent groups had been phoning the mayor's office, outraged at the idea of locating a motel near susceptible children. However, the public-hearing period was over, and a vote to extend it and let the parents speak was narrowly defeated. Mayor Kristensen joined the council majority in approving rezoning by a vote of eight to five. A front-page story announcing the vote was headlined, "First Step Set for Project Near Patricia Murphy's."[6]

Her own first step would need to wait a while. The zone changes would allow her to build her restaurant wing and gift shop and expand the parking lot. But she wanted nothing more to do with a hotel or motel. Those PTA members were her customer base.

Eager to escape the PTA's torches and pitchforks, Patricia took Rosie on a trip to their beloved London. There, they became central figures in a drama involving a prince, a television star, and female escorts. They went a long way from Yonkers and enjoyed every moment of it.

Their adventure began when their traveling companion, Helen B. Rich, decided to combine a little work with pleasure. Rich was a publicist and freelance journalist who ordinarily covered the socialite-and-celebrity beat in Palm Beach, but she also knew London. As her trip there with Patricia and Rosie drew to an end, she decided to interview Helene Cordet, an old friend of Prince Philip. Famous in England for hosting a top British TV show, *Café Continental*, Cordet had left television to run a popular restaurant in Piccadilly.

Rich returned to Patricia and Rosie with a hot investment tip: Cordet and her partner were set to open a new place at a posh address, but another buyer had outbid them at the last minute. It was now Friday, and their final offer was due on Monday. With the London banks closed for the weekend, they were desperate to find financial backing.

Checkbook in hand, Patricia and Rosie went to meet Cordet at the Society Restaurant on Jermyn Street, or "Chez Helene Cordet," as it was now called in ads featuring a candelabra logo eerily like the Candlelight's. Like Patricia at the start of her career, Cordet had taken over a twice-failed, boarded-up restaurant and turned it into a raging success, managing rather than owning it. But now she and her business partner, Peter Davies, were anxious to ditch it and start a place of their own. There were indications that their club was being used as a cover for illegal activity.

The Society Restaurant was connected, quite literally, to the neighboring Club Pigalle, a Vegas-style playground where patrons entertained by nearly nude showgirls might catch glimpses of Gary Cooper or Audrey Hepburn. Both clubs were owned by Al Burnett, a genial showman and entertainer who may have met Cordet on the set of Café Continental. Unbeknownst to most of their customers, a passageway connected the two, accessible from a concealed door in the Society Restaurant.

In his book about the British mafia, Douglas Thompson wrote that an elevator in the passageway allowed discreet exits onto Berkeley Square, with the Mayfair Hotel at one corner. "Some guests would have bedroom entertainment sent into the Pigalle, and if they were acceptable the next stop was a suite at the Mayfair," he said. Presumably, the Society Restaurant and its secret door also played a part in the activities described by Thompson, who also suggested that the club owner, Burnett, had financial dealings with a British mobster.[7]

It's unlikely that Cordet spoke of this in her meeting with Patricia and Rosie. In her autobiography, she cryptically mentioned "sabotage" and "fantastic scheming" at the club, which somehow led to a friend's suicide, convincing her that "I had to get out now!" She, in turn, convinced the visiting Americans to help her take over a supper club on Park Lane floundering under its current management by a French cultural institution.

"We had to lay our hands on several thousand pounds before Monday morning," Patricia wrote, adding that Rosie's ties to a top Barclays Bank official made it possible. Helene, too, was astonished that it happened over a weekend. "A miracle happened," she wrote, naming Patricia and Rosie as her benefactors and noting, with an excited exclamation point, that "Pat had started their prosperous business with $60!"[8]

Patricia did not return the favor. Proud of her interest in the supper club at No. 6 Hamilton Place, a stately mansion paneled in dark wood, Patricia described it to an American reporter as "veddy fahncy, my deah." She made no mention of Cordet, whose fame, talent, and connections had invigorated the Society Restaurant and made Patricia's investment an almost sure bet.[9] Born in France of Greek ancestry, Cordet had been friends since childhood with Prince Philip, a member of the Greek royal family. A cabaret singer and former Parisian model, the twice-divorced Cordet had often struggled financially to raise her two children. Philip was the godfather of her son. Gossip-mongers suggested a biological relationship, which she denied, although at times she seemed to capitalize on the rumors.

Tyrone Power, David Niven, and Stewart Granger patronized the Society Restaurant while Cordet ran it. At the Society, she'd sung almost nightly, encouraging audience participation. She wrote of her success in selecting men to join her act—and of the need to avoid female hostility as she did so. A flirt herself, Patricia might have sensed that Cordet was trying to pull Rosie into the act, as it were. That could explain Patricia's reluctance to mention her new female business partner.

She need not have worried. Rosie was devoted to her. They followed up their trip to London with a fall excursion to Honolulu.

In New York, they generally stayed at the Pierre, the hotel Patricia admired so when she first bought the Sixtieth Street restaurant. But one week after the Hawaii trip, they spent a night in Yonkers, possibly for reasons related to the Westchester expansion. They sometimes stayed at 1750 Central Park Avenue, close to the Candlelight. Tired of hotel living, they wanted to find a place for themselves in Manhattan near Central Park—not one on Central Park Avenue in Yonkers. Near the Yonkers house was one acre of land still restricted to residential use. Patricia needed the land to expand her parking lot, but for that she would have to petition the city.

Whether its cause was purely organic or related to these worries, a heart attack killed Captain James E. Kiernan at the Yonkers house on October 6, 1957. It happened at four o'clock on a Sunday morning; perhaps he and Patricia had slept there to give her a jump on the work week. News of his death ran in papers across the nation. Obituaries mentioned his graduate degree in naval architecture from MIT, his service during two world wars, and his supervisory work on the USS *Iowa*, *Missouri*, and other battleships. A paper in Hawaii, from where he and Patricia had just returned, said he was known to many navy people there.[10] It was a remarkable life for a man dead at age fifty-eight.

The *Herald Statesman* identified the Captain as the husband of Patricia Murphy, owner and operator of the Candlelight Restaurant. For the first time in years, the newspaper did not juxtapose her name with the word "zoning."

The funeral was held on Wednesday at St. Patrick's Cathedral, and the Captain was buried the next day with full military honors at Arlington National Cemetery.

Later that year, the *Daily Mail* of London reported that Helene Cordet's "chic new night spot in Grosvenor Place" had recruited five Buckingham Palace footmen to serve drinks at a New Year's party promising to be "the most exclusive affair in Town." Two columns of chatter, including an astonished comment from the palace and a mention of Prince Philip, completed this publicity coup. Patricia seemed to have made a solid investment.[11]

She didn't care—about that or anything else. "The lights went out," she wrote. Nine years earlier she had married her mate for life, and now one of their lives was over.

Yet even grief could not repress her generosity, energy, and attention to detail. Five weeks after Rosie's death, she was back at Kinsale, responding to a sympathy card from the American Woman's Association. On a green-edged notecard, she wrote in green:[12]

May I thank you all from the bottom of my sad and lonely heart for your great kindness to me since my beloved captain left me so suddenly—He was so proud of my being made "Woman of the Month" and I thank you again in his name.

I enclose a check for the scholarship, even though your leaflet did not say what it was for, but if you . . . are connected with it, it must be worthwhile. I'll be back in New York at the Pierre Hotel about December fifth for a month and please call on me if I can be of any help to you at the AWA.

Would you please telephone Mrs. Maynard at SP 9-5700 and tell her that you will pick up 1,000 of last year's tulip bulbs for the school, as I forgot before I left.

Patricia Murphy Kiernan

CHAPTER 12

Grieve. Drink. Expand.

Always remember to smile.

—Patricia Murphy's manual for employees, 1930

People annoyed Patricia by offering comfort, or by pressing her hand and recommending courage—a gesture she dismissed as "stupidity." A woman who had built her fortune in hospitality now wanted to push everyone away. The only people she could stand were Nana, Sheila, and a few friends, including one who phoned her daily without ever making the dreadful mistake of mentioning her loss.

Patricia wrote that her grief was nearly intolerable for "many, many months" until she turned to her usual tasks of ensuring perpetual gaiety at the Candlelight and pursuing her other interests, "but I was moving around like an automaton," she wrote.[1] If so, it was an automaton in high gear. After her stay at the Pierre, she escaped to New England at Christmas, probably to visit Kay Vincent and Howard Barnes at their Connecticut home. In late January, she hosted a meeting at Kinsale. The purpose was to plan a fundraiser for a hospital in Florida's Martin County.[2] Patricia had a new mission: supporting causes related to the heart disease that had killed Rosie. Dressed in black throughout most of 1958, she filled the year with a whirl of projects.

Perhaps suspecting that Rosie had not received all possible life-saving interventions in his final hours, Patricia donated mobile oxygen equipment to the Yonkers police. The proceeds came from coins tossed by her Westchester customers into the restaurant's wishing well; Patricia had quickly seized on the coin-tossing craze inspired by the 1954 film *Three Coins in the Fountain*.[3] In the past, she had divided the proceeds among three charities. Now all $10,000 in small change, collected over two years, would go to the new Kiernan Memorial Heart Fund. In February, Yonkers' public health commissioner came to the Candlelight to accept the first piece of oxygen equipment from John Rogers. Patricia was away in Europe.[4]

Her brief stay at Kinsale had sufficed to finalize plans for the tropical garden she would assemble in March at the New York Coliseum. It was to be her most ambitious entry yet, an entire tropical garden—one thousand square feet of exotic shrubs and flowers and a tree stripped of leaves, with orchids replacing them. To compensate for possible damage during the delicate process of transporting and setting up the show, more plants than needed for the show had to be brought into perfect bloom.

A week before the exhibition at the Coliseum, Patricia was back from Europe. However, she headed to Florida rather than New York. Two hundred people had bought tickets to spend the day at Kinsale.

This was the benefit for construction of the hospital, masterminded by Patricia in her meeting with a Stuart garden club shortly after Rosie's death. The *News Tribune* of Fort Pierce, Florida, wrote glowingly of her palatial house and the tables set on terraced gardens, where club officers poured beverages. While her gardeners crafted a jungle in New York, Patricia was treating Florida to a British tea time. Eight teenage girls in organdy aprons and bonnets assisted at the tea, while a woman dressed as a geisha served Asian food on a patio. In yet another section of this World's Fair in miniature, a table displayed objects collected by Patricia on her international travels.

A few days later, her garden was the hit of the Coliseum. The staging was completely novel. A tall hedge of camellias surrounded the exhibit so that it couldn't be seen from the aisles. People waited to enter, then were rewarded by the experience of strolling through the garden rather than simply viewing it. As at the Candlelight, hundreds of the curious willingly queued up, and Patricia took home the Horticultural Society of New York gold medal. She was in the major leagues: other gold medalists at the show were the Brooklyn Botanic Garden and the Jane Parker Division of the A&P supermarket company.[5] The awards were announced in *The New York Times* among other places.

After the show, the exhibit was reassembled at the Westchester Candlelight. Showcasing five thousand orchids, with more on stand-by in case of damage or wilting, the exhibit had cost $25,000 but was reaping revenue. Much of the credit belonged to Carlson, the chief gardener, who continued the work of constantly refreshing the display with fresh blooms. Although his name was not on the prize certificate, he felt proud of his work with Patricia, said his daughter, Diane Carlson Phillips. When he spoke of his boss, "there was no negativity," Phillips said.[6]

The gold medal had garnered invaluable publicity, and the exhibit itself became a destination—another reason for diners and tour buses to make a journey to Yonkers. The parking situation was becoming critical.

A week after the Coliseum flower show, the *Herald Statesman*'s front page announced that there would be no Candlelight hotel or motel after all. Instead, Patricia's Westchester corporation had leased five acres of the land from the would-be motel developer, Willow Cove, to expand her restaurant, erect a gift shop, and add parking.

By now, plans for the Jewel Box Gift Shop were well underway. Nathalie Rahv, divorced from the husband who had long overshadowed her, was now based in Boston. Whether for that reason or others, Patricia took her visions of a Regency-style crystal palace to another architecture firm, Ives, Turano, and Gardner. On its face, the choice seemed bizarrely inappropriate: her new architects would soon be associated with their jet-age design of the Pan-Am terminal at Idlewild Airport, often compared to a flying saucer. Patricia wanted something Jane Austen would have recognized. But just as Patricia had melded her own love of the past with Nathalie's modernism, she got what she wanted from these futurists.

The gift shop would be like "a large glass lantern," one of the architects told the *Herald Statesman* in May of 1958, when plans were being drawn. Designed along the lines of the Kinsale greenhouse, it would be octagonal, topped with a pointed spire and framed in aluminum painted white. Technology unavailable in the Regency period would illuminate it at night in seasonally changing colors. The Yonkers paper got an estimated cost, $60,000, from the architects, and quotes from John Rogers, who remembered to say that the gift shop would carry Patricia's new line of perfumes, soon to be launched.

Rogers also mentioned to the Yonkers paper that "the Candlelight restaurant in Manhasset has had a gift shop for some time." The Westchester menus still stated that the only restaurant Patricia personally owned and operated was the one in Yonkers. Rogers's unfortunate lapse, re-associating the restaurants in the public mind, could have reignited

Tavlin and Zimmerman's ire and renewed their request for an injunction. Although that didn't occur, the error suggests that Rogers—on whom Patricia was increasingly depending—lacked her savvy, or else was too busy with day-to-day management to deal skillfully with the media. Also, unlike Patricia, he did not constantly have publicists at his elbow, including publicists who were former or current journalists, like Kay Vincent and Helen B. Rich.

Either on her own, or at the suggestion of one of these publicists, Patricia took steps to heighten her social profile in New York, having focused mostly on Florida during her married life. In its obituary of Rosie, a Fort Pierce newspaper called Kinsale a "showplace" and "the scene of the most lavish benefit garden parties and other social activities given by the winter colony." New York society was a harder nut to crack. This time, Patricia would not forsake her Irish Catholic roots or Newfoundland origins by claiming ties to Betsy Ross, as she'd done in the thirties. Instead, she lent her money and talents to a civic-minded women's group called the Outdoor Cleanliness Association.

Although led by well-heeled women such as Zorah Gristede, daughter-in-law of the founder of New York's Gristede supermarket chain, the organization was not averse to dirty hands. The Outdoor Cleanliness Association worked closely with the New York City Department of Sanitation to correct health and sanitation violations and increase public awareness about litter, air pollution, and other urban problems that had spurred flight to the suburbs. Never mind that Patricia herself had fought, though unsuccessfully, for an environmentally threatening incinerator. She would lend her name and talents to the group's outdoor Flower Mart, a fundraiser held early each June on the steps of St. Patrick's Cathedral.

The mart was about to rise to a new level of professionalism as Patricia assumed her new role as honorary chairman. She arrived at dawn on a gloomy June day with her Westchester gardening staff. Donations had arrived from prestigious Manhattan florists, wealthy individuals, and such unlikely sources as Sing-Sing prison, where the warden was an avid horticulturist. Still, Patricia's task was formidable; the naive association hadn't purchased extra blooms to replace those that arrived bedraggled. Artistically disguising drooping flora, and braving rain showers, Patricia brought it off. The *Times* reported brisk sales in a piece that mentioned Patricia.

The article noted that Mayor Wagner had dropped by. In Florida, Patricia served watermelon spiked with booze at sybaritic pool parties, inviting the kind of guests who occasionally trashed the cabana. In the New York of the 1950s, where people voted Democratic and expected government to solve social problems, the dead-serious Outdoor Cleanliness Association was her ideal social vehicle.

It was far removed from the excesses of Kinsale. The association's records suggest prudent management, even a tendency toward nickel-and-diming. A few months after the 1958 flower mart, Patricia's chief horticulturist sent a letter in green ink—the Candlelight's typewriters used green ribbons—responding to a query from the group's officers. He said he'd been unable to locate the association's baskets, reported missing since the event, but he had located a piece of flannel they were worried about.[7] Net profits from the annual flower sale were typically below $2,000.

That was small change to Patricia, who soon exchanged New York's rainy days for the sunny skies of Spain. Her summer tour of Europe included a stop to Denia, Spain, a small town on the Mediterranean where *John Paul Jones* was being filmed. Cast as the naval hero was Robert Stack, a Hollywood leading man and former athlete, who was nearly every heterosexual woman's type. Despite the savings of filming in Spain, costs had soared to four million dollars, double the initial projections. Bronson, the producer, promised the film would be the epic of all epics. Patricia's investment was small, but she welcomed the chance to visit the set, where near-perfect replicas of Jones's *Bonhomme Richard* and the British *Serapis* bobbed in the harbor. In a scene shot at the Royal Palace in Madrid, Bette Davis made a brief appearance as Catherine the Great.

The European tour also gave Patricia a chance to stock the shelves of her soon-to-be-constructed gift shop. Embarking on her retail venture in earnest, she hired a buyer to look for items in Italy and Germany. Spain under Franco wasn't doing much business with foreigners—the filming was approved because the dictator thought it would present his country in a flattering light—but this was only one point on her itinerary. She gathered ideas at Expo 58, an international fair held in Brussels, before ordering French antiques. Also on her shopping list were china and furniture from Ireland and electric candelabra made in England.

She dropped in on Helene Cordet at the elegant Piccadilly club that she and Rosie had financed over a weekend. The posh spot, paneled in oak and swathed in drapes, was thriving. International celebrities, such as the American television sensation Milton Berle, carried membership cards showing a small crown over the club's full name: Helene Cordet's Cercle de la Maison de France. But people just called it Helene Cordet's. It was a place where Rita Hayworth might run into Cary Grant, or Kirk Douglas could be seated near Ingrid Bergman or Robert Mitchum.[8] Its elegant Louis Quinze party room was in demand for debutante parties.

Cordet had hoped to escape singing, as well as the Mafia, by breaking away from the Society Restaurant and its concealed door. Popular demand, however, had required her to perform here as well. Extremely thin, with a tiny waist, she entertained in gowns and was considered a London fashion icon. An American columnist had described the smoky-voiced Cordet as looking like a cross between singer Dinah Shore and dancer Vera-Ellen.

Weary of doing cabaret acts and prone to catching colds in her scanty attire, Cordet had not found exactly what she wanted in the new club. She was pleased with the catering operation, which didn't require her to stand at a microphone, but yearning to spend more time at home with her kids, relaxing in sweaters and slacks. There was also a unique problem in operating a London club in that era. Cordet wrote that many customers signed for enormous dinner tabs but failed to pay, with British law offering no legal remedy.[9]

It is highly improbable that Cordet expressed these quibbles to Patricia during her visit to London, supplemented by a journey to Ireland. There, Patricia placed orders for gift shop merchandise and conferred on plans for Treaty Stone. When she returned to New York, she proudly talked about her share in a London club. But while often mentioning her horse's name, she never once uttered Cordet's.

As for Cordet's secret preference for casual clothes over formal wear, Patricia would not have concurred. Social attitudes were changing in America, with the rising popularity of rock and roll and more open discussions of sex on film. Patricia said that Rosie's conservatism contrasted with her own personality, but she was referring to financial matters, over which he preferred to deliberate, while she was a self-described "born gambler." But regarding social propriety, she too was solidly conservative. Women in pants were barred from her restaurant.

Such attitudes invited the subtle ridicule of William I. Bookman, a *Herald Statesman* reporter who interviewed Patricia in late September

1958 about the Yonkers restaurant's expansion. With construction on the new wing and gift shop set to begin, Bookman seated himself on seal skin in the Candlelight's bar and began a devastating profile that began,

> Patricia Murphy, stylish but somber in a black dress and wearing a busy charm bracelet, walked with quick little steps into the cocktail lounge of her big restaurant on Central Park Avenue.

It was a little past noon, and the reporter noted with evident disdain that the luncheon guests were not only "mostly feminine," but "ripe in years." He said Patricia interrupted a "dreamy description" of the restaurant expansion when a woman in Bermuda shorts approached the door. She was turned away by "one of the Murphy arbiters of good taste," the reporter wrote, as are women in "slacks and 'Spanish pants' and any other garb indecorous by Murphian standards.'"

The less than reverent tone continued. As in previous interviews, Patricia claimed to be confused by amounts higher than one hundred dollars. Yet, as always, she had figures at her fingertips. The Westchester had served one million customers in the previous year. The new wing would increase seating to 1,200 from 1,052. Land for parking cost between $45,000 and $75,000 per acre.

None of this seemed to impress the reporter. Over the course of the interview, the restaurant filled, and the public-address system began to announce vacancies. Sampling the Candlelight's stuffed lobster, Bookman seemed more fascinated by Patricia's eccentricities than her success or his meal. He noted that she darted from one conversational topic to another, showing off Treaty Stone's medals, then boasting about her high perfume sales. Her description of "mystery tours," that brought out-of-towners to the Candlelight earned the reporter's mockery. She described the tourists' delight at seeing the restaurant and "paused to let the image sink in," he wrote derisively.

In the most startling moment of the interview, Patricia turned defensive about the heavy traffic that the Candlelight had generated on Central Avenue. "I kept out that motel that was going in behind us," she said. "Whoever started that lie that I was going to run the motel?"[10]

The *Herald Statesman*, of course, had reported on her negotiations with the proposed hotel or motel, which she hadn't denied in print. When first reporting the proposal, the Yonkers paper had not asked her for a comment. If their assertions were, in fact, inaccurate, she could have written a letter to the editor but did not. Nor, evidently, had she demanded and been refused a retraction, because here she was, granting the paper an interview over a lobster lunch. She was also leasing parking lot space from Willow Cove, one of the developers that had presented the Yonkers paper with an architectural drawing of a structure labeled "Candlelight Hotel."

Why had this interview spun out of control? For one thing, Patricia's preoccupation with traditional gender roles may have discouraged her from displaying her steel-trap business side, particularly now that her husband was gone. In addition to telling the *Herald Statesman* reporter that Rosie had built the Westchester Candlelight and set up the perfume business—none of which was true—she may have played up her femininity by acting ditzy.

"I loved Patricia, as crazy as she was," said Carleton Varney, the prominent interior decorator, who designed for Ethel Merman, Joan Crawford, and Judy Garland and helped Patricia prepare for charity functions. Varney compared her to Gracie Allen, the American comedian famous for playing a dizzy dame convinced of her own illogic.

Patricia's drinking could have been another factor. "She tippled," said Varney. "It was like a lady in the afternoon with sherry . . . it went with her personality." When drinking, he added, "she always got coquettish, and she was very coquettish. She liked men."[11] Perhaps none of this went over well with the reporter, apparently younger than the "ripe in years" women he described. He may have found Patricia rather ripe herself, aged fifty-three at the time.

In printing Patricia's stream-of-conscious ramblings—normally trimmed before print, or simply left in a reporter's notebook—the journalist rebelled against her dress code and her insistence on doing things properly. Once a visionary about suburban growth, she was falling out of step. Soon after this Yonkers interview, Patricia was given a national soapbox for her views. In an Associated Press piece headlined, "How Casual Can You Get?" Patricia—described by the AP women's editor as a "small but highly charged crusader," railed against the proliferation of barbecues. They were all right "on occasion," she conceded, but even hamburgers should be attractively plated and served by candlelight.[12]

Times were slowly beginning to change, and the interviewer's attitudes may have been a bellwether. *A Summer Place*, a movie that challenged conventional morality and examined the generation gap, was a hit at the box office.

But so was *Auntie Mame*, the Rosalind Russell film about a rich eccentric—with her own "busy" bracelet—who outwitted opponents foolish enough to underestimate her. In October, the year of mourning Rosie was over, not that she would ever forget her husband. "She was always talking about the Captain," Varney recalled, but she was ready to take some bold new steps.

Someone in Florida had told her about a tremendous new business opportunity. Ironically, it was in Fort Lauderdale, a cradle of the youth revolution, where propriety was thrown to the wind during hedonistic spring breaks. Patricia, however, would not be competing with beer joints that the college kids favored, like the Student Prince and the Elbo Room.

Spring break happened but once a year, and its participants came from afar. Typical diners in Fort Lauderdale would be eager for a jackets-required restaurant in lush surroundings, serving mainstream American fare and popovers.

Patricia knew this for a fact because popover girls and relish trays had preceded her to Fort Lauderdale. So had her name, albeit only in someone else's advertising. Michael Tavlin, accountant-turned-restaurateur, ran the popular Reef restaurant in that city. His Florida ads advised, "When up north, visit our other restaurants, Chimney Corner Inn, Stamford, CT, Patricia Murphy's Candlelight, Manhasset, Long Island, NY."[13]

Wouldn't it be sweet revenge all over again to open in Tavlin's market? But, first, Patricia had to craft a winning bid for the prime restaurant spot that was up for grabs. It would make sense to have two restaurants again. As she had discovered with her first two, in Brooklyn and Manhattan, economies of scale would reduce food prices, and she also expected to save on plants and personnel.

Of course, her first two restaurants had been in the same city. Now the two points on her chain would be New York and Florida. This enterprise would only work if she owned an airplane.

CHAPTER 13

Where the Yachts Are

Endeavor to please your guests in every way.

—Patricia Murphy's manual for employees, 1930

"Fast, pretty, roomy." That's how a headline in *Flying* magazine described the Cessna 310, the plane that Patricia bought in 1959.[1] John Bates, one of her pilots, said, "It was a very cool plane to fly," if perhaps not as well designed aerodynamically as later models. That was not the kind of thing that mattered to Patricia. It was a plane made famous by the television series "Sky King," in which a flying cowboy used the same model to capture bad guys or rescue children.[2]

In Patricia's case, the roominess was handy for transporting plants, rather than criminals, while she sat up front with Alexander E. "Al" Cabana, the first pilot to fly *Miss Tango*, as she'd christened the plane. For passengers, she'd had a white-leather couch installed in the rear. A proposal to affix orchid vases to the walls was nixed by Cabana, another of Patricia's ideal males—before taking the controls of *Miss Tango*, he had flown fighter jets in the Korean War.

Cabana, in turn, had tremendous respect for Patricia. "She was a great artist. Her restaurants were really fabulous. She was an artistic soul and a fabulous person," he said. However, he added, she never flew the plane, or even took flying lessons, to his knowledge.[3]

She was gaining altitude in New York social circles, however, continuing to serve as honorary chairwoman of the Flower Mart while still hosting garden party benefits and annual St. Patrick's blowouts at Kinsale. Up north, in the uppermost reaches of the Upper East Side, she had a lavish new venue for personal entertaining. Her new penthouse

147

at 1136 Fifth Avenue near Ninety-Fifth Street was a public garden in miniature, where dogwoods, dahlias, and begonias bloomed on three terraces. A small waterfall murmured over an artificial pool. At night, a chandelier fashioned of Venetian-glass grapes shone over dining and lounging areas separated by tubs of massive red flowers.

To maintain this thirteenth-floor conservatory, Patricia used what *Popular Gardening* dubbed a unique gardening tool, not accessible to others: her plane. Transported from Kinsale, a spectacular orange tree bloomed in a corner of tropical foliage overlooking the reservoir in Central Park.

If all went as planned, *Miss Tango* would become more than a flying trowel. Patricia was preparing to bid on the lease to a Fort Lauderdale restaurant situated on a yacht basin called Bahia Mar. It was in a prime location on the Intracoastal Waterway. The City of Fort Lauderdale, which owned the entire marina, would award the restaurant lease, and its youthful mayor was the man Patricia needed to impress.

Two years earlier, John V. Russell had been elected to the highest municipal office in Fort Lauderdale, at age thirty-one one of the nation's youngest big-city mayors. Russell, whose short hair was styled in a so-called Peter Gunn cut—named for a TV detective and popular in the Ivy League—had been in politics since his late twenties and had been elected city commissioner two years before becoming mayor. His knowledge of New York restaurants was limited, however.

In early August of 1959, Patricia's offer to pay $300,000 for the restaurant lease over ten years was splashed over the front page of the *Fort Lauderdale News*. Russell promised his constituents that he and one of the city commissioners would take a close look at Patricia's New York operation. Russell said,

> They asked us to come up and inspect their operation at their expense, and since this lease is a matter of great importance to the city, I think we should make sure of what we're getting into.[4]

It was no inconvenience to Patricia, who flew the two officials—one of whom was her attorney—up to the Candlelight in *Miss Tango*. She, her plane, and her pilot were becoming regulars at Westchester's Rye Lake airport. Nor was it a hardship for Fort Lauderdale's leaders to dine at the Candlelight, where on Patricia's less-crucial visits, "even the busboys had to look neat," recalled Nader James Sayegh, son of one of Patricia's executive chefs and a former busser himself.[5] One can only imagine the level of perfection demanded on this occasion.

Russell and James L. Leavitt—the city's engineer and deputy attorney, as well as a commissioner—returned "favorably impressed," as the mayor put it, or one might almost say floored. "It is the most unusual restaurant I've ever seen, with a definite woman's touch," Russell told the *Fort Lauderdale News*, praising the flowers. ("No plastic plants," reported a *News* entertainment columnist, who phoned the mayor for further details.) Russell rated the food and service highly, adding, "Every woman coming to the place gets either a corsage or perfume."

Or at least they did on the day of his visit. Normally, opening prices for the corsages were listed on menus, and there was a charge for perfume even when sold in single-dab vials. As it turned out, another city commissioner had visited the Candlelight on his own and was ready to give it the thumbs-up.

Hence, there was not much suspense as Patricia waited for results of the commission's September 1 vote, particularly because she was the only bidder. A brief flurry of interest had arisen from another airplane owner. This was the immensely popular television host Arthur Godfrey, who sent a local representative to evaluate the restaurant lease. Deciding he would only be interested in leasing the entire marina—an impossibility, due to legal complications—the star backed out, endorsing Patricia's bid as he went. His Fort Lauderdale representative told the *News* it would please Arthur Godfrey, known to millions of Americans, to have Patricia Murphy as a tenant.[6]

The vote passed, and the contractors moved in. After submitting her bid, Patricia had flown down to take a close look at what she called a restaurant in dire need of redesign and reconstruction. Her restaurant described the place once known as the Bahia Mar Yacht Club as "drabby," a coinage suggesting drab and shabby.[7] Nonetheless, she had agreed to pay the city $30,000 in each year of the ten-year lease, which came with an option to renew for another ten years, plus 5 percent of profits for each year of gross revenues exceeding $600,000.

What's more, she had committed to spending $50,000 on remodeling the place in return for the city's promise to pay for exterior repairs. After her walk-through, she knew the real costs would far exceed her estimate.

None of that mattered. Patricia had staked quite a claim on Florida's Gold Coast. The *Miami Herald* described Bahia Mar as "the plushest pleasure boat marina in the world," visited by 1,500 yachts annually. Cabin cruisers, charter-fishing vessels, and houseboats shared three miles of docks and more than four hundred slips with sleek sixty-foot yachts, some piloted by hired skippers and crews. A half-dozen sightseeing boats brought in tourists. Beachgoers could reach it by foot; the Atlantic was a short walk across narrow Route A1A.

The proximity of the public beach was a boon to boaters, as were Bahia Mar's marine repair yard and marine-supply center. Near a swimming pool was a strip of stores selling groceries, apparel, souvenirs, and sundries. The *News* described these outlets as "smart little shops," but Patricia knew she could do better. She would put a gift shop next to the restaurant and continue her father's tradition of providing sailors with everything from needles to anchors—or, in her case, cuff links, shawls, and Patricia Murphy–branded perfume.

Patricia was the beneficiary of Fort Lauderdale's troubled history of leasing public land for private gain. Bahia Mar had begun as a U.S. Coast Guard base, purchased by the city with municipal bonds. The marina was leased to a private operator in exchange for handshake promises, never honored, to pay $120,000 in annual rent and develop the site with new buildings. The city took a wink-wink attitude toward the situation until bondholders sued. The last of a chain reaction of cases reached the U.S. Supreme Court, which declined to review it. Meanwhile, the owner of the marina lease declared bankruptcy, but the sublet restaurant was not affected. Trios played music at its bar, people came to dance, and its revenues covered the administrative costs of the bankruptcy trustee.[8]

As a progressive, anti-segregation Democrat, Russell may have viewed Patricia as a potential Fort Lauderdale savior. Two years earlier, as a young councilman, he had cast a vote opposing the sale of a municipal golf course, long restricted to whites only, to private buyers who wanted to maintain that policy. The vote passed three to two. Fort Lauderdale sold the golf course for far less than its appraised value rather than comply with a federal judge's order to let black people use it.[9]

Patricia was hardly a civil rights activist, or even an equal-opportunity employer. Decades earlier, in Brooklyn, she had advertised for colored dishwashers willing to work for far less than her white waitresses and hostesses. Her continued employment of Filipinos as servers and cooks may have arisen from warmth and loyalty, but it also served her interests. Shortly after the Westchester Candlelight opened, immigration officials came to arrest a Filipino waiter who had overstayed his student visa. At the time, employers risked no penalties for hiring undocumented aliens, who tended to feel beholden to their bosses.[10]

Moreover, Patricia and Rosie had not hesitated to build their dream house, Kinsale, in the Jim Crow South. Patricia was amused when her Filipino groundskeeper, Victor de Leon, claimed to be a Native American. After the server's arrest in Yonkers, De Leon may have hesitated to reveal his immigrant origins, or he could have felt unsure about the legal status of Asians in segregated Florida.[11]

Nonetheless, Patricia had created a dining atmosphere in which African Americans felt comfortable. The New York Amsterdam News and the New York Age, African American newspapers, often reported on wedding and anniversary parties, as well as NAACP events, hosted at the Westchester Candlelight. Joyce Phillips Austin, an African American assistant to Mayor Wagner, chaired a professional women's dinner there. In 1959, as Patricia bid on the Bahia Mar restaurant, an Amsterdam News gossip columnist dished about lunching at Patricia Murphy's with the wife of Harold A. Stevens, the first black judge to sit on New York State's Court of Appeals.[12]

Patricia may have turned away women wearing shorts, but her "Murphian" standards were not based on race. That, added to the restaurant's obvious success, could have enchanted the mayor even more than the perfumes and corsages. At any rate, Russell tended to favor development, which he saw as a movement toward modernity, away from the South's racist past.

Most of Fort Lauderdale soon joined the Candlelight fan club, waiting excitedly for the results of the Bahia Mar restaurant's extensive facelift. An entertainment columnist for the News wrote that Al Sparks, a local performer, had returned "starry-eyed" from a visit to Patricia, "the gal-wonder of the restaurant world," at her Fifth Avenue penthouse, which was "like a Hollywood set."[13]

The projected November opening date was pushed ahead as the work progressed. There would be three dining rooms, one partially visible behind screens to the rear of an atrium with a fountain at its center and one wall almost entirely planted with flowers—an interior vertical garden. Patricia worked with noted interior decorator Edmund Motyka on this design. Architecture for the two-story renovation was by Leavitt and Henshell. The industrial designer and tastemaker Russel Wright, famous for his dinnerware, had chosen David Leavitt to design his own Hudson Valley home, Dragon Rock. Like Wright, Patricia sought Leavitt's modernist interpretation of Japanese-inspired nature themes. In her new restaurant, plants, water, and screens co-existed with enormous glass windows and sparkling electric lights.

A Bahia Mar lawn was torn up and replaced with formal and tropical gardens. City workers were provided, at no cost to Patricia, to assist with the landscaping. To promote the restaurant opening, Patricia assembled an orchid collection worth $30,000 from the Westchester greenhouse range and sent it to a Fort Lauderdale flower show in *Miss Tango*. Frost destroyed it all in transit. A second batch was sent and won a blue ribbon. To remind Floridians of the tulip honors she'd taken in Holland, Patricia sent the *News* a picture of herself planting bulbs in the Westchester gardens alongside that country's Tulip Queen.

Some Fort Lauderdale residents remained uncharmed. Among them was Vice Mayor Edward H. Johns, who had favored selling the lease to the marina, not just the restaurant. Following approval of Patricia's bid, the city commission had authorized $35,000 for added parking and landscaping. Johns objected, asserting that Patricia should have been asked to bid on the additional space.[14]

As unusually bad weather delayed parking lot construction, a parking crisis was anticipated at Bahia Mar. Even when the expansion was completed there would be a total of five hundred spaces for a restaurant planning to seat six hundred. After the mayor proposed introducing paid-parking concessions, Johns led the council in voting to require monthly financial statements of the Bahia Mar operation.

The skeptical vice mayor may have been one of the restaurant's first guests. City officials were invited to a quiet opening day on December 18, not publicly announced. It was a rehearsal for the staff as it prepared for the anxious hordes. Nana, now eighty-four, would have been invited had she not been in the hospital with a broken hip. A *News* reporter treated to a sneak preview on the previous day predicted that the "utterly breath-taking beauty" of the restaurant and gardens "should cause eyes to pop out of sockets."

Pop, they did. The Westchester Candlelight was expected to gross $4 million in 1959, and Patricia clearly had another hit on her hands with Bahia Mar, although on a smaller scale: even with its seating expanded, the Fort Lauderdale Candlelight was half the size of its northern counterpart. With the help of *Miss Tango*, Patricia put seasoned Yonkers hands in charge of her new eatery. Greg Camillucci had climbed far up the ranks since his student-job days. Discharged from the Air Force and about to be married, he had been given a lavish engagement party at Sky High and a new job as manager in Fort Lauderdale.

Skippers of ships operating out of the marina watched nervously as the changes were made to the restaurant's framework sign facing the Waterway, beckoning to sailors in need of food, razors, and recreation. For nearly a decade, the phrase "Bahia Mar Yacht Center" had loomed over the image of a giant anchor, with smaller letters announcing a restaurant and lounge. Now "Yacht Center," had shrunk to make way for "Patricia Murphy's Candlelight Restaurant," in a giant facsimile of Patricia's feminine signature. Boaters wondered if the basin's maritime services would shrink as well.

Elsewhere, another captain turned against Patricia. *John Paul Jones* had opened in mid-1959 to disappointing reviews. Director John Farrow, once a playboy but now a religious family man, had sanitized Jones's swashbuckling life to the point of boredom. Even Bette Davis's portrayal of Catherine the Great couldn't salvage this wreck. The four-million-dollar extravaganza grossed about one million, placing it near the bottom of a 1959 box-office list topped by *Auntie Mame*.[15] Small shareholders had lost two-thirds of their investment and, once other claims were paid, could expect nothing.[16] None of that mattered to Patricia the Great, who ruled her own empire.

Leaving Yonkers to capable John Rogers, who had proven more trustworthy than her blood relatives, Patricia had more time to relax at Kinsale. Occasional visits to Fort Lauderdale required only a short hop between that city's airport and Witham Field in Martin County, managed by Harold Strauss, who had sold *Miss Tango* to Patricia under a financing arrangement. On the cusp of the jet age, traffic at Witham was booming. Howard Hughes and Kennedy family members were frequent visitors, choosing the Stuart airport over larger ones to avoid media attention.

In November of 1960, John F. Kennedy became the first Catholic to be elected president, aided by two of Patricia's mayoral acquaintances. Wagner had stumped at his side in New York. Russell formed a friendship with JFK while leading the Democratic presidential campaign in Florida's

Broward County. Russell, however, was now an ex-mayor. In a surprising New Year's announcement, he had resigned from Fort Lauderdale's top job, saying he wished to spend more time with his family. Succeeding him was Edward Johns, slower to succumb to Patricia's pixie dust.

As the Bahia Mar Candlelight celebrated its first year in business—and its $1 million in revenues—even cynics took note. Interviewed in her garden, where five thousand poinsettias bloomed, Patricia reported that business had been brisk even in the summer, a notoriously slow time for South Florida restaurants. At Thanksgiving, when cars were parked by valets dressed in the Candlelight's notion of Native American attire, two thousand customers were served. Announcing expansion plans, she lamented having had to disappoint customers for lack of space. "We're here to serve them, not turn them away," she said.[17]

Allied with her in the push for expansion was Sam Shelsky, director of the marina. He told the News that the restaurant's popularity had business booming for all marina merchants. Shelsky's account of Patricia's investment showed it at a new high: $300,000 as of March 1960, with expansion plans for the following year likely to run another quarter-million. Acknowledging that $30,000 in public funds had already gone toward parking spaces and other accommodations for the Candlelight, Shelsky judged the cost reasonable "when you consider the new life that has been added to the center." He urged the city to spend again for yet more parking.

His gratitude toward Patricia was not universally shared. Regarding parking, "They gave her the whole darn lot," complained Howard Haines, owner of the Bahia Mar Groceteria. "I realize she has put a lot of money in that place, but she only pays $30,000 a year rent for all that space while I pay $9,000 a year for practically nothing," the grocer continued.[18] Boaters were also unhappy. Responding to a survey distributed by the city manager, some faulted the Candlelight for increased traffic as well as the parking crunch.

Traffic around the Westchester Candlelight was also becoming intolerable. There had long been talk of widening part of Central Park Avenue to make it part of an arterial-highway system that would ease congestion. Merchants and city officials were in favor; the problem was to find funding. New York Governor Nelson Rockefeller had recently approved the plan, moving it forward, but plenty of red tape lay ahead. Properties would be seized by the city and condemned, but the exact location of the reconstruction was still undergoing study.[19]

Unperturbed by this potential threat after years of talk and no action, Patricia enjoyed her triumphs. She didn't need to manage her restaurants any more than she needed to work their gardens with a hoe. The enlarged Westchester Candlelight was booming, with a Mercedes-Benz lounge car whisking customers from parking lot to entrance. In London, Vice President-Elect Lyndon B. Johnson had topped off talks with Harold Macmillan by spending a night dancing the cha-cha with Helene Cordet at her Patricia-financed club.[20] The Miss Patricia Murphy dahlia, named for her by hybridist Albert Parrella of the Bronx, had been featured in a full-page photo in *Life* magazine.

When not renting sumptuous homes in Ireland, or entertaining at Sky High and Kinsale, Patricia was buying her way into Palm Beach society. Regarding herself as a philanthropist as well as a businesswoman, she made large gifts to the Graham-Eckes school, a private school that enrolled male and female boarders. Founded by Inez Graham and her half-sister, Evelyn Eckes, the school aspired to become the Palm Beach equivalent of Andover or Laurelton Hall.

Described by one student as "regal," "imposing," and "impeccably dressed," Graham shared many similarities with Patricia. Raised in a small town with harsh winters—in Minnesota, in Graham's case—both had forged careers without the help of men.[21] In 1960, Patricia was elected to the board. Other members included Count Jean Pierre de la Valdene, a World War I flying ace descended from French nobility.

Although a stroke had sidelined Graham, Patricia planned further financial support of the school. Graham had brought opera star Lily Pons and conductor Leopold Stokowski to visit music classes. She also required students to study ballroom dancing and etiquette. Such things mattered to Patricia, no matter how younger people, such as the *Herald Statesman* reporter, might consider them cultural throwbacks.

Like Patricia, Graham was known for the jangling charm bracelet she wore when touring the school. "I think it's quite nice of me to announce my arrival with a jingle," the educator said. This could explain Patricia's bracelet as well. The two demanding women were belling the cat.

Patricia was about to remove her bell for a while to write her life story.

CHAPTER 14

Storm Over the Marina

Keep your clothes brushed and pressed.

—Patricia Murphy's manual for employees, 1930

The question Patricia had been waiting for was asked, and her answer appeared in a syndicated column carried by newspapers all over the country:

A New York career woman recently challenged Patricia Murphy. "We've both worked hard. But you've become rich, and I've stayed poor. What's the difference in us?" "I'm daring," Patricia Murphy answered promptly. "I've built my career on taking a gamble, and I believe opportunities are all over for anyone, if you see them, take a gamble and work hard."[1]

Patricia's promotion of her new book, *Glow of Candlelight*, was off to a good start, thanks in part to her latest gamble. That column by a Kings Feature syndicate writer was illustrated with a small line drawing of Patricia in the cockpit of a plane monogrammed "PM." Publicity materials describing Patricia as a "restauratrice, horticulturist, and aviatrix," had probably inspired it. There were also publicity photos showing Patricia at the controls of *Miss Tango*.

Patricia was making a safe bet that no one would find out she left the flying to Al Cabana. After all, "she had a plane, so it wasn't a lie, it was an extension of the truth," said Camillucci, who had flown for the Air Force before becoming manager of the Bahia Mar Candlelight. Perhaps Patricia was inspired by Jacqueline Cochran, who had been a guest speaker at her Fort Lauderdale restaurant. A native of Florida, Cochran was not only a record-setting female aviator, but also the operator of a cosmetics company.

Flying caught people's attention in a way that simply owning a plane didn't. Moreover, the book was filled with loving memories of Rosie and written, she said, to help her cope with the grief of losing him. Her fictitious descriptions of flying solo—"soaring high over the Florida coast or winging into Westchester"—were a better fit for the grieving-widow image than the reality of Patricia, single for the past four years, sharing those experiences while seated next to Al Cabana. "She especially liked to fly up to New York and watch the moonlight," her admiring aviator recalled.[2]

One paper that did not seem to swallow the fib, or where Patricia owned up to it, was the *Daily News* of St. John's, Newfoundland, the city that Patricia had left in 1928 "to conquer New York as few men have done," as the paper put it. A month before Patricia's book came out, the *Daily News* ran an extensive profile of her, including three photos from her press package. The Newfoundland paper ran a picture of Patricia standing next to *Miss Tango* while omitting another that showed her at the controls, and the story accurately reported that Cabana was the person who flew the plane. In her homeland, where nuns had educated her, Patricia may have felt uncomfortable lying.

The largest photo in the piece showed Patricia cuddling a small, short-haired dog, Little Miss Patricia, described in the caption as "her constant companion." Also included was the photo of the Jon Whitcomb illustration used on the book cover. Carleton Varney, then a young decorator who had helped design Patricia's Manhattan penthouse, thought the portrait captured Patricia's essence. "It was demure, and she was very demure," Varney said.[3]

Invited to the capital city of Newfoundland in October of 1961, Patricia was living out a real-life fantasy. The remote, stormy island where she had grown up had invited her to partake in a ceremony of state. Now a province of Canada, Newfoundland was about to celebrate the opening of Memorial University, and Premier J.R. Smallwood had invited her to the ceremonies. He introduced her as one of nineteen native Newfoundlanders who had gone out in the world to become "distinguished people." The others—all male—included a bishop, several presidents of banks and colleges, and an Antarctic explorer.

In his "My New York column," reprinted in scores of American papers, Mel Heimer announced that "Patricia Murphy has been given a four-star spangled salute" by being invited to the event, where "there will be more bigwigs and top educational brass than you can count, including Eleanor Roosevelt—the only other invited female guest."[4]

That wasn't exactly true. Some presidents of Catholic women's colleges had also been invited. Wives and other companions of men were also present. They looked on as Mrs. Roosevelt received a gift of Newfoundland, a mink stole. Patricia, who had a closet full of fur, probably approved.

She was a close match that night for her book cover. Dressed in an evening gown with a sheer shrug covering spaghetti straps, she waited for her name to be called. In lieu of allowing the distinguished Newfoundlanders from abroad to speak, the Newfoundland premier introduced them himself. Proud of his cheap haircuts, Joseph R. "Joey" Smallwood had been in Newfoundland politics since Patricia's departure and was the force behind its 1949 federation with Canada. He left his sole woman honoree until last, introducing her as "one of the world's great orchid growers" and the owner of "the great and famous Candlelight restaurants." He also briefly mentioned her father.[5]

Patricia shrugged off the shrug to bow, bare shouldered, before the assembled guests and Canadian Prime Minister John Diefenbaker. It was a great honor for her, and one her traitorous siblings were bound to hear about from friends in Newfoundland if they hadn't already seen it in the syndicated column.

In the role of a triumphant daughter, Patricia flew to Fort Lauderdale laden with gifts for her mother. As usual, she had overdone it, causing all kinds of inconvenience to baggage handlers as she changed planes several times. She had two enormous cartons filled with things one could only buy in Newfoundland, including codfish tongues, native partridges, and berries known as bake-apples. She knew Nana would love them.[6]

Lauraine, Maude, Jim, and Vincent would, of course, hear about the Newfoundland visit and the gifts. They were acutely aware that Patricia's book had been published, and that it had cut them out of the picture. The book was dedicated to their mother, as well as Rosie, and included full-page images of both the Captain and Nana. The chapter about Patricia's Newfoundland girlhood mentioned no siblings. Later pages referred only to Sheila, the "baby sister." The manuscript had included a sentence about setting up "one of my brothers" in the import-export business, but the published book omitted it.

The book jacket described *Glow of Candlelight* as "three books in one" because the recipe section is about the same length—one hundred pages—as the section titled "My Life," and there's a shorter gardening section. Patricia wrote that her friend and agent, Wilma Freeman, "envisioned" the book. The sectional scheme was effective for publicity, garnering mentions for Patricia in the food and gardening columns of scores of newspapers. Recipes for dishes served at Kinsale and Sky High—more adventurous than the Candlelight fare—were reprinted in the food columns of scores of newspapers. The horticulture editor of the *Trib* wrote a full-page feature about Patricia's New York penthouse gardens. *Popular Gardening* ran a three-page cover story on Patricia, written by John R. Rebhan, mentioned in *Glow*'s acknowledgments as one of her collaborators. Similarities between his magazine article and the book suggest he wrote the gardening chapters.

As for the autobiographical section—the "female Horatio Alger story," as Patricia described it—it was more likely to win a women's-page mention than a book review, except at book club meetings around the country, where it was a favorite topic for volunteer presenters. *Kirkus Review*, consulted by bookstores for advice on what to stock, savaged *Glow of Candlelight*. Not known for delicacy, *Kirkus* faulted Patricia for referring to property she'd owned during her marriage as "mine" instead of "ours." Her style "quickly palls," wrote the reviewer, because, in her "nouveau riche ingenuousness," "she prefaces everything with a quantity—5,000 chrysanthemums, 5,000 patrons." Financial literacy was vulgar, apparently, as was out-earning one's husband.[7]

Not that it mattered. Patricia was in far less need of reviews than most authors. A bookseller herself, she followed up the Macy's autographing session with others in Westchester and Fort Lauderdale, where her book was promoted on menus and had a permanent place on the gift store shelves. Her shops had already moved many copies of a self-published pamphlet of recipes, *Patricia Murphy Entertains*. At any rate, the women's pages gave glowing reviews to *Glow*. "Patricia Murphy believes in women," wrote the author of a column called "Beauty After Forty," which ran in many small-town papers.

It was a good year. The Bahia Mar Candlelight earned a recommendation from Duncan Hines in his influential book, *Adventures in Fine*

Dining, and the restaurant was featured in a book about restaurant design put out by the publishers of *Interiors* magazine. Patricia's elaborate orchid and begonia exhibits had won top honors at the International Flower Show, in time for her to include color photos of the flowers in her book.

In London, it was also a good year for Helene Cordet. She published her own life story, *Born Bewildered*, spiced with photos of her childhood friend Prince Philip, who had given Cordet's memoir his official blessing. The restaurant in the mansion at No. 6 Hamilton Place had closed, though it still housed Cordet's catering company. The former TV star and her partner, Davies, had moved their party into the mansion's former stables at No. 7. Finally rid of the slinky gowns she had grown to hate, Cordet had ditched live music and hired DJs. Modeled after the discotheques of Paris, the Saddle Club was an instant hit.

Cordet was twisting the night away with debs and rockers, dressed in slacks. Serving only bar food, the late-night spot raked in cash from drinks and membership fees. "Queen Helene of the Nightclubs," as the *Daily Mail* crowned her, was making a fortune by seizing new ideas and abandoning propriety.[8]

It is unclear whether Patricia had a vote on the sale of the plush London club, or whether she profited significantly from it. What's clear is that Cordet and Davies had made enough to buy 51 percent of the Saddle Room, while Tyne Tees TV, a major British television company, owned the rest of the shares. Although facile with numbers, Patricia was increasingly delegating responsibilities to John Rogers, identified in her book as general manager of the restaurants, without allusion to familial relationship through Vincent.

Varney recalled Patricia's anxiety regarding a machine installed by Rogers that spewed out checks pre-printed with her signature. The decorator remembered Rogers, whom he had thought to be Patricia's nephew, as nondescript—medium height, with glasses on a pale, rounded face, "sort of a nebbish."[9] Varney interpreted Patricia's nervousness as fear of technology. In the past, however, she'd embraced it, installing restaurant air conditioning in the 1930s and announcing table availability through public-address systems in the early 1950s. Instead, she may have been anxious about ceding control to Rogers.

Still fearless about gambling, Patricia prepared for her next step in Fort Lauderdale. The city-run marina in Bahia Mar was turning a profit, but problems lay ahead. Boaters accustomed to griping about the marina's telephone service now had a modern system. Consequently, phone installation costs had eaten into the yacht basin's earnings, and monthly bills had soared. Yachts gleamed in the sunlight, but corroded pipes and wood lay below the surface. Added to this were the heavy costs of debt service. Appraising the sales value of its celebrated yacht basin at $2.5 million, some Fort Lauderdale officials began wondering if they could unload it through sale or lease.

Patricia was well positioned to hear these rumblings. When John V. Russell suddenly resigned as Fort Lauderdale's mayor, he was expected to eventually occupy one of the Congressional seats added to Florida after the 1960 census. That didn't happen. For a time, he was city attorney of Opa-Locka in Dade County. In his private practice, he had represented Patricia on some legal matters. Now he was back in Fort Lauderdale's city hall, this time as city attorney.

When Patricia approached the city commission in March of 1962 with a proposal to lease not just the restaurant but the entire mainland of the yacht basin, she found receptive ears. "Many people, city commissioners included, feel it is Miss Murphy who turned Bahia Mar into the nationwide success it is today," reported the *News*, adding that her $800,000 improvements on the restaurant had far exceeded her lease obligations.[10]

Leasing the marina also involved obligations, though other than rent amounts, these were rather loose. The city expected $150,000 a year or 7.5 percent of gross revenues, whichever was greater, plus major improvements. Announcing her plans in late August of 1962, Patricia promised to transform Bahia Mar into a "Florida showplace." The Candlelight gardens would be extended, forming a park-like setting for a two-level shopping mall, a convention hall, two garden apartment buildings, and a pedestrian bridge to the beach over A1A. No longer averse to motels, Patricia proposed to build one—a steel-and-glass tower with two hundred rooms, three landscaped pools, and parking. Her contractor projected costs of four to five million dollars.[11]

This was going to be as big a production as the *John Paul Jones* movie.

In truth, she was not legally required to do all of this. In late August, following the city's approval of the bid, Patricia signed a fifty-year-lease to the Bahia Mar yacht basin, agreeing that

> . . . the leased premises shall be used as a first-class restaurant, cocktail lounge, liquor package store, yacht club, motel, hotel,

convention hall, retail stores, marine stores, marine service station, charter boat and sightseeing boat facility, apartments and other kindred and similar businesses. It is not the intention of the parties that the lessee shall be unreasonably restricted in the use of the leased premises other than the lessee is required to conduct a legitimate business or businesses . . .

The city had the right to review improvements made in the first three years. After that, the choice of businesses, as well as the timeline for construction, were left up to the Fort Lauderdale Candlelight Corp., for which Patricia signed as president and Camillucci as secretary.[12]

On September 1, a TV news camera whirred as Mayor Edmund Barry pressed symbolic keys to the marina into Patricia's white-gloved hand. "These are the keys to a gold mine," said Barry, who had opposed the lease. Also on hand were city commissioners, including Ed Johns, Patricia's vanquished former opponent. It was the day that the lease would take effect, "barring legal upsets," the *Miami Herald* added.

Legal upsets arose almost immediately. Patricia had a new nemesis: Robert Hayes Gore, Sr., a multi-millionaire developer, former governor of Puerto Rico and owner of the *Fort Lauderdale News and Sun-Sentinel*, as the *News* was now named. Described by a grandson as "a cigar chewer, a desk pounder, and a giver of orders,"[13] Gore saw himself as the guardian of Bahia Mar. His financial guarantees had backed the bonds that enabled Fort Lauderdale to buy the yacht basin from the Coast Guard. It was Gore who brought the suit that, after years of legal battles, canceled the city's lease with its initial derelict tenant.

As the ink dried on Patricia's lease, Gore used the front page of his newspaper to launch an attack on her and the city officials who had supported her bid. Headlined "Why the Bahia Lease Is Bad," the editorial began on the very top of Page One, above the name of the newspaper. His authorship is made evident by an accompanying news piece by staff writer Ray Wieland, in which Gore is extensively quoted, repeating the editorial's arguments.

It was an extraordinary move for Gore, a former beat reporter for small-town Midwestern newspapers. Up to this point, Patricia's business dealings had been covered fairly—one might say generously—by *News* reporters, and columnists had treated her with something like idolatry. Patricia, to be sure, was a *News* advertiser, regularly paying for columns titled "Comments by Henry Kinney for Patricia Murphy's

Candlelight Restaurant," that mixed snippets of local gossip with plugs for her business.

The Gore assault "wasn't personal," said his grandson, Paul A. Gore. "Anyone who wanted to take over Fort Lauderdale from up north, Granddad editorialized against."[14]

Calling the deal a "giveaway," Gore said nothing against Patricia's business expertise and did not mention her gender. Lists were his trademark, and here he enumerated thirteen points in the lease that, indeed, disadvantaged the city. The lease could be sold at any time with only nominal city review, he said, and the rent couldn't be adjusted for inflation. He noted that Patricia wouldn't likely be alive in 2012, when the lease ended and late payments were due, but—probably much to her relief—he didn't specify her age.

John V. Russell fared worse. Wieland's piece suggested that the city attorney had betrayed the public trust with a lease that favored his private legal client. Russell had announced his professional connection with Patricia in a formal statement made in April. He said he would step aside from the lease, leaving assistant city attorney Ronald V. Sladon to advise the commission and prepare it. The *News* didn't buy it, printing alongside Gore's castigation:

> Sladon was Russell's choice for assistant district attorney. Sladon has his desk in Russell's office in city hall, has additional space in Russell's law offices, and takes orders from Russell on all city matters except, presumably, this lease.[15]

With letters to the editors also suggesting a conflict of interest, Russell found the issue impossible to ignore. "Toleration of lies, innuendoes and deceit about one's professional conduct from ill-informed people is stupidity," he said as he asked the city commission to vote on their confidence in him and his legal staff. Urging them to "vote on integrity, not leases," he scored a 3–0 win. Mayor Burry abstained.

Gore took the city to court. Representing taxpayers, he argued that the marina—currently tax-exempt as a public facility—should pay real estate taxes if used for private enterprise. Taxation was not a point Gore had stressed in his editorial, but now he demanded it, skeptical that the Candlelight could keep up its rent payments. He also argued that the lease was invalid because bidding had violated the city charter.

Sixteen months of litigation ensued. Circuit Court Judge George Tedder, Jr. ruled that the lease was valid. However, he also ordered Patricia's company to pay taxes on the property for the 1963 tax year and the remainder of the fifty-year lease. Estimates of the tax bill were $30,000 a year, or $1.5 million for the lease term.

With the deadline for appealing the ruling passed, Patricia issued a statement indicating that she was pleased that litigation had ended. "Now we can proceed," she said.

Part of her mind was elsewhere. Gore, himself a native of Kentucky who was well into adulthood when he first came to Florida, considered Patricia a carpetbagger from New York. Lately, her thoughts had been traveling back there. Jim, Vincent, Maude, and Lauraine had bought a restaurant dating from Colonial times in Jericho, Long Island. It occupied ten acres of land, almost as much as the Westchester Candlelight, and Patricia had heard they planned to put up shops and bakeries. This could be the Eastern version of Knott's Berry Farm that Jim had always dreamed of.

There was a chance to outshine them. A chain of fine-dining restaurants called the White Turkey had recently gone bankrupt. They had some excellent locations in Manhattan, where Patricia sensed enormous possibilities.

One of Gore's dire predictions came true. Six months after the lease went into effect, Patricia sold control of it to Maryland Community Developers, Inc., or MCD, an investment group headed by her favorite kind of guy, a pilot. They probably saw one another often at Fort Lauderdale's Executive Airport, where James W. Campbell had his own twin-engined plane, as well as a private hangar.

A retired banker, he was also an aviation sportsman, hunting big game from the air. When not aloft, he lived right across the water from Patricia in the exclusive Harbor Beach section of Fort Lauderdale, where she stayed on business trips or while visiting Nana.[16]

The deal left Campbell and his Maryland-based partners with a controlling interest, but Patricia would continue to operate the Candlelight for them. They agreed she would handle food and beverage operations for their hotel, which they intended to build quickly.

Bahia Mar had changed hands. To the public, it barely mattered. Regardless of the corporate name on the lease, an iconic part of Fort Lauderdale was no longer theirs.

Satisfied with the terms, and leaving development headaches behind her, Patricia went on her own airborne safari. She was hunting White Turkeys in Manhattan.

CHAPTER 15

Manhattan Transfer

The more expensive banquets call for more detail in setting up.

—Patricia Murphy's manual for employees, 1930

The opportunity to buy restaurants in Manhattan came at an opportune time. Patricia now had more troops to inspect in New York, where she sometimes had to stay put. Her wings were clipped in 1964. Al Cabana was no longer her private pilot, and *Miss Tango* no longer belonged to her exclusively. Harold Strauss, the airport manager who had sold the plane to Patricia, no longer allowed Cabana to land at Witham Field near Kinsale. Cabana, who had formed his own business, sued, but in the end he stopped flying Patricia.

Miss Tango, bought on an installment plan, remained available to Patricia, who had faithfully marked her plane's "birthdays" by bringing cupcakes and champagne splits into its hangar for imaginary sharing. It was now part of Strauss's St. Lucie Skyways charter fleet. Patricia's Cessna, with its white-leather couch in the rear was now shared with other customers. Stripped down for fleet use—its autopilot system subscription had lapsed, and it lacked de-icing—the plane was no longer feasible for flights to New York. Now obliged to pay charter rates, Patricia used the plane mainly for short hops within Florida.

There were many of these, as Patricia kept an eye on the Fort Lauderdale restaurant, at least ceremonially, while organizing Stuart and Palm Beach charity events. Amid all this activity, she lost track of an $18,000 pair of diamond earrings. After a burglar scaled a Kinsale balcony and broke into an upper floor, Patricia reported the minor theft of a few pieces of jewelry, including a charm for her bracelet. Only weeks later did she notice the absence of the earrings, last worn at a Palm Beach ball she'd decorated with strands of faux gold coins covering windows and plumes on the chandeliers. As explained to the police, Patricia flew to Fort Lauderdale the day after the nocturnal theft. She hadn't planned to pack the earrings: diamonds were for charity events, charms were for business.

Left untouched was Patricia's closetful of furs. In that same year, she donated a mink stole and a Russian white fox for prizes at a fundraiser held at Kinsale. Patricia's cast-off furs helped raise money to beautify the city of Stuart.[1]

Despite Gore's characterization of her as a carpetbagger, Patricia was a proud ambassador for Florida, nearly stripping the state of native plants for her 1964 International Flower Show entry. Her so-called "jungle" garden included a thirty-four-foot live oak tree, chain-sawed in Florida for reassembly in New York, as well as Spanish moss, numerous palm trees, and an eighteen-foot illuminated waterfall.

Many wondered how the flower show could survive the demise of the great estates, with their armies of gardeners. Patricia's entry, of almost P.T. Barnum proportions, may have given them heart. So many Florida gardening centers took part in loading the display on a northbound tractor-trailer that the scene "took on the character of a nurseryman's convention," wrote the *News-Tribune* of Fort Pierce.

It was all part of her promotional budget. "Patricia Murphy used it as an advertising piece," said Diane Carlson Phillips, whose father maintained the exhibits once they moved to Yonkers.

A quarter-century earlier, Patricia's request to operate a concession at the 1939 World's Fair went ignored. Now she finally got her due. The Florida World's Fair Commission wanted her to operate its gift shop at the Florida State Commission, near its porpoise show and citrus tower.[2] With the country buzzing with anticipation, the Coliseum show was themed "the World's Fair of Flowers."

Patricia's jungle exhibit triumphed there, snagging the American Orchid Society trophy. Soon after, the World's Fair opened in Flushing Meadows, Queens. Three hundred protesters calling attention to civil right issues were arrested, including some staging a lie-in at the exhibit promoting Florida, where shortly after leasing her Fort Lauderdale restaurant, Patricia had advertised for "a white gardener to work and supervise one or two colored men."[3]

A few weeks after the opening, Jacqueline Kennedy and her daughter, Caroline, made a surprise visit to the fair, visiting the Florida pavilion, where they watched the porpoise show. Jackie left holding a copy of a Florida-cuisine cookbook purchased in one of the pavilion's gift areas.

Patricia brought Florida to New York and her magic back to Manhattan. In long white kid gloves and a beaded brocade gown, she turned opening night at the glittering new Patricia Murphy's on Forty-Ninth Street into a *Hello Dolly* moment. It was September 29, 1964. No one would have guessed that hours earlier she had been at Kinsale, mopping up the mess from a hurricane. As a magazine reporter wrote of the opening, Patricia Murphy "operates on vitamins and nervous energy."[4]

She would need plenty of both to compete in the hotly competitive restaurant scene of Manhattan in the 1960s. Cranes groaned overhead, erecting office buildings, apartment complexes, and hotels while a Godzilla-sized culinary corporation prepared to court their occupants. Fourteen years earlier, when Patricia sold her city restaurants, Restaurant Associates was a workaday chain of lunch counters, cafeterias, and airport concessions. Now it was a publicly owned behemoth grossing fifteen million dollars annually[5] and opening and acquiring eateries to suit every taste and budget. While still operating snack bars and hot dog stands at stadiums and air terminals, Restaurant Associates' innovative president, Joe Baum, had taken it into the glamour business. His innovative Manhattan creations, including La Fonda Del Sol, at the base of the Time-Life Building and the Forum of the Twelve Caesars in Rockefeller Center—a stone's throw from Patricia's place on Forty-Ninth Street—had bedazzled the public and the press.

Even as Patricia donned opera-length gloves for her restaurant opening, *The New Yorker* was preparing a thirty-page profile of Restaurant Associates, with ample space devoted to its premiere accomplishment, the Four Seasons restaurant. Dick Kelly, who had lit the dining rooms and interiors of Patricia's Yonkers and Manhasset restaurants, subsequently illuminated not only the Four Seasons, but also the landmark that housed it, the iconic Seagram Building. *The New Yorker* article would quote Restaurant Associates founder Abraham F. Wechsler, speaking of the Four Seasons: "Who ever thought before of spending fifty thousand dollars a year on plants and flowers, as they do here?"[6] The answer, of course, was Patricia, now overseeing the plantings at her own Manhattan eatery, which would change with the seasons, as they always had in Westchester.

Despite those similarities, the upscale Four Seasons, where even the least expensive dinners topped ten dollars, was not competing with the Radio City Candlelight, where $2.95 could buy a complete dinner. However, Restaurant Associates also owned Leone's—known to all as Mamma Leone's—a 1,200-seat tourist draw just four blocks from the Forty-Ninth Street Candlelight and a rival for the same theater-going and special-occasion market. A red-sauce Italian restaurant known for its five-course, five-dollar Famous Dinner and an array of statuary inviting comparisons to Forest Lawn, Leone's was louder and brasher than Patricia Murphy's elegant place nearby, and perhaps less likely to be frequented by locals. However, both angled aggressively for the out-of-town customer.

It was a market worth courting. Leone's and its unlikely sibling, the Four Seasons, were the major moneymakers of Restaurant Associates. Each grossed about four million dollars a year, but Leone's was far more profitable.[7] Founded in 1906 and well established on the tourist map by the time RA bought it, more than a half-century later, it was a must-see for visitors to the city. Its predictable menu choices reduced waste and made it easy to run.[8] Hoping that happy diners would spread the word, Mamma Leone's provided free postcards with its menus, as the Candlelight had always done.

Patricia was undaunted by her tourist-trap neighbor. For one thing, her food was better. Craig Claiborne, the notoriously discriminating food critic of The New York Times, awarded her Forty-Ninth Street restaurant two stars, noting that although they "may look a trifle prim and proper to some guests, the quality of the food is excellent and it is cooked with care and some sophistication."[9] He graced Leone's with only one star, writing that "the sheer abundance is most impressive on an initial visit. Thereafter it may begin to pall."[10]

The Murray Hill Candlelight had its own Italian-themed Restaurant Associates rival. Just blocks away from the new Pan Am building, which hulked over Grand Central Terminal, Patricia's temple of Quiet Good Taste on Madison Avenue faced off against Trattoria, one of three RA restaurants serviced by a single kitchen in the fifty-nine-floor skyscraper. Another was Zum Zum, part of Baum's popular new fast-food chain, where customers ate at counters, choosing from a vast array of sausages and beer. The third was the noisy, pub-styled Charlie Brown's Ale and Chophouse, with a seemingly mile-long bar for whiling away the inevitable wait for tables.

Of these, the beautifully decorated Trattoria posed the most direct threat to the Candlelight. No red-sauce groaning board like Leone's, Trattoria aspired to replicate the casual yet elegant counter-and-table dining spots of Florence and Rome in the 1960s.

In this it failed, however, according to Claiborne. "If only it were possible to eat the scenery and ignore the kitchen," said the *Times* critic of Trattoria, admiring the posters and the mosaic-faced rotunda but savaging the "hopelessly mediocre" food and dismissing its mozzarella in carrozza as a "poor and overcooked joke."[11]

Patricia felt confident of thriving in this culinary thicket. The purchase of two bankrupt White Turkey eateries simply reintroduced the Murphy magic to a city she had never really left. Her name remained on the slightly sagging awning of the restaurant on Sixtieth Street, still recommended in magazine pieces aimed at budget-minded tourists, along with other visitor favorites such as the Oyster Bar at Grand Central Terminal and Angelo's on Little Italy's Mulberry Street.[12] Her old Brooklyn Heights place was officially called the Candlelight, but in borough vernacular it remained Patricia Murphy's. Unlike Michael Tavlin, the buyers of these restaurants were unperturbed by the disclaimer she continued to print on her menus in Westchester, as well as Bahia Mar. As she had told the court, it was nothing but the truth: she personally owned and operated only the restaurants in Yonkers and Fort Lauderdale.

A line on a menu didn't stop Sam Mandelkern, owner of the Brooklyn Candlelight, from delighting in Patricia's visits to his establishment. The feeling was mutual. "My mother sensed there was something between them. There was an attraction, big time," said his son, Peter Kern. (The family eventually shortened its surname.) Handsome and muscular, Mandelkern was not Patricia's usual military man or pilot. However, he knew how to run a restaurant. Taking over from a first, disappointing buyer, he met Patricia's standards in more ways than one. They had even talked about opening another restaurant together, much to his wife's displeasure.

Andy Kern, another of Sam's sons, recalled his mother saying with irritation, "So! Open it with her!" Andy recalled Patricia as a "statuesque, beautiful woman"—statuesque at least to Andy, who was then nine or ten. "There weren't that many famous business women in that day and age," he added.[13]

Fame, however, was increasingly linked to television. Other than the paid radio lunchtime programs broadcast from the Westchester Candlelight, Patricia lacked broadcast exposure. A rare moment arrived when Sam Mandelkern was invited to "The Joe Franklin Show," a popular talk show carried on a local New York station. More typical guests were stars like Barbra Streisand and Liza Minelli, alternating with tap-dancing dentists and other small-time phenomena. However, Franklin sometimes sought opportunities to promote his sponsor, Canada Dry, whose soft drinks were served at the Brooklyn Candlelight. The guest spot allowed Mandelkern to plug both ginger ale and Patricia Murphy's.[14]

The camaraderie of Patricia and her city successors was in stark contrast to the lawsuit brought by Meyer Zimmerman and Michael Tavlin. While still an accountant, Tavlin had done the books not only for Patricia, but also for Harry and Dorothy Davega, owners of the bankrupt White Turkey restaurants that Patricia wanted to take over. Through Tavlin, she was familiar with their operations. Like Patricia, Dorothy Davega had a knack for table settings and interior decoration. Dorothy and her husband kept an eye on service by hiring the professional snoops of the Willmark Service to pose as diners while checking the wait staff for efficiency and clean fingernails. Willmark's spies did not wear jangling bracelets to warn of their approach. Nevertheless, the White Turkey's fortunes fell.[15]

Tavlin, the accountant for both restaurant chains, might have done some cross-pollination in 1955, when the Davegas purchased the tired Red Barn restaurant in Westport, Connecticut, and rejuvenated it with impressive flower beds planted by a Swiss-born gardener. Patricia had taught the suburban-restaurant garden trick to Tavlin. He could have suggested it to his other accounting clients.

The Davegas had not brought botanicals to their failed urban restaurants in midtown Manhattan. Patricia, however, made the flooring bloom at her site near Radio City, where throngs lined up daily for movies and concerts. Her six-hundred-square-foot jungle at the New York Coliseum had been a dress rehearsal for Forty-Ninth Street. It was as if a slice of Central Park had moved over to take root behind two stories of storefront glass. Inside, the White Turkey's bentwood chairs and hunting murals made way for trees, shrubs, and flowering plants. A velvet-lined elevator carried guests to the upper floor, all crystal chandeliers and tall candelabras—the kind of posh décor Helene Cordet had escaped in London to operate her stripped-down disco, where record promoters were now debuting their new releases.

The East Forty-Ninth Street restaurant was "a ladies' rendezvous," wrote a male columnist for a New Jersey newspaper, while hastening to add, "although no man would feel out of place."

The columnist felt more at home in Patricia's second new location in Murray Hill. Sprawled over half a blockfront, the new Candlelight at 260 Madison Avenue had an elegant bar "designed with the businessman in mind," the columnist wrote, with small tables perfect for martini-fueled conferences. However, flowers and candlesticks reigned here, too, in an oval dining room with stage-width red curtains and lighted panels, and along the sides of a broad staircase sweeping down to a banquet room.[16]

Close to department stores and airline offices as well as Grand Central, the Murray Hill restaurant was an almost-perfect neighbor for the J.P. Morgan library and museum across the street. A Chippendale-style cornice topped the door, bent aluminum railings suggested bay windows, and a tall planter draped in hanging plants ran its length. Only the emerald-green façade and a bas-relief sign with the Murphy name asserted the founder's Irish roots.

Patricia was flaunting her brand like never before. On Forty-Ninth Street, enormous three-dimensional electric-blue letters spelled out her name in cursive. She may have lacked Radio City Music Hall's gigantic Wurlitzer organ, as well as its ballet company and orchestra, but her glowing signature rivaled its marquee.

New Candlelight menu covers included color photos of all four of her restaurants. The slogan remained, "Enjoy luxury dining at budget prices." Dinner prices ranged from $2.95 for chopped sirloin to $5.75 for filet mignon. The entire inside cover was devoted to the Westchester restaurant, with a detailed calendar of monthly celebrations.

There was also a photo of Patricia, looking dazed and unwell in the Bahia Mar gardens, and a message: "To answer many inquiries from our friends, we can say there *is* a Patricia Murphy," followed by a synopsis of her rags-to-riches story. Once Patricia had argued that her customers, who likely knew her, shouldn't expect to see her in Manhasset. Now she felt the need to announce she was not, like Betty Crocker, a fictional character. She may have been right. America was entering an era in which fame required TV appearances, and she had had only a mention on the Joe Franklin show, and even that by proxy.

She continued printing the message that had so upset Tavlin, but now it took on an almost fantastical quality. "Miss Murphy personally owns and daily supervises the New York, Westchester, and Florida Candlelight Restaurants, between which she commutes by plane," said the legend. The word "daily," with its suggestion of super-powers, might have raised eyebrows for the rare diner who stopped to read the notice rather than focus on dessert choices.

In truth, her managers ran the business, said Greg Camillucci, who came up from Fort Lauderdale to take charge of the city restaurants. For business reasons, the Candlelight was split into many corporations; the Murray Hill site, for example, was owned by the Madison Avenue Candlelight Corp. However, the managers viewed the organization as a single entity. "I used to go back to Fort Lauderdale, and I once sent a guy from Forty-Ninth Street to manage Fort Lauderdale," said Camillucci.

Despite her pop-up visits to the restaurants, Patricia "didn't take part in the operations," he said. Delighting in the surprise factor, she always used the same driver from the Carey Limousine Service, never revealing, even to him, where she was heading next.[17]

On the other side of the family schism, Lauraine Murphy Jericho, Inc., was operating Lauraine Murphy's in Manhasset and the Milleridge Inn in Jericho. Its owners, the Murphy siblings, were aware of Patricia's Florida business dealings. All of them—and Sheila, still neutral in the feud and close to Patricia—owned homes in Fort Lauderdale at one time or another, initially drawn there by Nana's presence. They also knew that Patricia expected her White Turkeys to turn into gold. They, however, were placing their bets on the future of Long Island.

The Milleridge purchase arose, almost accidentally, from the Long Island lifestyle of the sixties. Once a busy hotel bookkeeper, then a Lockheed department head, Monica McDonough Murphy now had time to play cards. Her bridge partner was married to a restaurant broker who knew that the current Milleridge owner, recently arrested for drunk driving, faced revocation of his liquor license. Over seventy years old now, he was looking to sell, but he wanted two million dollars.[18]

Jim was interested. It was a historic property on a huge lot. A patchwork of additions had been built around tiny rooms dating back to 1672. There was plenty of room for parking, and new highway construction was improving the location. Routes 106 and 107, which met near the restaurant, were being widened, and an extension of the Long Island Expressway would create a nearby exit.

Nonetheless, two million was a lot for a restaurant that Jim called "a hodgepodge" with no defined entrance. Instinct told him it could anchor a Knott's Berry Farm East, but he didn't know how to begin. One day he was eating at the Milleridge with a son, James McDonough Murphy—one of the nephews who, years before, had received Christmas cash from Aunt Patricia with a mandate to spend it in her gift shop. Lunching with the younger James, now college-aged, Jim had a brainstorm: he could remove walls and construct an entrance around a roaring fireplace.

After months of negotiations, the owners accepted his one-million-dollar offer—$125,000 down, with the rest in notes payable over ten years. The siblings had banked $150,000 from the sale of the original Lauraine Murphy's in Great Neck, but bills piled up as the refurbished Milleridge underwent a colonial revival. It reopened in early 1964 with three remodeled dining rooms and an expansive bar staffed by servers in period attire.

Unhappy with the restaurant staff inherited from the previous owner, Jim grumbled that he should have replaced all of them. That's what he had done at the Manhasset Lauraine Murphy's, sparing none of the former Louis Sherry's workers except the baker. However, the Milleridge workforce numbered in the hundreds, and a mass firing wouldn't have gone down well in the socially conscious sixties. Jim kept a close watch on the staff, however, guarding against food theft and fashioning part-time workers' schedules to avert a legal requirement to provide them meals.

The first year, with its heavy construction expenses, was rough. Jim discovered that the previous owner had cooked the books, showing the restaurant taking in $100,000 a month when the actual amount was $40,000. Jim needed to find an additional $10,000 to meet the bills, and neither he, Vincent, nor their sisters took anything out of the business.

But soon the picture brightened. Even as the Milleridge décor harked back to the past, the nation's rush into the space age ensured its success. Electronics companies had flocked to Long Island, attracted by its quality of life, fine school systems, and proximity to major airports. Big companies like Sperry Gyroscope, Hazeltine, and Airborne Instruments, joined by small startups, made electronics the leading industry on the island. Jim credited these midcentury tech firms for keeping the Milleridge's thousand seats filled.[19]

In stark contrast to Patricia's "ladies' rendezvous" restaurants, the Milleridge had a men's grill, one of only a handful on Long Island. This taproom-themed mancave became a surprise hit, and not for its historical values. Restricted to males at lunchtime, presumably to promote the efficient conduct of business, it admitted women later in the day. Every Friday night, young people packed the bar solid. Unwittingly, Jim and his siblings had created an after-work hot spot for Long Island singles.

Revenues quickly doubled. The new Milleridge owners took in one million dollars in their second year, and things snowballed from there. An old stable on the property had previously been used for storage. Jim cleaned out the junk, removed the horse stalls, and put in a bakery. Soon it was turning out two thousand loaves a day, for use in the restaurant and customer purchase. Jim had taken his first steps toward a Knott's Berry–inspired combination of dining and theme park.

There was one setback, however. A glass cottage was constructed to sell packaged liquor. This simulated "grog shop" tanked, taking in only a few dollars a day. "No one would go out to dinner and buy liquor," said Jim, who was undoubtedly aware of Patricia's liquor store in Bahia Mar—also named the Grog Shop. Copying, generally so profitable for him, failed him in that one instance. No matter. After a visit to another historically themed restaurant in New Jersey, the Smithville Inn, he successfully duplicated its figurine shop. The Milleridge became a place to spend the day, enjoying pot roast and popovers at the restaurant, then strolling the lanes of a recreated village.[20]

As for Patricia, "She never copied anyone," said Carlton Varney. "She was fabulous at setting tables," the decorator said, adding, "If a strawberry came through that wasn't right, she'd throw it back at the vendor." While Milleridge employees privately complained about their mock-colonial uniforms—a plastic clerical-style collar mandated for shop-clerk wenches drew particular ire[21]—at least one Candlelight employee seemed happy with the hostess gowns created for Patricia by Evelyn Dawson Winn, designer of the moderately priced Suzy Perette label then popular in department stores.

Samantha Harper, an actress who appeared in the Broadway hit *Oh, Calcutta!* fondly remembered working at the Forty-Ninth Street

Candlelight soon after her arrival in New York. "Patricia Murphy's provided me with food, work clothes (hostesses wore green velvet dresses), a social life, and a feeling of family," she wrote.[22]

The new Patricia Murphy establishments proved popular, particularly the Forty-Ninth Street location, where tour buses combined a stop at the Candlelight with a show at Radio City. Patricia wasn't the only one with a stake in the venture. While Jim's business was a partnership of brothers and sisters, Patricia had long been a sole proprietor, as the Tavlin lawsuit had made clear. Now, however, John Rogers had a piece of her business.

A refinancing agreement involving a mortgage on the Sixtieth Street property bears Rogers's as well as Patricia's signatures. Both of Patricia's key managers, Rogers and Camillucci, had previously signed several corporate documents—along with Patricia, signing as president—over the words "secretary" or "treasurer," titles that do not necessarily indicate ownership. In a new twist, however, the refinancing document refers to a 1962 meeting of the directors—in the plural form—of Westchester Candlelight Corp. and Candlelight Orchid Corp. and a vote taken by shareholders, also newly plural.

Still generating rent from tenants (including the Candlelight restaurant operated by Patricia's buyer), the building on Sixtieth Street, formed of two fused brownstones, remained a valuable property. The Westchester Candlelight Corp. took out two mortgages on the property in 1960 and 1962.[23] Leaving such decisions to her managers, Patricia continued wintering in Florida before returning in spring to Manhattan to entertain at Sky High and chair the Outdoor Cleanliness Association's Flower Mart.

New York City's dashing new mayor, John V. Lindsay, snubbed an invitation to the Flower Mart, sending his sanitation commissioner instead. Distributing air pollution complaint forms at its annual flower sale and advocating for apartment dwellers sick of filthy streets, the Outdoor Cleanliness Association did what it could for a troubled city. Operating city restaurants in the mid-sixties, Patricia was taking a gamble again.

The Depression-era daffodils she had bought in lieu of dinner gave her yet another opportunity to tell her life story. In 1966, the inspirational Christian magazine *Guideposts* invited her to write a Lenten column in which her path to selling fifty million meals over thirty-five years became a spiritual message. Recounting her early struggles in Brooklyn, she wrote, " 'Seek ye first the kingdom of God,' Christ said. Afterwards, He promised, a real abundance would follow." The column was reprinted in dozens of small-town newspapers.

Abundance had made Patricia a prominent Florida socialite. For several years she had chaired the Heart Ball held at The Breakers hotel in Palm Beach, a position requiring heavy donations from her own purse. Carleton Varney, who helped her with the decor, said, "She had reached the pinnacle of society, and that cost." Chairing the ball elevated Patricia to the level of Mary Sanford, a Palm Beach grand dame married to a business mogul who had once played professional polo. Patricia "had certain trepidations about being on that list, but she was on it. I thought she always had a sense of being timid or afraid or insecure," Varney added.

Those feelings could have stemmed from a rebuff. An even higher pinnacle, perhaps, was membership in the Everglades Club, where prep-school founder Inez Graham had entertained, and where she and Rosie had long ago attended a party. In 1958, a year after Rosie died, the admissions committee of the Everglades wrote to the American Women's Association. The letter said an applicant for membership, Mrs. James Eugene Kiernan, had named the AWA "as one of her Clubs" and asked for information, which would be held in the "strictest confidence."

In a swift reply, AWA president Dorothea Hopfer said the woman-of-the-month award had cited Patricia as "a humanitarian, a woman who has made a phenomenal success in business, and for her notable contributions to horticulture." She concluded, "Fortunate, indeed, is any organization in which she is interested."[24]

The interest wasn't mutual. The hyper-exclusive Everglades Club evidently declined Patricia's application. Social climbing in Palm Beach had taken Patricia to nearly the highest ledge, but finally a foot came down on her bejeweled fingers. The secretive club's membership rolls have included names like Hilton, Cabot, and Pillsbury, but apparently not Patricia Murphy Kiernan. While Patricia never wrote or spoke publicly of rejection by the club, neither did she mention acceptance, a social coup she'd scarcely have kept secret. She hosted planning sessions for the Heart Ball in the Everglades Club's meeting rooms, but she might have been invited to those rooms as a guest. Evidently, her application hadn't survived the Everglades' stringent screening, said to include a blackballing process.[25]

Famed for its exclusion of blacks and Jews, the Everglades Club admitted women, but they tended to be wives or descendants of wealthy or distinguished men. Among these were Mary Sanford, Patricia's co-star on the charity-ball circuit. Patricia's working-woman friend, Inez Graham, was a less typical club member. Inez's 1963 death capped a long career in education, but, unlike Patricia's, it was a career free of kitchen grease.

The sting of rejection could explain Patricia's vacillation as she considered selling Kinsale and moving to Palm Beach, where she sometimes paid for extended stays at the Colony Hotel. Wobbling down Lake Trail on a tricycle, past the backyards of the Palm Beach rich, she discussed this dilemma with an interviewer. Something held her at Kinsale, where her Japanese-born maid, Matsuyo "Missy" Koike, had become her friend and constant companion. Wife of Kinsale's chief gardener, Missy often accompanied Patricia on charter flights around Florida.

Apparently, Patricia did not think reconciliation with her estranged siblings would bring her comfort or solace. While visiting Lauraine and Maude in Fort Lauderdale, James M. Murphy—Jim's son—went on his own to the Bahia Mar Candlelight. Knowing his Aunt Patricia was on the premises, he asked a hostess to inform her of his presence. Patricia failed to materialize, and the hostess passed by again, avoiding the young man's glance.

The chairwoman of the Heart Ball was guarding her own heart.

CHAPTER 16

Desperate Measures

Remember you are bidding goodbye to guests who have been dining in your tea room—your imaginary home.

—Patricia Murphy's manual for employees, 1930

The Candlelight empire was going to have to change or die.

The writing had appeared on the wall in early 1965, when the State of New York announced it would pick up the entire tab for widening ten miles of Yonkers road. No longer required to pay for land purchases, Yonkers dropped its opposition to the project. The state would seize the land—very likely including the area around the Westchester Candlelight.[1]

Aware that the government moved slowly and that plans weren't finalized, Patricia and her managers continued to milk their cash cow. Ironically, the replacement of Central Avenue's four lanes with a six-lane arterial road was designed to alleviate suburban traffic generated by places like the Candlelight.

There were signs of alarm, but not panic. In 1967, a classified ad ran in the *Wall Street Journal* headlined, "For Sale. Patricia Murphy's Fabulous Waterfront Home." Twenty lines described Kinsale in detail, including the dance patio behind a "shimmering lagoon," the private island, "magnificent" gardens, and the greenhouses and staff cottages on its twenty-eight acres.[2]

"Price reduced for immediate sale," said the ad, but there were no immediate takers. A year and a half later, Kinsale appeared in a wire-service news piece describing "white elephant" mansions in Florida

181

and elsewhere that had gone out of style. Locating Kinsale in the price range between $300,000 and half a million, the article reported that such estates were moving slowly, even when priced at a fraction of their building costs. Labor costs were rising, dream-house concepts were changing, and Kinsale's location wasn't for everyone;[3] one of her orchid growers described it as "out in the swamps."

So, Patricia stayed put, still a faithful customer of St. Lucie Skyways, where five pilots now flew *Miss Tango* and the other planes of the charter fleet. There was a party buzz at the Stuart airport in those days, as celebrities passed through, as well as the occasional drug plane, swiftly followed by the FBI. Bates, the former St. Lucie Skyways pilot, compared the scene to an aviation comic strip, *The Adventures of Smilin' Jack*, that ran in newspapers at the time, featuring he-men aviators and bodacious ladies called "de-icers." The eponymous hero was a square-jawed, mustachioed pilot bearing an uncanny resemblance, Bates said, to a St. Lucie Skyways pilot, James H. Stuart, who Patricia routinely requested as her preferred pilot and who sometimes escorted her to social functions.

Single, slim, and leathery, Jim Stuart was "very cool and suave, very tan," said Bates, recalling what he called Stuart's "pseudo-tuxedo," discount formal wear worn on fly-and-dine outings with Patricia. A former Pan Am pilot, the white-haired Stuart was considerably older than Bates, who began flying Patricia at age twenty-five. Nonetheless, Mrs. Kiernan, as Bates knew her, always addressed him as "Mr. Bates."

"She was eccentric, a character, but very generous and kind," said Bates. On prolonged visits to the Candlelight in Fort Lauderdale, she would have one car pick her up, then send another for the pilot, instructing the wait staff to give him any meal he wanted. Then a young father of baby twins, living with his family in an airport administrative building, Bates was appreciative. Returning home, Patricia would often present him with a twenty-dollar bill and a box of lobster tails, a rare tip for a charter pilot.

Such generosity made it easy to overlook Patricia's behavior in-flight, when she had "no unuttered thoughts," Bates recalled. If there were lightning strikes off the coast, she might cross herself repeatedly, chanting "Are you afraid, Mr. Bates?" in rapid-fire staccato. Her aging, overweight dachshund, Honey Girl, sometimes sat in front with him, once jumping on his instrument panel as he prepared for a challenging bad-weather landing. Muttering, he shoved the dog away, as Patricia scolded, "Are you cursing, Mr. Bates?" Even under stress, Murphian standards applied.

Nevertheless, he admired his "always entertaining" passenger, who Bates said, was "never abusive," unlike a significant number of his other wealthy clients.[4]

An even younger pilot was Richard A. Strauss, son of the airport manager and charter-company owner Harold Strauss, who had sold Patricia *Miss Tango*. When eighteen-year-old Dick began flying Patricia, he had already known her for years. As a child, he had been delighted by invitations to stay overnight at Kinsale, a treat for a boy who, like Bates, lived at the airport. Patricia's kitchen was larger than his family's apartment, he said. He'd marveled at the estate's overhanging trees that formed a half-mile canopy.

He remembers Patricia fondly, apart from one quirk. "She doused everyone liberally with that Green Orchid perfume," including the dachshund, "but she was always generous, not only financially, but with hugs and love." He was always laden with cheesecake and lobster salad on return flights from Fort Lauderdale, where Patricia taste-tested popovers, chatted with customers, and holed up for hours in the office.[5]

Winter tourism was booming in Fort Lauderdale, but still plagued by parking problems, the Patricia Murphy's in Bahia Mar battled other restaurants for visitors' dollars. Among these were the Polynesian-themed Mai Kai and Muriel's Exotic Jade Room, where Muriel Hanford Turnley greeted guests with a monkey on her shoulder, and then performed Gay Nineties routines for audiences dining on Iowa roast beef. Patricia's personality earned her comparison with Muriel, a veteran of the Midwestern vaudeville circuit.

Perhaps the biggest threat, though, came from Creighton's on Sunrise Boulevard. Owned by Charles Creighton, a community leader who had arrived in Fort Lauderdale a decade before Patricia, this restaurant housed a veritable museum of antiques, a lure for the same customers she wooed. Creighton's answer to the popover was an apple pie billed as the world's best. Customers sampling this delicacy for the first time were given certificates dubbing them "Knights of the Round Table."[6]

Leaving an indelible mark on Fort Lauderdale by locking up public land for private use, the Candlelight had sold the yacht basin lease for "enough money," said Camillucci, choosing a phrase that does not suggest a fortune. Camillucci said Patricia's corporation had sought the lease, in part, to reduce the rent it was paying to the city. The restaurant's new Maryland-based landlord, now renamed the Bahia Mar Yachting Center, had likely offered the restaurant a sweetheart deal for the rent, perhaps charging nothing. The Maryland company was also promoting Bahia Mar heavily, always mentioning Patricia Murphy's Candlelight Restaurant.

The restaurant remained the main attraction. At Bahia Mar, as in Yonkers, bold construction plans were moving slowly. The promised $8 million hotel-mall complex failed to materialize quickly. By 1967, the only major change was a new Bahia Mar Motor Inn with 115 rooms and its Patricia Murphy's Patio Café, serving three meals daily. Patricia no longer operated the Grog Shop liquor store, copied by her brother Jim with disappointing results. It had been turned into a forty-seat addition to the restaurant cocktail lounge, furnished Old English style and dubbed the Captain's Quarters.

The outlook became cloudier in New York. In September of 1968, the state transportation department served John Rogers with a notice of property appropriation.[7] The Westchester Candlelight's landlord, Central Arcade, was also served. Because of Yonkers's zoning changes or other issues, Central Arcade had never built the shopping center envisioned around Patricia's restaurant. Patricia had spent more than a million dollars to build the flagship Candlelight and nearly half a million to expand it, but only the landowner would be paid for the appropriation.

The notice surely rattled Rogers, living luxuriously after decades of toil. Five years before the arrival of the process server, his family had moved into an impressively large home on Soundview Avenue in White Plains. One of the youngest of the eight Rogers children remembered it as "like a small hotel," staffed with cooks and housekeepers.[8] Upkeep was not cheap. However, the Yonkers restaurant was still standing, and there were high hopes for the new Manhattan restaurants on Forty-Ninth Street and on Madison Avenue.

Meanwhile, Westchester was a good place to raise a family and within easy commuting distance to the city. There, Rogers had more financial plans for Sixtieth Street. Patricia had bought the building to sell liquor. The owners of the independent Candlelight still advertised popovers and "wholesome food" in the *Christian Science Monitor*. The landlords were cooking up something more sensational.

In 1967, Patricia's name appeared on a building-permit application for a $320,000 conversion of 33–35 East Sixtieth Street into a four-story restaurant measuring 20,230 square feet—comparable in size to Mamma Leone's.

Had Patricia planned to cover at least part of the costs of this ambitious project with proceeds from the sale of Kinsale? The advertisement offering her estate for immediate sale appeared around this time. Kinsale, however, remained unsold, and the Sixtieth Street Candlelight Corporation took out bank mortgages to cover construction costs in 1968 and 1969. This was followed by an intricate web of mortgages involving the Candlelight, a realty company, and a New York corporation involved in the financing of restaurant equipment.

The Candlelight was the borrower in some of these transactions, but the lender in others. Three companies were involved, including a realty company named Legaret. If there had been grand plans for a multi-floored restaurant on Sixtieth Street, these were abandoned, either for profit or under duress. In the end, Candlelight no longer owned the Sixtieth Street building, and it had assigned a $275,000 mortgage on the building to a New York company, Keybro Enterprises, headed by a man named Leonard Schlussel.[9]

Schlussel had a hand in building Patricia's restaurants, though not as an architect or engineer. He was a principal in Keybro Enterprises, a financial enterprise, as well as two companies involved in restaurant construction and equipment, Wellbilt Equipment Corp. and South Key Restaurant Corp. Schlussel would lend to restaurants that pledged their assets as collateral. He also sued or foreclosed on establishments that failed to make payments. For the alterations, Candlelight had borrowed from a bank, but now it was dealing with Schlussel's company.

With Rogers in charge, the Candlelight was negotiating a lease for another Manhattan restaurant, this time in Greenwich Village near the downtown campus of New York University. Something had to be done; road-digging in Yonkers had begun. Another Florida restaurant would be good, too, to capitalize on the value of Patricia's name there.

∾

Acutely aware of her high name recognition—not only in New York and Florida, but back in her homeland—Patricia expected admiration from a young Newfoundlander she met around that time. In 1968, Anne Marie Murray was singing in the Sea View hotel in Miami, which she described as "truly extraordinary, out of filmdom," when she got a call from Patricia, who was, indeed, still much discussed back home.

Murray remembered that Patricia began the conversation by asking, "Do you know *where you are?*" referring not to the hotel's location, but rather its status. The hotel was partly owned by mining magnates who'd heard Murray sing in St. John's and arranged the engagement. At the Hotel Newfoundland, her version of "When Irish Eyes Are Smiling" reduced a millionaire to tears. It also earned her an invitation to entertain at a Hialeah race celebration.

Patricia invited her young compatriot to her Fort Lauderdale home in Harbor Beach. "I liked her. She was a lovely person," said Murray, remembering Patricia, then in her early sixties, as quite attractive. Seeing her for the first time, "I honestly never thought of the word 'old,' Murray said." However, she did notice eccentricities, in this case, Patricia's repeated comparisons of herself to Coco Chanel.

Patricia seemed to believe "she had every right to think that both she and Chanel, were talented geniuses, that the two of them were cut from the same cloth," said Murray. As a well-traveled young person who'd recently been in Europe, Murray found it strange that Patricia talked "as though she were in the top-tier of restaurateurs. I thought perhaps she was living in the past, when she was at her height."

Speaking about Rosie, gone for more than a decade, Patricia seemed so sad that her young guest supposed she had been recently widowed. Accompanying herself on Patricia's piano, Murray played, "Jack Was Every Inch a Sailor," a tune that every Newfoundlander knew.[10]

That was the song Patricia used to play at her home at Placentia, for Jim and her other little brothers and sisters. Now their Milleridge Inn was grossing more than $3.5 million a year, and its shops were pulling in a couple of million more.

Hoping to attract young people while deploring the way they dressed these days, John Rogers prepared to open Patricia Murphy's Candlelight Restaurant in Greenwich Village. He employed some of his own children on Forty-Ninth Street and Madison Avenue during their school breaks. They were nothing like the guitar-playing hippies hanging around Washington Square, one block from the new restaurant in the One Fifth Avenue Hotel.

Yet this was Rogers's brainchild, the idea of bringing the Candlelight downtown. It was all about the deal. Months of negotiations had finally produced a ten-year lease with the landlord, New York University. With the help of the Sixtieth Street proceeds, Patricia's business was about to pour a lot of money into a hexed location where several others had failed. Convincing NYU that the main problem was aesthetics, Rogers had persuaded the university to advance $150,000 toward remodeling costs. Rent would be a percentage of the gross, with no minimum specified.

The deal was initially worked out with the hotel's managing agent. However, NYU was the landlord and had the final say. In the last phases of the haggling, Rogers sat across from John O'Mara, a university vice president. Hesitant to agree to Rogers's ultimatum regarding the advance against remodeling costs, O'Mara sought a second opinion from Laurence "Larry" Tisch, a giant in the Manhattan real estate and hotel worlds. In a letter to Tisch, he described the hotel as a "tough pull," for the university, with its food and beverage operation posting an operating deficit of $78,000 the previous year. He attached Rogers's final offer. The hotel king concluded that it looked like the best possible deal NYU could make under the circumstances, so it would be best to take it.

The next step was to sell the proposal to the university's executive committee. O'Mara wrote a memo blaming the failure of previous restaurant operators on "drab décor" and obsolete food preparation equipment.[11] Betting that Candlelight's famed flowers and furnishings would provide an answer, or simply relying on O'Mara's assurances, the committee approved. On July 15, 1969, Rogers alone signed the lease for the Candlelight. It was summer, an unlikely time for Patricia to be in Florida. She was leaving One Fifth in the hands of Rogers. As her brother Vincent's brother-in-law, he was the closest thing she had to family.

Moreover, Patricia had gotten her own version of a Rogers final offer. That is why he was now a Candlelight shareholder.

Perhaps unaware of this, in memos, O'Mara referred to Rogers as a "representative" of the "Murphy chain," now holding the lease to a large chunk of the hotel. In addition to the existing restaurant and bar, the Candlelight would occupy two first-floor hotel areas formerly used for private functions and entertainment, the mezzanine, a second-floor banquet office, and parts of the basement. The lease allowed a gift shop, and a rider gave NYU a small share of sales of Patricia Murphy–branded merchandise.[12] Patricia's name was still considered bankable.

Leonard Schlussel of Keybro Enterprises, involved in the intricacies of the Sixtieth Street finances, also had reason to celebrate. As soon as the lease was signed, Candlelight ordered restaurant equipment from Wellbilt Equipment, another of his companies. Shortly before Christmas, Schlussel sent Rogers another bill, adding,

> After reviewing the work performed to date we felt that the requisition should be more sizable than that spoken about. It also appears that we are progressing at a fairly good clip, in fact, we are quite pleased . . . considering that this is the Holiday, and workers seem to find it an unusual [sic] good time of year to rest their weary bones. I'll have to anticipate that we will be requisition [sic] you at the rate of $25,000 a week if all goes well.[13]

Weary bones and all, the workers forged on. Using some of the old hotel furniture, but rejecting much of it, the Candlelight completed the renovations in March. A month later, Patricia Murphy's reopened at One Fifth. Within weeks, the people at No. 2 Fifth accused the restaurant of illegally operating a cabaret without a zoning variance. NYU quickly squelched the complaint, pointing out that live music was nothing new at the hotel.

Long past fighting zoning battles, Patricia was mingling with New York theater royalty. Her decorations adorned a champagne-supper fundraiser for the Museum of the City of New York's theater collection.[14] Costumes worn by Edwin Booth and the Barrymores were on display amid Patricia's white, gold, and red decorations. Truman Capote was there, along with actors Cyril Ritchard and Joan Bennett. Mayor Lindsay, always too busy for the Outdoor Cleanliness flower mart, found time for this Stars of the Theater gala.[15]

Patricia had reasons to raise her champagne glass. Even if Rogers was in charge at One Fifth, she still got top billing. The new place in the Village was the ninth restaurant to open under her name—No. 9, like the Chanel perfume. Florida had two Patricia Murphy's restaurants now, following the launch of one in Deerfield Beach. That one was a lush, tropical paradise with a moat and a stream. Best of all, it was a turnkey operation. A developer had built this extravaganza, trying out other operators before handing Patricia the key.

Holiday celebrations continued as usual in Westchester, where so many people came for Easter dinner that some gave up waiting for tables and were served on the bus.[16] At Christmas time, a sheep escaped from the crèche. A crewman for the electric company spotted it in the parking lot of Roosevelt High School, and a truck was sent to pick it up.[17]

As it turned out, the sheep was prescient. In February, Patricia's showplace in Yonkers closed its doors, ostensibly for remodeling. By August of 1971, the Yonkers *Herald Statesman* sent a reporter out to check on rumors that it was closed for good. Rogers told the paper that the restaurant would be back in full swing once minor differences with the landlord were worked out.[18]

But the lease had already been surrendered, without Patricia's signature. It was over.[19]

CHAPTER 17

Ignominy

We are guardians of the public health.

—Patricia Murphy's manual for employees, 1930

It was the era of the fern bar, and the Cascades Gardens in Deerfield Beach, Florida, had plenty of ferns, as well as "orchids by the ton," in the words of one of Patricia's gardeners. There were also waterfalls and fish ponds, as well as palm and ficus trees stretching almost sixty feet to the ceiling of the dining room, through which a stream flowed. Plexiglass windows wrapped around the Grotto bar looked out on the moat, where an uninvited infant alligator temporarily took up residence. Animal Control was called, disappointing customers who had come to catch a glimpse.[1]

Even without the gator, crowds flocked to Patricia Murphy's Cascades. That was the restaurant's new official name, although everyone just called it Patricia Murphy's. The greenery alone had cost one-quarter of a million dollars, paid by Southern Bydale Corp., a developer constructing several other expensive projects along U.S. 1. A five-minute drive from Boca Raton, the spot was already popular for proms, anniversary celebrations, bat mitzvahs, or simply drinks in the Grotto bar with its view of the moat.

With Rogers and Camillucci overseeing the New York restaurants, Patricia signed the lease to the three-hundred-seat Cascades space. Ads and menu covers for Patricia Murphy's listed a half-dozen locations for what was now a full-blown chain. Transferring a longtime manager from Fort Lauderdale to Deerfield Beach, she costumed the hostesses in long gowns, adorned the tables with flora, and passed the celery and watermelon pickles. The waterfalls were new, but the formula was the same: crisp linens, fine china, and sharp service. The food and prices had not changed much either: lamb, turkey, duck, prime rib, or seafood dinners for between four and seven dollars. With Julia Child's public-television show, *The French Chef* introducing fine cuisine to the masses, some diners regarded Patricia Murphy's as a "peas and carrots kind of place," as a review put it. One item, though, remained eternally popular: people became irate if not quickly provided with popovers.

It was a good, albeit demanding, place to work. Slowness and slovenliness were not tolerated. Patricia's managers ran a tight ship, and Patricia continued to fly in unannounced, chartering planes to hop the short distance between Fort Lauderdale and Boca Raton, near Deerfield Beach, then hiring limos to pick her up at those city's airports. Her pilot, Bates, coined the term "The Arrival" to describe these elaborate air-and-land operations. Given the unpredictability of traffic, Patricia's mode of travel also gave employees at the second restaurant less time to prepare, even if alerted by the first one.

Staff members presented themselves for inspection as if for royalty. Employees who passed Murphian muster felt confident of their employment chances elsewhere; competitors knew they'd been well trained. However, there were compelling reasons to stay. Many employees had health benefits, sick leave, and paid vacations, the former gardener said, adding that servers could make hundreds in tips and the kitchen staff was well paid.[2]

Eight years earlier, an attempt to organize Patricia's Bahia Mar workers had failed. Local 133 of the Hotel and Restaurant Employees Union gathered enough support from staffers there to force a vote on representation. Ultimately, the workers rejected the union, 92 to 26. Despite losing elections at other south Florida restaurants that year, the union persisted.[3] Veiled threats of firing often shroud such elections, resulting in union losses. It is possible, however, that Patricia's pay and benefits were already considered fair, or—as often happens—that they were improved to stave off further organizing efforts.

Costs in general were rising for restaurants, and across the United States revenues and profits were falling. The once mighty Restaurant Associates was now a "besieged empire," wrote *New York* magazine food critic Gael Greene, reporting the removal of its visionary leader, Joe Baum, after losses exceeded one million dollars in the first quarter of

1970. At the Four Seasons, carpets were dirty, holes appeared in table-cloths, and flowers were absent for weeks. On the lower rungs of the empire, Zum Zum—a high-priced version of the hot dog stand—had proved disappointing, and RA's Citgo Village truckstops ended up on the wrong side of a new Atlanta highway.[4]

Closings of iconic spots like Toots Shor and the Colony in New York, as well as local favorites in Houston, New Orleans, and Atlanta, prompted *Fortune* magazine to conduct a survey. In every town, it found, restaurant sales in 1971 declined 5 to 15 percent from the mediocre levels of the previous year. Profits were taking hard hits, and losses growing common.[5]

The *Fortune* piece focused on gourmet landmarks with prized chefs, not places like Patricia Murphy's, where a cook named Shorty Orpano had baked popovers for thirty years. Still, in all price ranges, after "a glorious decade of prosperity," as the magazine put it, the industry was going through a shakeout.

Rogers had calculated labor costs into his deal-making for the new place in the One Fifth Avenue Hotel. New York City was a union town, and Local 11 of the Chain Restaurant and Luncheonette Employees Union represented workers at Patricia Murphy's, Howard Johnson's, Schrafft's, Childs, and dozens of other eateries. Salaries and benefits had improved over the years, and despite mounting charges of collusion with management, the local's oft-indicted leadership remained entrenched. Union benefits, not unusual in Manhattan, appeared in the One Fifth Candlelight's books under "adjustments."

Labor was not One Fifth's worst problem. The restaurant was losing money because no one was going there. A year and a half after it opened, Rogers wrote a three-page letter of complaint to O'Mara, reminding the university president that "Miss Murphy made a very substantial investment." Laying blame for the failure squarely at NYU's door, Rogers began,

> Although we realize that no one has control over the neighborhood, we have great difficulty inducing people to come into the Washington Square area because they are actually afraid of some of the people walking the streets. I myself have not been able to enter the Restaurant in the past two weeks . . . without being accosted by loiterers and panhandlers.

Placing NYU students in much the same category as the "loiterers and panhandlers," Rogers said their presence in the hotel's lobby and near its entrance "discourages many diners from entering or returning to the presence." Other complaints involved the location of the restaurant sign, pipe leaks that had ruined a carpet, and unfulfilled promises to promote the Candlelight to the Faculty Club and NYU alumni.

The need to keep restrooms locked was a source of particular annoyance. With perhaps a whiff of homophobia, Rogers traced this practice to the assault of a man in the men's room, also mentioning destruction of property and "abuse of these facilities in every imaginable way" by "users from the lobby and the street" when attendants were not on duty.[6]

Before replying, O'Mara forwarded this litany of woes to Morton Wolf, the hotel's managing agent. It did not find sympathetic ears. No one can control the type of people in an area, the hotelier wrote in a letter to O'Mara. He excused the pipe leaks as inevitable in "any high-rise building," and asserted that his staff had cleaned the restaurant carpet "perfectly." Bristling at Rogers's implication of the hotel in his failures, Wolf countered by describing the Candlelight's service as "wholly inadequate," crediting this to "mismanagement."

"It is very simple for them to write a 3-page letter attempting to find fault. We would suggest that they search their own faults first," the hotelier concluded.[7]

Consequently, O'Mara carefully composed a letter to Rogers in a tone both cordial and stern. He began,

> I think that you may agree with me, after you have had time
> to reflect, that your letter was somewhat of an exercise in
> overkill. I, myself, am frequently guilty of the same thing,
> so don't feel bad.

Addressing each complaint at length, he gently chided Rogers's distaste for the Village denizens. "I have never been bothered at all by panhandlers," the university vice president wrote, adding, "Maybe you suffer from looking much more affluent than I." As for the students, O'Mara said, "One can see young people of similar appearance all around New York, including the lobbies of some of our better office buildings."

Mailings to alumni and faculty would make no difference because "I can tell you flatly that the majority of people who work at Washington Square know that . . . the Patricia Murphy's Restaurant is there," O'Mara wrote. In softer words than Wolf's, he spoke of the "irritatingly slow" service he had received on his regular visits to the restaurant, and the absence of personnel "to greet the guests and come to know them and . . . give them the recognition that frequently is important in developing repeat business."

Along with his complaints, Rogers had expressed a desire to jettison the restaurant entirely and turn it over to NYU as a student dining facility. O'Mara rebuffed the proposal as unneeded, reminding Rogers of the need for "supervision of service" before closing with a friendly, "Let's get together."[8]

Late submitting checks to NYU, and still owing most of the $150,000 construction loan, Rogers wasn't in the mood for a get-together. Even with Camillucci sharing management tasks in New York, Rogers was stretched thin and could not be at One Fifth daily. In his letter to NYU, he mentioned visiting the restaurant "several times" over the previous two weeks, as if this were more frequent than usual.

Trouble was brewing at the other Manhattan restaurants as well. The big draw around the Forty-Ninth Street location, Radio City Music Hall, reached its fortieth birthday with signs of wear. The landmark was struggling to fill its 6,200 seats with a potpourri of ballet, classical music, opera, and the Rockettes. Changes in film distribution had limited its film showings to G-rated family fare. As the queues shortened, the nearby Patricia Murphy's had fewer show-goers to feed.[9]

Amid the rise of city magazines and alternative newspapers, journalists had turned snarky, and the lunch crowds at Patricia Murphy's were locked in their sights. One line in *New York* magazine was sufficient for its capsule review of the Madison Avenue Candlelight: "popovers, little old ladies." A *Times* feature characterized the Forty-Ninth Street location as "wall-to-wall ladies."[10] No matter that the *Times* piece, written by a woman, went on to praise the restaurant's lighting and service; the damage was done. Second-wave feminists—like Patricia herself, decades earlier—sought to distance themselves from idle wives and clubwomen.

The food, too, came in for a drubbing. A 1972 *Women's Wear* Daily review of the two midtown restaurants grudgingly praised their "elegant" interiors and "eyeball-grabbing seasonal cuttings" before launching into an attack. A "gelatinous" chopped-liver appetizer preceded a "dry and stringy" breast of Cornish hen; a veal cutlet was "lukewarm, greasily crumbed and ill sautéed," and broccoli arrived "tasting of a frozen food carton."

Patricia Murphy's is "all floral decor and no culinary technique," concluded the *WWD* food critic, Doris Tobias. The popovers escaped unscathed, however, and dinner prices were judged "reasonable," opening at $3.75 for a fruit and cottage cheese entrée and topping out at $7.75 for lobster tails.[11]

Those were also the prices in the Florida restaurants, where things looked brighter. Big ad buys can protect eating places from hostile reviews, and the Bahia Mar Yachting Center continually advertised Patricia Murphy's in southern Florida papers. Moreover, lower overall costs may have helped maintain food quality. In New York, where Patricia's greenhouses were gone, those eyeball-grabbing displays may have grown costly. In Florida, just a short charter flight from the restaurants was Kinsale, with 50,000 orchids available for decoration and a large vegetable garden for salads and sides. Also, the Fort Lauderdale restaurant apparently paid no rent, a benefit of the sale of the Bahia Mar lease.

No longer in control of her image in New York, Patricia could still spin a story in Florida. In early December of 1972, she persuaded the *Boca Raton News* to run two stories—thinly disguised advertisements—about her new policy at the Cascades. The subterranean lounge area of the bar, the Grotto, would admit men only during weekday lunchtimes. Telephones with long extension cords would be available for those conducting business, but the real purpose was to let men "be men," Patricia said.

"I enjoy being a woman, dressing pretty and all that, but when it comes to running things, I think men are the bosses," Patricia told the Boca Raton paper. After some quick plugs for her orchids and perfume, she added, "Men make the world, and as long as I can work in it and get what I want, I'm happy." Ending with, "One thing is sure—she doesn't want Ms. before her name," the piece was headed, "Look Out Women's Libbers, Murphy's is for Men Only."

On the following day, in what was almost certainly a publicity stunt, the paper ran a front-page article about two women allegedly denied admission to the lounge. Raising no objections, the women retreated—presumably to dine elsewhere in the restaurant, though mentioning this would have stripped the piece of drama. Reporting the "incident" with not a hint of criticism, the piece admiringly described the Grotto's décor and quoted two businessmen happily enjoying their female-free surroundings.

Writing her autobiography a decade earlier, Patricia had cast herself as the working woman's champion. Now she was she was spouting the anti-feminist line, even advising the Boca Raton paper to call her "Mrs. Murphy." Had her thinking really changed? In the words of a Fort Lauderdale friend, Linda Schaefer, "Patricia was all business."[12] Eager to shed the ladies-who-lunch stigma—or finally copying Jim, after his many years of copying her—she was probably looking to boost her lunch trade.

Still, Patricia was a bit late to the party. Famously restricted to males for decades, McSorley's Old Ale House had served its first woman customer two years earlier, after New York City passed an ordinance prohibiting gender discrimination in public places. Inspired in her youth by trailblazers like the Ware sisters of the Tea Room Management school, Patricia had chosen a strange time to oppose women's rights.

From a marketing standpoint, it may have worked, however. Located outside the fiercely competitive Fort Lauderdale market, the Cascades shared none of One Fifth Avenue's problems. Indeed, one of the businessmen interviewed inside the Grotto said he liked the men-only hours because it spared him the trouble of waiting in line.

Far from the savage New York press, Patricia continued to shine on the Treasure Coast social scene. In the spring of 1972, she chartered a plane to fly up north, but only to bring in a team of New York decorators. They were to transform St. Lucie Country Club suite into a Parisian street for an April in Paris ball. The event was a benefit for Martin Memorial Hospital, which acknowledged Patricia's hefty donations by naming her to its honorary board that year, alongside Ralph Evinrude of motor boating fame.[13]

Money was flowing at Bahia Mar, as well, affecting her relationship with the yachting center landlord. A $5.7 million mortgage had finally been obtained for remodeling the entire basin, including its shopping center, and erecting a hotel. Plans unveiled in Fort Lauderdale had changed from years before, when Patricia sold control of Fort Lauderdale Candlelight Corp. to the group led by aviator sportsman James W. Campbell. Acknowledging the growing importance of the maritime industry to Fort Lauderdale, a good portion of the loan would go toward marine facilities. The motel, where Patricia had the Patio café, would remain, supplemented by a new fifteen-story hotel with meeting areas and a dining room.

Reporting this, the *Fort Lauderdale News* wrote, "The entire complex is owned by Patricia Murphy."[14] Such was her reputation in the city. However, that hadn't been true since Campbell first worked out his deal with her, telling the *News* she'd be in charge of food and beverage operations at the prospective hotel. Years had passed, and Campbell had stepped down from the presidency of Maryland Community Developers, now holding the long-term lease. Pronouncing the shops "in terrible shape," MCD began reconstructing some and demolishing others. Patricia Murphy's Candlelight Restaurant would be left intact, it announced.

As the hotel opened, Patricia's name figured prominently in increased Bahia Mar advertising. Her name glowed, as always, over the restaurant, and she continued to materialize there from time to time. Young new hires at the restaurant, like Carol Nossett, caught curious glimpses of this legendary lady, now nearly seventy and needing assistance to emerge from her car. However, Patricia "really wasn't involved with the restaurant when I was there," said Nossett, then a valet parking attendant. "It was owned and managed by the hotel."[15]

Changes were also afoot in New York, where Rogers was exhibiting signs of desperation. In August 1974, NYU sold its lease on the One Fifth Avenue Hotel to an investor incorporated as Washmews, after a nearby street called Washington Mews. The new landlord seemed interested in taking over the restaurant, but there was no deal as yet. Struggling to repay NYU $15,000 a year on the remodeling advance, Rogers turned once again to Leonard Schlussel, mortgaging his White Plains home to Schlussel's Keybro Corp. for $110,000, soon followed by a second mortgage for $40,000 more.

Greg Camillucci had left to become general manager of the Russian Tea Room. Instead of worrying about the demise of Radio City, he'd be greeting celebrities and assigning tables in order of status. Patricia had plucked him from the ranks in Westchester, sent him on a grand tour of Europe, feted him at her penthouse, and been godmother to his son. As Patricia presided over charity balls in Florida, her protégé escaped the ruins of her northern empire.

Rogers was shopping for a savior for the two East Side restaurants and seemed close to finding one. In December of 1974, *New York* magazine took a break from making wisecracks about Patricia Murphy's— "candlelit and corny" was one—to run a business item about it. A vice president of National Restaurants, a corporation binging on acquisitions of troubled eateries, told the magazine's business columnist he was "on the verge" of buying the two Candlelights. He "told me papers should be signed shortly clinching the deals," wrote the columnist, Dan Dorfman.[16]

But negotiations didn't go quite so fast, perhaps because Patricia didn't want her brand tarnished by connection with the Riese brothers' downmarket eateries. The Fifth Avenue Candlelight Corp., owner of the Forty-Ninth Street location, and the Madison Avenue Candlelight Corp. declared bankruptcy in March of 1975. Evidently, there was an agreement to assign leases to National, though not immediately. The plan seemed to call for closing the restaurants after Christmas. National would make alterations, reopening in January with a new format.

Sorrows and worries progressed through that year. The Candlelight changed settings with the seasons, but these varied only by shades of darkness. In April, Missy Koike died. An obituary most likely written by Patricia described her beloved late employee as "a devoted companion and longtime friend of Patricia Murphy," who "worked closely with Miss Murphy in her many charitable endeavors in Stuart, Palm Beach, and many other places." She was survived by her husband, Kinsale's head gardener, as well as the mother and nine siblings she had left in Japan.

Soon after the funeral, Patricia fired Missy's husband, Walter. A dispute had arisen over the medical bills related to Missy's terminal illness. Walter alleged that Patricia had reneged on promises to pay the expenses or provide insurance to cover them. Perhaps to even the score, Walter tried to remove 681 orchids valued at $6,810 from the estate, claiming them as personal property. When he was forcibly restrained from removing the flowers, Walter sued Patricia for the orchids and the broken promises. In Palm Beach, where Patricia carefully cultivated her philanthropic image, the lawsuit appeared in the paper.[17]

With summer came a note of cheer, as Rogers surrendered the One Fifth lease. The new hotel operator would take over the restaurant. In negotiations, Rogers had neglected to mention the $90,000 still owing on the construction advance, and the $15,000 payment he had just missed. The restaurant, which the new owners would run under a different name, was now theirs.

The last Christmas at the Patricia Murphy's on East Forty-Ninth Street was merry. The holidays cloaked Radio City in its former glory as out-of-towners thronged to see the Rockettes. A hit musical called *Shenandoah*, playing nearby at the Alvin Theater, was an even bigger draw. In mid-December, the restaurant had seventy-eight people on staff, many of them unaware of their impending change of employer. Some workers had never seen one another before: temporary staff was hired to handle the crowds.

As always, popovers helped ease the wait for a table. The hot breads earned the enthusiastic applause of members of a Waltham, Massachusetts, theater group and their chaperones. Spending a few days in New York, forty-two high school and college students had convened at Patricia Murphy's for the sole dinner shared by all. It was a special opportunity to get together with a Waltham native who had landed a part in *Shenandoah*.

Still in line, almost every member of the group ate a popover, and some ate several. A vegetarian declined, unsure of their animal-product content. Eventually the large group was seated, and the actor joined them. It was December 13, one of many busy nights before the holidays.[18]

Servers who worked in the Forty-Ninth Street tended to dread groups like this, with everyone asking for separate checks. However, soon there would be a long break. The restaurant was planning to close to the public between Christmas and January 19, ostensibly for remodeling. Some of the staff knew, however, that the management was about to change.

The restaurant was already locked and dark on January 11, as health officials arrived to chain it closed. Shortly after their Broadway outing, several members of the theater group, including the actor, had fallen ill. Returning to Massachusetts, they were diagnosed with typhoid. Other cases were reported in New Hampshire and Connecticut. Health officials conferred across state boundaries, and the New York City Health Department announced it had "very strong evidence" that traced the infection to Patricia Murphy's, where all the stricken had dined between December 12 and 14.[19]

Perhaps because the restaurant ownership was in transition, some employees reported back to work in advance of the scheduled reopening. They were greeted by health officials demanding stool samples. Typhoid cases had been rare in New York for the previous quarter-century except among travelers returning from less developed countries. Newspaper accounts conjured memories of Typhoid Mary, the cook who had knowingly infected others while not suffering symptoms herself.

Epidemiologists and other so-called "medical detectives" stood in the spotlight as a carrier was sought. "The search narrows," wrote the *Times*, also calling it "the hunt." An exhaustive AP feature carried in papers across the nation introduced Patricia Murphy's to readers who had never been near the Eastern Seaboard. The Waltham vegetarian had not taken sick, the wire story noted. Could the infection have been popover-borne? Unlikely, said a health official, because they were cooked. In that case, perhaps the salad dressing?[20]

Rogers was apparently not asked for comment, shielded by workers who told reporters—perhaps honestly—they were unsure who owned the place. One newspaper report mentioned a mortgage foreclosure. It is possible that Rogers had relinquished the restaurant to the Riese brothers under pressure related to the Candlelight's debts.

In the end, all fifteen people definitively diagnosed with typhoid were treated with antibiotics and recovered. No equivalent cure was available for Patricia's name, publicized for the first time in *Morbidity and Mortality Weekly*. More than seventy Candlelight food handlers were examined and cleared. Locating workers hired off the books, with social security numbers and addresses unrecorded, was a challenging task, particularly when so many employees fell under suspicion. The scope narrowed, however, as the city health department identified the source of contamination. It had to be the popovers.[21]

Patricia's famous bread items were baked at high temperatures, but they passed through the hands of several workers before reaching eager customers. In the absence of what the health officials refer to as "rigid handwashing and personal hygiene," a kitchen employee removing the popovers from the oven, or assembling them in a basket, could have turned them into menaces.[22]

Only three kitchen workers had handled the popovers on the fateful day the theater group dined at the restaurant. A man from the Bronx was tested and found negative. Another had gone to Venezuela, and health officials there were able to locate and clear him. A third, also from South America, remained elusive. New York health officials concluded he had fled the country, perhaps aware he was a typhoid carrier.

With no culprit found and the restaurant closed, the newspapers lost interest. The definitive link to the popovers was never publicized. Nevertheless, Patricia's New York era was over. In the nation's greatest metropolis, she had fallen as spectacularly as she had risen thirty-six years before.

The Riese brothers of National Restaurants reopened the East Side restaurants under their old name, White Turkey. In White Plains, the Rogers family packed up their mortgaged home. They were bound for Florida.

CHAPTER 18

The Party's Over

When going off duty, make sure that your assigned duty is complete.

—Patricia Murphy's manual for employees, 1930

Reviewing the Cascades in December of 1977, a food critic wrote, "This establishment is no longer owned by Patricia Murphy, but I am told the proprietor is John Rogers."

The typhoid stain had faded in the sunlight of Deerfield Beach, where the Cascades was still packed. Writing for the *Boca Raton News*, Arnold Goodman liked the food and loved the décor, while conceding that "some men may dislike the tea room atmosphere." He griped only about his long wait for a table and delayed attention from the busy servers.

Assuring his readers that the popovers still abounded, Goodman wrote, "Mrs. [*sic*] Murphy has sold her two Florida restaurants (the other is at Bahia Mar in Fort Lauderdale) and now operates only the gift shops in both places." The name, of course, was eternal: his piece ran under the headline, "Patricia Murphy's Fare is a Good Bet."

Not a safe bet, however—not for Rogers. The piece was written in the winter, the height of the tourist season, but there were slow times as well. Now controlling Boca Raton Candlelight Corp., Rogers remained embroiled in the financial mess at One Fifth, where it wasn't only the carpet that had never come clean. He had turned over the lease to the hotel while still owing NYU most of the money advanced for renovations. Despairing of recovering the entire $90,000, the university sued for one-third of the amount. A trial court awarded NYU the amount of one missed payment, $15,000.[1]

Both NYU and Candlelight were appealing the judgment, with NYU arguing for double the amount and Candlelight asserting it no longer owed anything. There were legal fees, and mortgage payments for Schlussel, but from outward appearances, Rogers was living in comfort.

His family had a home in Lighthouse Point, overlooking the Intracoastal Waterway. Lacking for nothing, the family of ten enjoyed frequent meals at the Cascades and other dining spots. If in Washington Square, Rogers's polished attire made him a panhandler magnet—as NYU's O'Mara suggested—around Boca Raton he fit right in.

As for Patricia, even if her Fort Lauderdale restaurant was in other hands, her involvement remained as intense as ever. Her accountant, Charly Schaefer, heard the phone ring late one night. Patricia's agitated voice was on the other end of the line. The operator of the new hotel was advertising her restaurant with big display ads headlined "Pop over to Patricia's for dinner tonight." Evidently created by an agency, the ads indicated an image makeover. A sketch showed two figures clad in bell-bottomed pants entering the restaurant—not a skirt or jacket between them—over text describing Patricia Murphy's Candlelight as "elegant without being stuffy."

It was the "pop over" pun that prompted Patricia's nocturnal call. "She *hated* it," recalled Charly's wife, Linda. There was nothing her accountant could do about it, just as he could do nothing about the people who were always trying to rip Patricia off, as he told his wife. The restaurant was no longer hers. She owned only the gift shop at Bahia Mar, paying nearly $20,000 to lease it at the yacht basin. As the hotel had risen, so had the rents.

The ad continued to run in the *Fort Lauderdale News*, annoying Patricia while proving she was too iconic to require a surname. To the young restaurant employees, she looked old and frail, but she was still throwing grand parties at her rented Harbor Beach home, with its high green walls reaching to a ceiling painted a shade called Martini. Over marble flooring were fabrics in muted blues, greens, and oyster white. A gallery ran the entire length of the house, painted a bold emerald and showcasing the Asian art objects she and Rosie had collected on their travels.[2]

"Oh, what a magnificent table she set there," recalled Linda Schaefer.

Soon, only one setting was needed. Five years earlier, Patricia was hosting a shamrock festival at Kinsale to benefit the hospital. Since then, the Southern Colonial house and most of the grounds had been sold. Some of the orchid collection remained, however. By 1975, as the Bahia Mar parking attendant noted, Patricia required assistance getting in and out of a car. The Kinsale staff was dispersing, and Patricia needed someone to tend the orchids until she decided where to take them next. Packing up in New York and Stuart, Patricia's staff put everything into storage. It wasn't so simple to stow cattleyas.

She, or her grounds staff, located the perfect orchid babysitter. Dr. Greg J. Harrison, a Palm Beach County veterinarian, was a fellow orchid collector with thousands of plants in Lake Worth. After conversations with a groundskeeper, probably Victor de Leon, Patricia's orchids were moved sixty miles south for what was intended to be a short stay.

Months passed, the flowers were not retrieved, and Harrison's bills for extended floral care were ignored. His suit for payment provoked a countersuit, and then a lawyer invited him to meet Patricia to try to work things out. Residing some distance from the Broward County restaurants, and a generation younger than Patricia, Harrison had never been to a Candlelight. Still, he knew of Patricia as "the lady with the fancy restaurants" and was eager to meet her. His wife accompanied him to a meeting place he described as a care facility.

Patricia had suffered a stroke, one of a series. In the opinion of her estranged siblings, who knew of her condition, the strokes were a consequence of her heavy drinking. Harrison said Patricia was conscious but never rose to her feet during his visit. It seemed the orchid-care bills had gone unpaid because no one knew what they were for. The grounds crew was apparently gone, and others around Patricia might have suspected a scam.[3]

The case ended with a court judgment in Harrison's favor. In July of 1979, Patricia was ordered to pay her fellow orchid collector $2,500 immediately and $5,000 more in September. The second payment was collateralized by Patricia's property, for which Harrison's attorney demanded copies of deeds and mortgages. The lawyer might have been skeptical about collecting payment from the former Palm Beach socialite, now gravely ill.[4]

Not long after Harrison met her, Patricia slipped into a coma. Seeking guardianship, Sheila joined in early August with her two sisters, Lauraine and Maude, and their brothers, Jim and Vincent, to have Patricia declared incompetent. A notice was sent to the sumptuous home in

Harbor Beach, where her estranged siblings had set up round-the-clock nursing for her. Bedridden and unconscious, Patricia lay beneath the martini-colored ceiling. She was summoned to a hearing on her physical and mental competence.

Before the scheduled hearing, a court-appointed lawyer for the incompetent was sent to visit her. "Although she was awake, she was unable to answer any questions or show any acknowledgment that questions were asked," he wrote on August 18, 1979, adding that she had been like this for several months. The hearing was canceled.

There was nothing to do but wait for the end. The court declared Patricia incompetent due to organic brain syndrome arising from a severe cerebral vascular accident. Sheila was appointed guardian, and the others helped arrange payment for the day-and-night nursing. Patricia's papers were in disorder. One thing was clear, however: she had not left a will.

She evidently hadn't left many assets, either. In the process of helping Sheila seek guardianship, the siblings had been shocked to find Patricia's kingdom in ruins. The Boca Raton food critic's information was right: Patricia was merely a gift shop proprietor. All her other wealth fit into a few jewelry boxes. Her fine earrings, bracelets, and brooches were appraised at $50,000, but that was outweighed by medical costs. Facing mounting nursing bills, Sheila sought and received court approval to sell the jewelry. Aside from that, guardianship papers estimated the value of Patricia's property at roughly $45,000. There was a chance that more would be located, but the siblings weren't hopeful. Jim, Vincent, Lauraine, and Maude were doing well in their restaurant business, but they were disappointed for Sheila and more than a little shocked.

After years in diamonds and fox, Patricia appeared to be broke.

The siblings who had been estranged from her for thirty years decided to waive their rights as beneficiaries. Everything would go to Sheila, the one Patricia loved. With medical bills still piling up, a decision was made to transfer Patricia to a cheaper rental.[5]

With the court's consent, the unresponsive Patricia and her nurses were moved to a more affordable house in Coral Ridge. It was in a desirable location near the waterway, if not even remotely a showplace. Two decades earlier, the *New York Tribune*'s horticulture editor had written of Patricia,

> Her love of plants has paid off handsomely, but after talking with her at lunch I am convinced that she would never be

happy unless surrounded with growing and blooming plants. All other things are incidental.[6]

A woman always precisely tuned to her surroundings was now totally unaware of them. Lawns outnumbered gardens here, but what did it matter? Her orchids were gone anyway.

On November 23, 1979, Patricia passed away. She had lasted only two months after the move and the jewelry sale. Five days later, she was buried in Arlington National Cemetery, next to Captain James Eugene Kiernan, the love of her life. During her lifetime, she had been known by a half-dozen names. In the guardianship hearings, she had been Ellen Murphy, aka Eleanor Patricia Murphy. Socially, she had been Mrs. J.E. Kiernan, and in her later years, Mrs. Murphy. Her gravestone at Arlington reads simply, "Patricia Murphy, His Wife."

Probate began. Sheila's attorney was Paul A. Gore, a grandson of the recently deceased R.H. Gore, the onetime newspaper publisher who had fiercely opposed Patricia's Bahia Mar lease. Convincing Sheila he could fairly represent her despite the connection, he took on a case that would prove memorable "It was one of the worst estates I had ever seen for records and confusion," he said.

The remains of Patricia's many recent moves were in six Fort Lauderdale warehouses. Gore heard from Sheila soon after she opened the storage units. "She said, 'Good God, do you know what's in there? They're full of refrigerators and rotting food. They smell to high heaven.'" Preparing the probate documents, Gore told her to get appraisals or submit her best estimates.

He also got an urgent call from Martin County, ordering him to cap an artesian well on Patricia Murphy's property. Rock had given way, and the water was shooting up. Investigation revealed that Patricia had died owning other lots in Martin County. Four had since been sold by the local government to collect delinquent taxes.

An attorney-client conflict arose, with Sheila asserting that Gore should have known of the Martin County real estate, and Gore maintaining he had had no way of knowing. He had three of the four tax-deed sales overturned, arguing that if the county could find him to fix a well, they could have found him before selling land.[7] The real estate was valued at $175,000, bumping the value of the estate up to $195,000. Sheila sold some of Patricia's crystal and china in estate sales and took over the gift shop.

Filing last papers in 1983, Gore wrote an asterisked note:

From the date of her appointment as Guardian . . . [Sheila] was unable to assess a complete and accurate inventory of the assets of the ward because of the confusion of the ward's records of ownership and because of the wide disbursement of assets between New York, Stuart, Florida, West Palm, Florida and Ft. Lauderdale, Florida.

Speaking of Patricia—whose Bahia Mar restaurant he knew from his college years, but had not been impressed by, Gore said, "I thought she was high society, an Auntie Mame, not a normal person who would dot the i's and cross the t's." In those days before Google, had he and Sheila failed to find buried treasure?

Camillucci, Patricia's former restaurant manager, found it plausible that Patricia had simply spent it all. "She liked to live very high on the hog," he said, although she had also made massive donations to the Martin Memorial Hospital, the Graham-Eckes School, and many other causes. John Rogers had actually run the restaurants, he said, adding, "We ran into difficult times and did the best to keep it going."

∽

In 1982, John Rogers called his two youngest children into a room. He told them to prepare to leave southern Florida, immediately. Their mother, Frances O'Meara Rogers, had died in 1978. Rogers had a new wife, a former Cascade gift shop employee with connections in North Carolina. Rogers grabbed the hands of his school-aged kids and took off for the Tar Heel State.[8]

Lawsuits seeking payment for seafood, produce, groceries, and linen had been piling up. The IRS had a lien against Rogers for withholding payroll taxes from employees and failing to turn them over.[9] There were state tax liens as well. Rogers had been playing a dangerous game of lending himself government money.

Through complex financial arrangements involving another of Schlussel's companies, South Key Restaurant Corp., Rogers had kept the Cascades going under a new name, Trees and Me. Appropriately enough, a tree service was among the plaintiffs naming both Rogers and South Key as defendants. Now Rogers was headed for the woods of Watauga County, high in the Blue Ridge Mountains, fleeing creditors, making a fresh start, perhaps delaying the inevitable encounter with the IRS.

One of Rogers's children, Jim, then twelve, remembered the shock of adjusting to rural Boone, North Carolina. "We were South Florida and New York people," he said. The years of spacious homes and dining out were over. After years of overseeing fine restaurants, Rogers was scrambling to find more humble jobs. For a time, he managed a yogurt store in Banner Elk. The family moved from house to house, and Rogers drank heavily.

Another habit Rogers never quit was soliciting infusions of cash from Schlussel, whom he seemed to regard as a friend, his son said. Several federal and state tax liens were eventually released or satisfied. At age seventy, Rogers stopped running. The cause of death was a perforated esophagus, possibly caused by alcoholism.[10]

∽

There were no obituaries for Rogers in newspapers across the nation, as there had been for Patricia. He wasn't part of the myth. Like the protagonist of *Mildred Pierce*, both Patricia and her general manager had finished their lives where they started. Like her father long ago in Newfoundland, Patricia was left with a bit of property and some store inventory. Rogers, born to an Irish immigrant father working for a Brooklyn ice cream company, ended up running a yogurt stand.

The end, however, did not define the journey. Bucking prejudices that barred female names from commercial leases, deemed Al Smith too Irish, and banned career women from the Social Register, Patricia got what she wanted. Sweat and imagination helped her succeed in the male-dominated restaurant world, and she did it on her own. Her parents gave her a good education, a nose for business, and a trip to New York. The rest was up to her, and she seized the chance.

Her embellished life story and extravagant floral displays brought thousands to her restaurants. Midcentury diners were happy with her standard American food and thrilled with the popovers. At restaurants run by her siblings and successors, these remained on the menu long after her death.

For better or worse, she left her mark on the many cities in which she operated. Hiring a woman as her architect, she was something even rarer, a female developer.

Her siblings competed with her, and a trusted manager proved unworthy of her trust. Tragedy abbreviated her loving marriage. In the end, her closest companion was a household employee, while a pilot squired her to parties. But like her fictitious counterpart Mildred Pierce, Patricia was unsinkable. Casting off her traitorous daughter, Veda, forever, Mildred shouted, "To hell with her!" Mildred's last words might well have been Patricia's: "Let's get stinko."[11]

Notes

Chapter 1

1. Eugenia Sheppard, "It's Chic to Be Corny," *New York Herald Tribune* (hereafter *NYHT*), Dec. 1, 1961.

2. Edyth Thornton McLeod, "Beauty after Forty," *Dunkirk Evening Observer*, Dec. 26, 1961.

3. R. John Bates, interview with author, Apr. 28, 2015.

4. J.W. Johnston, "Garden Treat at Restaurant," *NYHT*, Oct. 18, 1959.

5. Display ad, *NYT*, Nov. 16, 1961, 20.

6. Westbrook Pegler, "Soviet Genius a Fraud," *Montana Standard* Aug. 17, 1959.

7. McLeod, Dec. 26, 1961.

8. Agnes Murphy, "At Home with Patricia Murphy," *New York Post*, Nov. 26, 1961.

9. Ibid.

10. Carleton Varney, interview with author, Feb. 1, 2017.

11. Dorothy Roe, "How Casual Can You Get?" AP, *Blytheville (AK) Courier News*, July 24, 1959.

12. Clementine Paddleford, "Two Restaurants Found through Bachelor's Tip," *NYHT*, June 1, 1946.

13. Richard Kluger, *The Paper: The Life and Death of the New York Herald Tribune* (New York: Knopf, 1986), 488 and 624.

14. "Movie Critic's Car Hits Pole," *NYT*, Aug. 27, 1939.

15. "Yonkers's Patricia Murphy to Run Lauderdale Bahia Mar Restaurant," *Herald Statesman* (hereafter *HS*), Sept. 8, 1959.

16. Rosa Tusa, "Candlelight and Popovers," *Palm Beach Post*, June 21, 1973.

17. "Initial Celebration," *New York Age*, May 28, 1955.

18. Patricia Murphy, *Glow of Candlelight*, unpublished manuscript, n.d., ca. 1961, 82.

19. Patricia Murphy, *Glow of Candlelight* (hereafter *Glow*) (Englewood Cliffs, NJ: Prentice-Hall, 1961), 5.

20. Patricia Murphy testified that she often heard comments like these. "Affidavit of Eleanor Patricia Murphy Kiernan Read in Opposition to Motion," Munsey Candlelight Corp. v. Eleanor Patricia Murphy Kiernan, aka Eleanor Patricia Murphy, New York Supreme Court, Appellate Division, First Department, 155 N.Y.S.2d 504; 1956.

21. "Macy's Sets Record for Autographed Copies Sold," *Publishers Weekly*, Dec. 18, 1961, 24–25.

22. Gregory Camillucci, interview with author, March 11, 2015.

Chapter 2

1. W.J. Chafe, *I've Been Working on the Railroad*, 55.

2. Murphy, *Glow*, 30.

3. Clayton D. Cook, *Tales of the Rails: Volume IV*, 63.

4. Murphy, *Glow*, 34.

5. Paul Murphy email, Feb. 18, 2015.

6. Newfoundland Fisheries Enquiry Commission, Interview with Frank Murphy, Newfoundland Hotel, Apr. 17, 1936.

7. *The Western Star*, May 1, 1918.

8. *Census of Newfoundland*, District of Placentia and St. Mary's, Book 1, 1921.

9. Kathrine E. Bellamy, RSM, *Weavers of the Tapestry*, 324.

10. James F. Murphy, interview with Paul Murphy, Sept. 9, 1995.

11. Ibid.

12. Ibid.

13. Murphy, *Glow*, 39.

Chapter 3

1. "100-Mile Gale Lashes City," *NYT*, Jan. 26, 1928.

2. *Murphy's Good Things*, Feb. 1922.

3. *NYT*, Jan. 26, 1928.

4. Robert McWhirter, *The Citizenship Flowchart* (Chicago: American Bar Association, 2007), Part C, Nos. 32–35.

5. John C. Street, ed., *The Journal of Oliver Rouse*, ix.

6. James F. Murphy, interviewed with Paul Murphy, Sept. 9, 1995, interviewer's transcript. Note: It was often reported that Patricia arrived with sixty dollars, although she spoke of that amount as her "nest egg." One obituary gave the sum as $400. In *Glow*, she wrote that she had a "roll of bills."

7. "Brilliant Non-Scholastic Records of Princeton Men," *Brooklyn Daily Eagle* (hereafter *BDE*), Jan. 15, 1924, and "Princeton Degrees Go to 21 Brooklyn Men," *BDE*, June 19, 1928.

8. Martin Spollen, email to author, Sept. 16, 2016.

9. Ibid.

10. Murphy, *Glow*, 11–12.

11. Ross Westzsteon, *Republic of Dreams, Greenwich Village: The American Bohemia 1910–1960* (New York: Simon and Schuster, 2007), 389.

12. Murphy, *Glow*, 12.

13. Ibid.

14. Marion R. Casey, "From the East Side to the Seaside: Irish Americans on the Move in New York City," in *The New York Irish*, ed. Ronald H. Bayer and Timothy J. Meagher (Baltimore: Johns Hopkins University Press, 1996), 404.

15. W. Herbert Blake, "Three Arts Club Is New York Home for Stage Novices," *Los Angeles Herald*, June 25, 1909.

16. Help Wanted: Female, *NYT*, Feb. 17, 1925. Note: Patricia would have seen a later ad, but this same Foster's ad appeared in many papers during the 1920s.

17. Murphy, *Glow*, 12–13.

18. Ware School of Tea Room Management, *A Course in Tea Room, Cafeteria and Motor Inn Management*, ca. 1927.

19. Murphy, *Glow*, 12.

20. Murphy, *Glow*, 14–17.

21. Jan Whitaker, "Marketing the Anglo-American Home," in Avakian and Haber, eds., *From Betty Crocker to Feminist Food Studies*," 92.

22. *BDE*, Mar. 13, 1900, 9.

Chapter 4

1. James F. Murphy, interviewed by Paul Murphy, Sept. 9, 1995.

2. Ware School, "Dining Room Personnel," 3.

3. Murphy, *Glow*, 17.

4. Jean Piper, "100,000 Filipinos in U.S.; 1,000 in Brooklyn, Many Come for Higher Education," *BDE*, July 1, 1928.

5. Newfoundland Fisheries Enquiry Commission, Apr. 17, 1936.

6. Lew Sheaffer, "Lew's Talk," *BDE*, Jan. 10, 1947.

7. Robert W. Ruth, "'Axis Sally' Tells of Oath to Reich, *Baltimore Sun*, Feb. 24, 1949.

8. "Heights Café Is Robbed of $350," *BDE*, Dec. 24, 1930.

9. James F. Murphy, interviewed by Paul Murphy, Sept. 9, 1995.

10. MacDougall, *The Secret of Successful Restaurants* (New York: Harper Brothers) 1929, 161.

11. Frank R. McGregor, letter to Charles Green, Oct. 28, 1936, New York World's Fair 1939–1940 records, Manuscripts and Archives Division, The New York Public Library.

Chapter 5

1. Murphy, *Glow*, 41.

2. "5 Schrafft Stores Ask Liquor License," *BDE*, March 31, 1934.

3. Murphy, *Glow*, 42.

4. James F. Murphy, interviewed by Paul Murphy, Sept. 9, 1995.

5. U.S. Department of Commerce, *Census 1940*, E.D. 41-612, Apr. 15, 1940.

6. Murphy *Glow*, 45.

7. Paddleford, "Two Restaurants Found through Bachelor's Tip," *NYHT*, June 1, 1946.

8. "Society," *BDE*, Feb. 22, 1932.

9. "Miss Murphy Engaged to Schuyler Robinson," *NYHT*, Nov. 14, 1939.

10. Newfoundland Fisheries Enquiry Commission, Interview with Frank Murphy, Newfoundland Hotel, April 17, 1936.

11. "Miss Patricia Murphy to Be Wed to E. Schuyler Robinson," *BDE*, Nov. 14, 1939.

Chapter 6

1. "DeCourcy Browne Sues W.B. Pierce for $250,000," *NYHT*, Nov. 19, 1929.

2. City of New York, Certificate of Marriage Registration, No. 17420, Nov. 28, 1939.

3. U.S. Department of Commerce, *Census 1940*, E.D. 31-4347, April 20, 1940.

4. "Luncheon and Lifestyle Show on Wednesday Will Assist French Refugees in England," *NYT*, Oct. 20, 1949.

5. Murphy, *Glow of Candlelight*, unpublished manuscript, 94.

6. "Ceremony Marks Passing of Old Wallabout Market," *BDE*, June 14, 1941.

7. Murphy, *Glow*, 54–55.

8. "More Women Wanted for Jobs at Brooklyn Navy Yard," *BDE*, June 5, 1944.

9. James F. Murphy, interviewed by Paul Murphy, Sept. 9, 1995.

10. "Couple Lose in Suit against Restaurant," *BDE*, Mar. 16, 1938.

11. Saroyan, *Across the Board on Tomorrow Morning* in *Three Plays* (New York: Harcourt Brace, 1941).

12. Classified ads, *BDE*, May 20, 1943, and June 21, 1943.

13. Owen T. Smith, interview with author, notes, Feb 17, 2015.

14. "Quake Throws Bomb Scare into Brooklyn Residents," *BDE*, Sept. 4, 1944.

Chapter 7

1. James F. Murphy, interviewed by Paul Murphy, Sept. 9, 1995.

2. Murphy, *Glow*, 52.

3. "Manhattan Transfers," *NYT*, Jan. 13, 1947, and June 23, 1948.

4. *BDE*, Jan. 14, 1947.

5. Daniel Kahn, "Cooking Up More Than a Restaurant," *Newsday*, Oct. 18, 1973.

6. Lew Sheaffer, "Lew's Talk," *BDE*, Jan. 10, 1947.

7. "Manhattan Transfers," *NYT*, June 23, 1948.

8. Dana, *Where to Eat in New York* (New York: Current Books, 1948), 118–119.

9. "Boro's Restaurants Please Every Palate, *BDE*, Dec. 27, 1940.

10. Murphy, *Glow*, 57–65.

11. City of New York, Certificate of Marriage Registration, No. 21413, July 7, 1948.

Chapter 8

1. James F. Murphy, interviewed by Paul Murphy, Sept. 9, 1995.

2. "Mrs. Kiernan's Country Home: It Gives Her a Busboy's Holiday," *Interiors*, Vol. CX, No. 81, Mar. 1951, 88–93.

3. "Mrs. Kiernan's Country Home," 89.

4. Paul Murphy, interview, notes, May 30, 2015.

5. James F. Murphy, interviewed by Paul Murphy, Sept. 9, 1995.

6. Owen T. Smith, interview, notes, Feb 17, 2015.

7. "To Open Manhasset Restaurant," *NYT*, Nov. 5, 1949.

8. Clementine Paddleford, "Bigger, Brighter Candlelight," *NYHT*, May 20, 1950.

9. Owen T. Smith, interview, notes, Feb 17, 2015.

10. Paul Murphy, interview, Apr. 9, 2015.

11. "Woman Leases Place Near Waldorf for Restaurant," *NYHT*, Jan. 1, 1931.

12. James F. Murphy, interviewed by Paul Murphy, Sept. 9, 1995, interviewer's transcript.

13. Goldstein, *Inventing Great Neck*, 39.

14. James F. Murphy, interviewed by Paul Murphy, Sept. 9, 1995.

Chapter 9

1. "Mrs. Kiernan's Country Home: It Gives Her a Busboy's Holiday," *Interiors*, Vol. CX, No. 81, Mar. 1951, 88–93.

2. "Restaurant Lighting in Manhasset, Candlelight Restaurant," *Light*, Vol. 22 (1953), 9–14.

3. Westchester County Records, Liber 5226, 334, May 1953.

4. Lowell, "Man and Wife," poets.org, www.poets.org/poetsorg/poem/man-and-wife

5. Joseph Dorman, *Arguing the World: The New York Intellectuals in Their Own Words* (Chicago: University of Chicago Press, 2001), 102.

6. Straus, *Palaces and Prisons* (Boston: Houghton Mifflin, 1976), 68–69.

7. Lowell, *The Letters of Robert Lowell* (New York: Macmillan, 2007), 300.

8. Carol Brightman, ed., *Between Friends: The Correspondence of Hannah Arendt and Mary McCarthy, 1949–1975* (New York: Harcourt Brace and Co., 1995), 29–30.

9. Andrew James Dvosin, *Literature in a Political World: The Career and Writings of Philip Rahv*, unpublished PhD dissertation, New York University, 1977, 104.

10. "9–4 Vote Adopts New Zoning Ordinance," *HS*, Sept. 1, 1953.

11. Murphy, *Glow*, 86.

12. *HS*, July 7, 1937.

13. Kelly, Day Book entries July–Sept. 1954, Richard Kelly Papers (MS 1838). Manuscripts and Archives, Yale University Library.

14. "Candlelight Restaurant: Luminous Pavilion Touched by Orient," *Interiors*, Vol. CXIV, No. 12, July 1955, 76–79.

15. Kelly, clippings and Day Book entries.

16. James F. Murphy, interviewed by Paul Murphy, Sept. 9, 1995.

17. Advertisement for Lauraine Murphy restaurant, milleridgeinn.com/portfolio-type/milleridge-history

18. Lowery, "Happy Housewife Feeds 4,000 Every Day," Associated Press *Index-Journal* (Greenwood, SC), Jan. 13, 1955.

19. "No Greenhouse Ruled for Patricia Murphy's," *HS*, May 21, 1955.

20. "Management: Charms in the Kitchen," *Investor's Reader*, Vol. 25, No. 1, June 29, 1955, 21–22.

Chapter 10

1. Leone King, "Party Parade Begins Here," *Palm Beach Post* (hereafter *PBP*), Dec. 30, 1964.

2. "Zoning Board Grants Two Greenhouse Permits," *HS*, June 22, 1955, and "Special Use Permits Get Council OK, *HS*, June 30, 1955.

3. Munsey Candlelight Corp. v. Eleanor Patricia Murphy Kiernan, aka Eleanor Patricia Murphy, New York Supreme Court, Appellate Division, First Department, 155 N.Y.S.2d 504; 1956.

4. Munsey v. Kiernan, affidavit of Meyer Zimmerman.

5. Neal M. Rosendorf, "Hollywood, Tourism and Dictatorship: Samuel Bronston's Special Relationship with the Franco Regime 1957–1973," in *The United States and Public Diplomacy: New Directions in Cultural and International History*, Kenneth Osgood and Brian C. Etheridge, eds. (Leiden: Nijhoff Publishers, 2010) 105–111.

6. Murphy, *Glow of Candlelight*, unpublished manuscript, 151.

7. Nader James Sayegh, interview with author, notes, Feb. 1, 2017.

8. "Bronxville Junior League Program Is Subject of Interview on Radio," *Review Press-Reporter*, Sept. 27, 1956.

Chapter 11

1. Murphy, *Glow*, 82.

2. "Democrats Retain 9–3 Council Control; Kristensen Gets Fourth Term as Mayor," *HS*, Nov. 9, 1955.

3. "Grand Union Has Realty Corporation," *Troy Record*, May 8, 1956.

4. Owen T. Smith, interview, notes, Feb. 17, 2015.

5. "$3 Million Development Planned for Central Avenue," *HS*, June 12, 1957.

6. "First Step Set for Project Near Patricia Murphy's," *HS*, June 26, 1957.

7. Douglas Thompson, *Shadowland: How the Mafia Bet Britain in a Global Game* (Edinburgh: Mainstream Publishing Co., 2011), 128–129; Frankie Fraser with James Morton, *Mad Frank's London* (London: Virgin Books, 2001), 57–58.

8. Cordet, *Born Bewildered* (London: Peter Davies Ltd., 1961), 170–171.

9. William I. Bookman, "Operator of Restaurant Here Tells of Still More Expansion," *HS*, Sept. 24, 1958.

10. "Capt. Kiernan Dies in NY," *Honolulu Star-Bulletin*, Nov. 14, 1957.

11. Paul Tanfield, "Tanfield's Diary," *Daily Mail*, Dec. 3, 1957.

12. Patricia Murphy, letter to Dorothea Hopfer, Nov. 14, 1958, American Woman's Association Records, 1911–1981; Box 21, Barnard Archives and Special Collections, Barnard Library, Barnard College.

Chapter 12

1. Murphy, *Glow*, 95.

2. "To Host Auxiliary," *News Tribune* (Fort Pierce, FL), Jan. 3, 1958.

3. Sherwood D. Kohn, "H2$: Fountains and Pools are Pelted with Millions of Dollars a Year," *NYT*, Nov. 13, 1964.

4. "Wishing Well Aids Health Program Here," *HS*, Feb. 20, 1958.

5. "County Exhibitors Win at Flower Show," *HS*, March 11, 1958.

6. Diane Carlson Phillips, interview with author, tape transcript, Mar. 30, 2017.

7. Carlson, letter to Mrs. William R. Coleman, Aug. 6, 1958; Outdoor Cleanliness Association records, Manuscripts and Archives Division, The New York Public Library.

8. Cordet, *Born Bewildered*, 178.

9. Cordet, *Born Bewildered*, 190.

10. Bookman, *HS*, Sept. 24, 1958.

11. Varney, interview, Feb. 1, 2017.

12. Dorothy Roe, "How Casual Can You Get?" AP, *Blytheville (AK) Courier News*, July 24, 1959.

13. Display ad, Reef restaurant, *Fort Lauderdale News* (hereafter *FLN*), Nov. 22, 1959.

Chapter 13

1. "Used Plane Report: Cessna 310," *Flying*, Vol. 123, No. 6, June 1996, 76–78.

2. R. John Bates, interview with author, notes, Apr. 28, 2015.

3. Alexander E. "Al" Cabana, interview with author, notes, Apr. 20, 2015.

4. "300,000 Rental Bid for Bahia Restaurant," *FLN*, Aug. 4, 1959.

5. Sayegh, interview, Feb. 1, 2017.

6. Bill Tarleton, "Restaurant Lease at Bahia Nearer," *FLN*, Aug. 28, 1959.

7. Murphy, *Glow*, 111.

8. City of Fort Lauderdale v. D.D. Freeman, as Trustee in Bankruptcy for Bahia Mar Corp., Supreme Court of the United States, October Term, 1956.

9. "Florida City Sells Links to Bar Play by Negroes," *NYT*, July 10, 1957.

10. "Waiter Held on Alien Count," *HS*, Nov. 8, 1954.

11. Murphy, *Glow*, 79.

12. Thomasina Norford, "On the Town," *New York Amsterdam News*, Oct. 3, 1959.

13. Dick Hoekstra, "The Night Watch," *FLN*, Oct. 2, 1959.

14. "New Parking Lot Plans Approved," *FLN*, Nov. 10, 1959.

15. "1959: Probable Domestic Take," *Variety*, Jan. 6, 1960.

16. C.D. Jackson, Memo to Shareholders, Dec. 27, 1960, C.D. Jackson Papers, 1931–1967, Dwight D. Eisenhower Library.

17. "Candlelight Passes $1 Million Mark," *FLN*, Dec. 18, 1960.

18. "Lack of Parking Raises Tempers at Bahia Mar," *FLN*, Feb. 19, 1960.

19. "Arterial Plan for Yonkers Becomes Law," *HS*, Apr. 23, 1959.

20. Paul Tanfield, "Visiting Senator Lets His Hair Down," *Daily Mail*, Nov. 28, 1960.

21. Leone King, "Colorful Career Ends for Headmistress," Oct. 31, 1963.

Chapter 14

1. Rhonda Fleming Roesch, "Restaurateur's Career Began with a Gamble," *Athens Messenger*, Nov. 2, 1961.

2. Cabana, interview, Apr. 20, 2015.

3. Varney, interview, Feb. 1, 2017.

4. Mel Heimer, "My New York," *Kane Republican*, Sept. 16, 1961.

5. Newfoundland Public Relations Company, *Commemorating the Official Opening of the New Campus of Memorial University of Newfoundland: Oct. 9 and 10* (St. John's, Government of Newfoundland, 1961).

6. Agnes Murphy, "At Home with Patricia Murphy," *New York Post*, Nov. 26, 1961.

7. Review of *Glow of Candlelight*, *Kirkus Review*, Nov. 3, 1961.

8. Eve Perrick, "Queen Helene," *Daily Mail*, Dec. 30, 1961.

9. Varney, interview, Feb. 1, 2017.

10. Bob Kerr, "Bahia Mar's Fate Hangs in Balance," *FLN*, July 15, 1962.

11. "'Showplace' Promised at Marina," *Miami Herald*, Aug. 23, 1962.

12. Broward County records, Official Record Book 2870, 538.

13. Paul A. Gore, *Past the Edge of Poverty: A Biography of Robert Hayes Gore, Sr.* (Fort Lauderdale: R.H. Gore Co., 1990), 1.

14. Paul A. Gore, interview with author, notes, May 2, 2016.

15. Ray Wieland, "Why the Bahia Mar Lease is Bad," *FLN*, Sept. 2, 1962.

16. Ray Wieland, "Marina Changes Started," *FLN*, Sept. 23, 1964.

Chapter 15

1. "Garden Club Has Planted a Total of 932 Trees in City," *The Stuart [FL] News*, Mar. 12, 1964.

2. "Patricia Murphy Participates in Fair," *PBP*, Nov. 17, 1963.

3. Ad, *FLN*, Jan. 14, 1960.

4. Virginia Palmer, "Patricia by Candlelight," *Pictorial Living*, Jan. 24, 1965.

5. Robert Sheehan, "Four Seasons: A Flourish of Food," *Fortune*, Feb. 1960, 220.

6. Geoffrey T. Hellman, "Profiles," *The New Yorker*, Oct. 17, 1964.

7. Ibid.

8. Paul Freedman, *Ten Restaurants That Changed America* (New York: Liveright, 2016), 201.

9. Craig Claiborne, *The New York Times Guide to Dining Out in New York* (New York: Atheneum, 1969), 195.

10. Ibid., 145.

11. Ibid., 257.

12. Bill Leonard, "It's a Wonderful Town!" *Woman's Day*, July 1955.

13. Peter and Andy Kern, interview with author, notes, Feb. 18, 2017.

14. Ibid.

15. Harry S. and Dorothy R. Davega v. Commissioner, U.S. Tax Court, Dockets 30506 and 30507, Mar. 31, 1952.

16. Ken Haynes, "It's Only Natural," *Madison Eagle* (NJ), Apr. 29, 1965.

17. Camillucci, interview with author, Mar. 11, 2015.

18. James F. Murphy, Sept. 9, 1995.

19. Francis Wood, "Murphy's Menu a la Midas," *Newsday*, Dec. 21, 1967.

20. James F. Murphy, Sept. 9, 1995.

21. Silo Pegbottom, "Milleridge Inn," *Jericho High School Class of 1972 Thirderly On-Line Newsletter*, Fall 2006, jhs1972.net/The%20Library%20(newsletters)/Fall%202006%20Newsletter%20(No.%2014).pdf

22. Samantha Harper, "Loving Men, No. 14," samanthaharpermacy.word press.com/2013/04

23. New York City Department of Finance, mortgage index and Liber 6460, p. 264.

24. D'Arcy Rutherford, letter to AWA, Dec. 15, 1958, and Dorothea Hopfer, letter to Rutherford, Dec. 21, 1958, American Woman's Association Records, 1911–1981, Box 21, Barnard Archives and Special Collections, Barnard Library, Barnard College.

25. Mark Seal, "How Donald Trump Beat Palm Beach Society and Won the Fight for Mar-a-Lago," *Vanity Fair*, Feb. 2017.

Chapter 16

1. C. Allyn Van Winkle, "City Will Save $3 Million," *HS*, Jan. 6, 1965.

2. Classified ad, *Wall Street Journal*, Apr. 7, 1967.

3. "Dream Home Costly to Build, Many White Elephants Are Still for Sale," *News Press* (Fort Myers, FL), Oct. 13, 1968.

4. Bates, Apr. 28, 2015.

5. Richard A. Strauss, interview with author, notes, Feb. 20, 2015, and email to author, Feb. 26, 2015.

6. Joy Wallace Dickinson, "Dining-out Memories Come with Slice of Fine Apple Pie," *Orlando Sentinel*, May 10, 2015.

7. New York State Department of Transportation records, Liber 6806, 283, Sept. 9, 1968.

8. Jim Rogers, interview with author, notes, Feb. 28, 2015.

9. New York City Department of Finance, Register of the City and County of NY, Reel 157, pp. 1787–1798, Nov. 18, 1969 and Reel 157, p. 1792, Dec. 1, 1969.

10. Anne-Marie Murray, interview with author, notes, Oct. 10, 2015.

11. John M. O'Mara memo, June 10, 1969, Records of the Office of Administration and Facilities (Eileen Buckley), RG 8.0, New York University Archives, New York University Libraries (hereafter NYU Archives).

12. Rider to lease, New York University, landlord and Westchester Candlelight Corp., tenant, July 15, 1969, NYU Archives.

13. Leonard Schlussel, letter to John Rogers, Dec. 23, 1969, NYU Archives.

14. "Dance at City Museum to Benefit Theater Collection," *NYT*, May 3, 1970.

15. *Annual Report 1970*, Museum of the City of New York, report on "Stars of the New York Stage 1870/1970" gala, n.p.

16. Kevin J. Gonzalez, interview with author, Feb. 19, 2015.

17. "Sheep Strays from Live Creche," *HS*, Dec. 1, 1970.

18. "Restaurant Plans to Open Again," *HS*, August 6, 1971.

19. Westchester County Records, surrender of lease, Central Arcade, landlord and Westchester Candlelight, tenant, July 30, 1971.

Chapter 17

1. Kevin J. Gonzalez, interview with author, Feb. 19, 2015.

2. "ludwig" (user name), Patricia Murphy forum, roadfood.com, staging.roadfood.com/Forums /m/tm.aspx?m=156360&p=4

3. "Hotel Group Nixes Union as its Agent," *FLN*, Mar. 16, 1962.

4. Gael Greene, *Bite: A New York Restaurant Strategy for Hedonists, Masochists, Selective Penny Pinchers and the Upwardly Mobile* (New York: Norton, 1971), 214.

5. Eleanore Carruth, "Restaurateurs Need Some New Recipes for Survival," *Fortune*, Vol. 85, Mar. 1972, 90–92.

6. Rogers letter to O'Mara, Nov. 9, 1971, NYU Archives.

7. Wolf letter to O'Mara, Nov. 18, 1971, NYU Archives.

8. O'Mara letter to Rogers, Dec. 10, 1971, NYU Archives.

9. Camillucci, interview with author, Mar. 11, 2015.

10. Barbara Hudgins, "Suburban Babes on Broadway," *NYT*, July 1, 1971.

11. Tobias, "At Table," *WWD*, Sept. 28, 1972.

12. Linda Schaefer, email, Apr. 26, 2016.

13. "Martin Hospital Seeks Addition Permit," *PBP*, Apr. 26, 1972.

14. "Bahia Mar Complex Has a February Due Date," *FLN*, July 28, 1973.

15. Carol Nossett, email, Feb. 17, 2016.

16. Dorfman, "The Bottom Line," *New York*, Vol. 7, No. 52, Dec. 23, 1974.

17. "Gardener Files Suit Over Firing," *PBP*, Dec. 25, 1975.

18. Associated Press, "Typhoid Outbreak Traced to NYC Restaurant," *Amarillo Globe-Times*, Jan. 23, 1976.

19. David Bird, "Patricia Murphy's Here Linked to Typhoid Cases," *NYT*, Jan. 16, 1976.

20. Associated Press, "Typhoid Outbreak Traced to NYC Restaurant," *Amarillo Globe-Times*, Jan. 23, 1976.

21. Pascal Imperato, MD, former New York City deputy health commissioner, interview with author, tape transcript, Apr. 10, 2017.

22. Ibid.

Chapter 18

1. NYU v. Westchester Candlelight Corp., Supreme Court of NY, Appellate Division, First Department, 64 A.D. 2d 581; 407 NYS 2d 168, July 20, 1978.

2. Diana Aitchinson, "Designers Pitch in on Old House for Good Cause," *Sun Sentinel*, Apr. 19, 1987.

3. Greg J. Harrison, interview with author, notes, Mar. 10, 2015.

4. Greg J. Harrison v. Patricia Murphy Kiernan, Circuit Court of the 15th Judicial Circuit of Florida, Palm Beach County, Case No. 78-4388-CA(L).

5. Probate Division, Circuit Court for Broward County, File 79-3905, In Re: Guardianship of Ellen Murphy, aka Eleanor Patricia Murphy.

6. J.W. Johnston, "Garden Treat at Restaurant," *NYHT*, Oct. 18, 1959.

7. Paul A. Gore, interview, Apr. 2, 2016.

8. Jim E. Rogers, interview, notes, Feb. 28, 2015.

9. Internal Revenue Service, Notice of Federal Tax Lien, John E. Rogers, 6672 tax, Sept. 19, 1983.

10. Rogers, Feb. 28, 2015.

11. James M. Cain, *Mildred Pierce* (New York: Random House, 1941), Vintage Books Edition, 2011, 298.

Selected Bibliography

Baylor, Ronald H., and Timothy J. Meagher, eds. *The New York Irish*. Baltimore: Johns Hopkins University Press, 1996.

Bellamy, Kathrine E. *Weavers of the Tapestry*. St. John's, NL: Flanker Press, 2006.

Cain, James M. *Mildred Pierce*. New York: Vintage Books, 2011.

Chafe, W.J. *I've Been Working on the Railroad: Memoirs of a Railwayman, 1911–1962*. St. John's, NL: Harry Cuff Publications, 1987.

Cook, Clayton D. *Tales of the Rails, Vol. IV: The Newfoundland Railway, 1881–1988*. St. John's, NL: Flanker Press, 2005.

Cordet, Helene. *Born Bewildered*. London: Peter Davies, 1961.

Fraser, Frankie, and James Morton. *Mad Frank's London*. London: Virgin, 2002.

Freedman, Paul. *Ten Restaurants That Changed America*. New York: Liveright, 2016.

Goldstein, Judith S. *Inventing Great Neck: Jewish Identity and the American Dream*. New Brunswick, NJ: Rutgers University Press, 2006.

Gore, Paul A. *Past the Edge of Poverty: A Biography of Robert Hayes Gore, Sr.* Fort Lauderdale, FL: R.H. Gore, 1990.

Haber, Barbara, and Arlene Voski Avakian, Eds. *From Betty Crocker to Feminist Food Studies: Critical Perspectives on Women and Food*. Amherst: University of Massachusetts Press, 2005.

Murphy, Patricia. *Glow of Candlelight: The Story of Patricia Murphy*. Englewood Cliffs, NJ: Prentice-Hall, 1961.

Nadal, Kevin L. *Filipinos in New York City*. Charleston, SC: Arcadia Publishing, 2015.

Thompson, Douglas. *Shadowland: How the Mafia Bet Britain in a Global Gamble*. Edinburgh: Mainstream Publishing, 2011.

Whitaker, Jan. *Tea at the Blue Lantern Inn: A Social History of the Tea Room Craze in America*. New York: St. Martin's Press, 2002.

Index